TERRORS OF THE NIGHT

RECENT BOOKS OF RELATED INTEREST

TERRORS OF THE NIGHT

CANADIAN ACCOUNTS OF EERIE EVENTS AND WEIRD EXPERIENCES

JOHN ROBERT COLOMBO

THE DUNDURN GROUP
TORONTO

Copy-Editor: Lloyd Davis
Design: Andrew Roberts
Printer: Transcontinental

Library and Archives Canada Cataloguing in Publication

Colombo, John Robert, 1936-
    Terrors of the night: Canadian accounts of eerie events and weird
    experiences / John Robert Colombo.

Includes bibliographical references.

ISBN-10: 1-55002-576-7
ISBN-13: 978-1-55002-576-7

    1.Parapsychology--Canada. I.Title.

GR113.C645 2005   130'.971   C2005-904878-6

1   2   3   4   5   09   08   07   06   05

We acknowledge the support of the Canada Council for the Arts and the Ontario Arts Council for our publishing program. We also acknowledge the financial support of the Government of Canada through the Book Publishing Industry Development Program and The Association for the Export of Canadian Books, and the Government of Ontario through the Ontario Book Publishers Tax Credit program, and the Ontario Media Development Corporation.

Care has been taken to trace the ownership of copyright material used in this book. The author and the publisher welcome any information enabling them to rectify any references or credit in subsequent editions.

J. Kirk Howard, President

Printed and bound in Canada.
Printed on recycled paper.

www.dundurn.com

Dundurn Press
3 Church Street, Suite 500
Toronto, Ontario, Canada
M5E 1M2

Gazelle Book Services Limited
White Cross Mills
Hightown, Lancaster, England
LA1 4X5

Dundurn Press
2250 Military Road
Tonawanda NY
U.S.A. 14150

To those who believe,
no explanation is necessary.
To those who do not believe,
no explanation is possible.

Joseph Dunninger

Dedicated to Doris and Ted Davy

Contents

Preface

TERRORS OF THE NIGHT is a collection of more than one hundred accounts of eerie events and weird experiences. The highly readable accounts are told-as-true stories of incidents that have happened to Canadians from all walks of life, and from all across the country, over the last century. The events are mainly objective in nature, and the experiences are more or less subjective in nature. Cumulatively, such incidents raise issues that vex and perplex the rational mind. The questions they beg are related to the "terrors of the night." They are not concerned with the "problems of the day" — such mundane matters as work, health, illness, family, taxes, etc. Instead, they are concerned with mystical and meta-physical matters, worries of the spirit — "things that go bump in the night," as the Scottish saying has it.

This collection is an outgrowth of my ongoing interest in Canadian mysteries. I define a "mystery" as an experience (psycho-logical) or an event (physical) that is so out of the ordinary as to defy reason and common sense. Whether they do in fact defy reason and sense is a matter that I leave to the reader to consider. Are there ghosts? That question still cannot be answered with certainty. Are there ghost stories? That question may be answered with assurance. Yes, there *are* ghost stories, and they tell us about ghosts, about which there is no direct evidence.

The following true story may illustrate this paradox. Some years ago, my late friend Robert Zend, a brilliant poet with a lively imagination, asked me the following seemingly silly question: "John, do unicorns exist?"

Robert was serious. He was knowledgeable about the literature of his native Hungary, and he had a wry sense of humour, but I was aware that he knew surprisingly little about classical mythology, and nothing at all about zoology.

Much to his disappointment, I assured him that unicorns do not exist and that they never did. Yet behind his query is an interesting one that draws attention to the paradoxical nature of the unicorn, which becomes apparent in the form of questions and answers:

> Q. Does a unicorn have a single horn that grows
>   from its forehead?
> A. Yes.
> Q. Does the unicorn exist?
> A. No.

So the category (the unicorn) exists, but not the category's content (one unicorn). Ghosts, spirits and other mysteries may be like unicorns: they exist conceptually, but they will be found to exist concretely only if and when someone succeeds in capturing a member of their ghostly host.

No unicorns dance across these pages, but there are mermaids, witches and ogres; indeed, a herd of beasts and beings thunder across these pages. There are accounts of earthly powers, reports of mysterious events and enduring traditions, aboriginal beliefs and practices, descriptions of wild beasts and semi-human beings, not to mention stories of omens and prophecies, miraculous cures, and a range of bizarre incidents that seem impossible, yet are recorded in earnest.

The accounts come from the newspapers of the past, both daily and weekly. What impresses me most about these instances of reportage is the fact that the journalists have generally taken pains to report what they have seen and heard and been told, generally without editorial comment.

Some comment might be called for. Certainly the events and experiences related in these stories are baffling and defy common sense. The episodes range from the illogical through the improbable to the impossible. On the surface, the events and experiences that are described are preposterous. If the illogical episodes occurred at all, they certainly "beat the odds." If the improbable ones occurred, there "might be some mistake." If the impossible ones occurred, "something has to be wrong." Whether or not they took place as described, they are wonderful and weird. They are full of wonders, for the word *weird* is related to ancient words for "fate" and "destiny." Today the word generally refers to "providence," but it has a whiff of the supernatural, the mysterious and everything "out of the ordinary." Perhaps these weird stories will cause readers to pause and wonder about human nature, belief and disbelief, life and death, the world, fate and destiny, and the cosmos. These are not matters that are discussed in broad daylight.

Such, then, are the terrors of the night.

Acknowledgments

IN THE PREPARATION of the present work, I am pleased to acknowledge the assistance provided by researcher Alice Neal and librarian Philip Singer. Fellow inquirers who helped me along the way include Dwight Whalen and W. Ritchie Benedict. Discussions about issues raised here were held with Cyril Greenland and David A. Gotlib. The late Marcello Truzzi is much missed; discussions with him were always enlightening. Also helpful were (and are) Matthew James Didier and Jennifer Krutilla, who founded The Ghosts and Hauntings Research Society. (The G&HRS has an impressive website.) I remain in the debt of Tony Hawke of Hounslow Press, part of the Dundurn Group, who ushered this book into print. Editing and production fell into the capable hands of Lloyd Davis, Barry Jowett, Jennifer Scott, and Andrew Roberts.

The epigraph is based on the words of illusionist and mentalist Joseph Dunninger, who would introduce his popular stage performances with these wise remarks. The words have outlived the man, and they will continue to do so... at least as long as magic and mystery cast their twin spells over the human mind.

I remain on the lookout for firsthand reports of strange events and eerie experiences. If you wish to share your accounts with me for future publications, feel free to write to me care of the editorial department of the publisher. You may also use my e-mail address — *jrc@ca.inter.net* — or my website: *http://www.colombo.ca.*

1 Witchery and Magic

WITCHES COME TO mind at least once a year, with the approach of Halloween. That is October 31, otherwise known as *Walpurgis Nacht*, "the night the witches ride." The principles of ancient witchcraft are honoured in the contemporary practice of wicca. Wiccans keep alive what are quaintly described as "pagan practices," "primitive religion," "sympathetic magic" and "shamanism." The latter word refers to the customs, beliefs and ritual practices of the world's indigenous peoples.

The power of wicca may be defined broadly as the practice of causing changes to occur in conformity with the will. Such practices were and are central to the culture of the Native peoples of Canada. This section examines some exciting expressions of witchery and magic.

A CERTAIN PAGAN POW-WOW

Peter Jones (1802–1856), who was known as Kahkewaquonaby (Sacred Feathers), was a Methodist minister of Native background. He is remembered for his ministry, as well as for a major work with a long title and subtitle: *History of the Ojibway Indians with Especial Reference to their Conversion to Christianity... With a Brief Memoir of the Writer and Introductory Notice by the Rev. G. Osborn, D.D., Secr. of the Wesleyan Methodist Missionary Society* (1861, 1970).

Jones's book preserves much Ojibwa lore and communicates a sense of the importance and power of the spiritual traditions of his people. With respect to the latter, Jones described his attendance at "a certain pagan pow-wow." He was not really impressed with this "pow-wow," which took the form of a performance of the rite of the shaking tent, and this sense of disappointment is apparent in the passage that follows.

Yet Jones might well have been more impressed. The conjuror, or *jessuhkon*, seemed to be a knowledgeable and honest person. By consulting the "familiar spirits," or *munedoos,* or by listening carefully to a concealed confederate, he ascertained the fact that there were Native Christian observers among the rite's pagan participants. As well, the conjuror gave Jones a careful account of what the "spirits" had conveyed to him about the wisdom of the Indian people embracing Christianity. On this issue, the voices of the "spirits" were divided.

On the 9th of August, 1828, I was engaged in preaching to the Indians at Lake Simcoe, at which time the Great Spirit began in a very powerful manner to convert them from paganism to Christianity. During the day some of the Christian Indians informed me that a certain pagan pow-wow had intimated his intention of consulting his *munedoos,* to ascertain from them whether it was right for Indians to forsake the religion of their fathers, and to take hold of the white man's religion. I requested them to let me know when he would begin his performance, as I wished to go and hear him for myself. Shortly after dark they brought me word that the pow-wow had gone towards the pine-grove to commence his incantations. I immediately accompanied them in that direction, and we soon heard the rattling of his conjuring wigwam, called in Ojebway *jessukhon;* which is made by putting seven poles in the ground at the depth of about a cubit, in a circle of about three or four feet in diameter, and about six feet high, with one or more hoops tied fast to the poles, to keep them in a circle. The sides were covered with birch bark, but the top was left open. Into this the pow-wow had entered, and was chaunting a song to the spirit with whom he wished to converse. The *jessuhkon* began to shake as if filled with wind.

Wishing to see and hear his performance without his knowing we were present, we proceeded towards him as softly as we could, and placed ourselves around the *jessuhkon.* On our approach we heard the muttering talk of one of the familiar spirits, in answer to questions he had put to him. This spirit told him that it was right for Indians to become Christians, and that he ought to go to the meetings and hear for himself. The next spirit he invoked spoke decidedly against Indians becoming Christians, and exhorted him to adhere to the religion of his fathers. The third spirit spoke nearly as the first; with this addition,— that he, the conjuror, was quite wrong in supposing the Christian Indians to be crazy, as if they were under the effects of the fire-waters; that they were not as they appeared to be, but that all the time they were crying and praying, they were in their right minds and worshiping the Great Spirit in their hearts, and according to His will. The fourth spirit informed him that shortly one of his children would be taken from him by death.

One of the Christian Indians standing near whispered to me, saying, "If we kneel down and begin to pray to the Great Spirit, his enchantment will be broken, and all his devils will have to fly." I replied, "We had better not disturb him," as I wished to hear the end of it. My friend then in a low whisper prayed that the Great Spirit would have mercy on this poor deluded Indian. That very instant the *jessuhkon* ceased shaking, and the muttering talk stopped, as if the evil spirits had all been put to flight.

The juggler then spoke to himself: "I suppose the Christian Indians are praying at my wigwam?" He then began to sing with all his might, and presently his *jessuhkon* was filled with wind, and began again to shake as if it would fall to pieces. Then a grumbling voice spoke and said, "The Christian Indians are standing all around you." Upon this the conjuror came out of his *jessuhkon*. We then asked him what news the spirits had communicated to him? He replied, "Some have forbidden me to become a Christian, and encourage me to live as my forefathers have done; but others inform me that it is perfectly right to be a Christian, and that I ought to go and hear the missionaries for myself; this I shall now do, and to-morrow I shall go and hear you at your meetings."

I have now stated what came under my own observation in this one instance, and I leave the reader to form his own judgment as to the power by which these deluded Indians perform their incantations. This Indian, according to promise, attended worship the next day.

AN INDIAN CURSE

"The Curse of Mahingan" is reprinted from the May 5, 1890, edition of the *Winnipeg Free Press*. Apparently this account first appeared in the Buffalo *Express* as a letter written from Lake Temiscamingue, Quebec.

17

THE CURSE OF MAHINGAN
A Bit of Indian Legendry from the Upper Ottawa
Manahchinty Tomahawked Mahingan
Because the Latter Ate the Sacred Lamb;
A Curse that Lasted through Several Generations
Ended in a Dog's Death

When the first white missionaries endeavoured to explain to Indians the Christian religion, the effect was at times rather startling. The Indians mistook the substance for the symbol, the objective for the subjective. It is not surprising therefore that an Ogibeway chief, who once travelled in the early dawn of Canadian civilization as far as Montreal, and met there a Jesuit missionary, having received from him a lamb as a present, mistook it for the Lamb of God, concerning whom the missionary had talked much, and taking it with him when he returned to his people, impressed upon them the sacredness of this wonderful, and to them, strange beast, enjoining upon them the necessity of worshiping it with honour and reverence. A small island was chosen as a suitable dwelling place for this new Manitou, and the Indians were happy in possessing an animal at once so sacred and so easily kept.

Unfortunately the owner was the object of much jealousy on the part of the one who had always laid counter claim to the position of a leader of the people. The name of this man was Mahingan. He was a good hunter and a bold man, but he had the reputation of being what is called a "Bad Indian," a very vague term of disapprobation, but very common amongst Indians. He saw that the possession of this lamb gave much power to his rival, and he determined to deprive him of it; and being somewhat of a utilitarian he considered that the best way to do this was to eat it, which he did surreptitiously, and at night. On the following day consternation reigned amongst the Indian camps; the sacred lamb was gone.

The owner was furious, but tried to turn the mishap to account by stating that no Manitou of such importance would stay where "Bad Indians" were allowed to live with impunity, which explanation was

18

accepted as satisfactory until the bones of the lamb were found, clean picked and bearing unmistakable evidence of having been boiled. This upset the supernatural translation theory altogether, and evidently pointed to the murder of a Manitou, but the question arose, "Who was the sacrilegious wretch who had dared to fill himself with a god?" Manahchinty, the owner, openly accused Mahingan to his face, but Mahingan laughed at him, saying:

"No one can eat a real Manitou. The Manitou would more likely eat him. If your animal was a truth, then it would have saved itself; if a fraud, then the sooner it was eaten the better."

So true did this saying appear that some of the Indians sided with Mahingan, for all recognized that it was he who had eaten the lamb, and there were not wanting those who began to murmur at Manahchinty for inducing them to worship false gods; and Manahchinty saw that strong measures were necessary in order to maintain his reputation of "Big Injun," so he tomahawked his rival on the sly, and the people at once returned to their allegiance, probably fearing lest they themselves should be tomahawked. Strange to say, after this Manahchinty became listless and depressed; some thought it was on account of the loss of his sacred lamb; but finally it leaked out that Mahingan, before dying, had found time to curse his murderer, to threaten him with his vengeance even though he were dead, and to promise him that he would pursue him and his heirs relentlessly for many generations. Strange to relate, Manahchinty soon joined his victim, having been upset from his canoe and drowned during a loon hunt. For several generations his descendants in the male line died violent deaths, and it was generally conceded among Indians that a curse was upon them.

One evening about six years ago, during the month of July, a small band of Indians were encamped upon the island whereon had lived and died the sacred sheep. The ever-encroaching white man had usurped the heritage of the Indians, who now had dwindled into a few families in place of the powerful tribe who had once held undisputed sway in the land. The curse of Mahingan had been almost forgotten, and that very evening as they sat around the camp fire an old crone with shaking head related to the younger folk in substance that which I have above written. Amongst them stood a boy intently listening with more than

19

an ordinary interest. He was a direct descendant of Manahchinty. Scarcely had she finished when a fiendish howl was heard in the bush close by.

The Indians started to their feet in fright and still another cry awoke the echoes of the summer night; at the same time an enormous dog, with eyes like balls of fire, bounded into the midst of them and, seizing the boy, the descendant of Manahchinty, by the throat, bore him to the ground. Luckily one man at least preserved his presence of mind. He snatched his rifle from his tent and with good aim sent a bullet crashing through the skull of the weird beast. It was all over in a moment and the boy rose up unhurt, except for the wound in his throat where the dog had seized him.

That night the Indians did not sleep, but sat discussing the event until daylight, when one of them took the carcass of the dog and threw it to the pigs of a white man who lived close by. The pigs made short work of the dog and soon had it all devoured except the heart, which they left untouched; and there it lay in the hot summer sun for two consecutive days, until, impelled by curiosity, one of the Indians examined it to find out why the pigs would not eat it. It seemed to be as hard as stone, and, impelled still further by curiosity, he took his ax and cut it in two. What was his astonishment at finding it nothing but a solid lump of ice. The discovery spread like wildfire and caused a great sensation among Indian circles.

The shaky-headed crone at once pronounced it to be Mahingan, and assured the Indians that the vendetta was ended by the death of the dog, or, rather, the second death of Mahingan. Whether she was right or wrong, the boy still lives, nor has he experienced any great and especial ill luck. So let us hope that Mahingan's curse is a thing of the past, a mystery snuffed out by a "Winchester" with the latest modern improvements.

These things are hard to believe. I myself doubted if they were true, and expressed those doubts to my informant, a most respectable and pious Indian, as Indians go. I even dared to laugh, but he assured me of their truth, and rebuked me for laughing, saying, "It is not right to laugh at such solemn, sacred things."

BLACKFOOT MAGIC

"Magic of the Blackfeet" appeared in the *Times-Herald* (Moose Jaw, Saskatchewan), on April 30, 1897. Sir Cecil Edward Denny (1850–1928), its author, recounted these and similar experiences in articles and chapters of his colourful 1905 memoir titled *Riders of the Plains: A Reminiscence of the Early and Exciting Days in the North West*. True to his Irish background, he could tell a good tale.

MAGIC OF THE BLACKFEET
Wonderful Feats of Jugglers among the Indians;
A Medicine Man's Dance in a Red-Hot Kettle;
A Lodge Shaken and a Bound Man Released by an Unknown Agency;
Pet Rattlesnakes of Medicine Men

"In the days long previous to the advent of the white men into the Northwest Territories of Canada and into the Western territories of the United States," says Capt. C.E. Denny, who went out to the Northwest with the Mounted Police in the early seventies, and since then has been Indian agent and has held other offices under the Canadian Government, "the Indians used to practise their medicine ceremonies, and many of their medicine men were adepts in the use of roots and herbs, and were looked upon as having intercourse with spirits, and accordingly greatly feared by the tribes among whom they practised their rites.

"On my arrival in the Northwest Territories, with the Northwest Mounted Police in 1874, I was curious to find out how far these medicine men carried their arts, and also what these arts consisted of. I heard from Indians many tales of wonders done by them, but it was a long time before I got a chance to be present at one of these ceremonies. The Indians were reluctant to allow a white man to view any of their medicine ceremonies. As I got better acquainted with the several tribes, particularly the Blackfeet, I had many chances to find out the truth regarding what I had heard of them, and I was truly astonished at what I saw at different times. Many of the medicine feats done by their medicine men before me did not allow of any jugglery, the man being naked, with the exception of a cloth around his loins, and I sitting within a few feet of him.

21

"All Indians believed in their familiar spirit, which assumed all kinds of shapes, sometimes that of an owl, a buffalo, a beaver, a fox, or any other animal. This spirit it was that gave them the power to perform the wonders done by them, and was firmly believed in by them all. On one occasion I visited a lodge where a medicine smoke was in progress. There were about a dozen Indians in the lodge. After the smoke was over a large copper kettle, about two feet deep and the same or a little more in diameter, was placed empty on the roaring fire in the middle of the lodge. The medicine man, who was stripped, with the exception of a cloth around his loins, was all this time singing a medicine song in a low voice.

"The pot after a short while became red-hot, and a pole being passed through the handle, it was lifted in this state off the fire and placed on the ground so close to me that the heat was almost unbearable. On the pole being withdrawn, the medicine man sprang to his feet and, still singing his song, stepped with both naked feet into the red-hot kettle and danced for at least three minutes in it, still singing to the accompaniment of the Indian drums. I was so close, as I have before said, that the heat of the kettle was almost unbearable, and I closely watched the performance, and saw this Indian dance for some minutes with his bare feet in it. On stepping out, he seemed none the worse; but how he performed the act was and is still a mystery to me.

"On another occasion I was sitting in an Indian tent alone with one of the medicine men of the Blackfeet Indians. It was at night and all was quiet in the camp. The night was calm, with a bright moon shining. On a sudden the Indian commenced to sing, and presently the lodge, which was a large one, commenced to tremble, and the trembling increased to such a degree that it rocked violently, even lifting off the ground first on one side and then on the other, as if a dozen pair of hands were heaving it on the outside. This lasted for about two minutes, when I ran out expecting to find some Indians on the outside who had played me a trick, but, to my astonishment, not a soul was in sight, and what still more bewildered me was to find on examination that the lodge was firmly pegged down to the ground, it being impossible for any number of men to have moved and replaced the pegs in so short a time. I did not enter the lodge again that night as the matter looked, to say the least, uncanny.

"I have seen the loosening of a man, when strongly bound with ropes, as done by some of our own jugglers, but with different variations. In one case, in the centre of a large lodge a smaller one was pitched, the small lodge being just large enough to hold one man sitting down. All over the ground covered by this small tent, and about six inches or even less apart, dozens of wooden pegs were driven into the ground. They were about six inches high and all sharply pointed. A small bell was also bound to one of the poles at the top of the lodge. The medicine man was tightly bound with rawhide ropes, and was then carried by two Indians to the door of the small tent, which was all this while wide open, and was thrown all doubled up, into the centre of it, and of course on to the sharp-pointed pegs. The blanket was quickly drawn over the door, and for about five minutes no sound was to be heard inside the tent, when, of a sudden, the little bell at the top of the tent commenced to ring, as it seemed without human agency. The blanket was thrown back and the medicine man stepped out freed from the ropes and without a scratch. I looked into the tent and found the ropes lying among the pegs, not one of which seemed to have been moved.

"I will give you one instance that came under my own observation, among many curious things performed by Indian medicine men. I had long heard of a Blackfeet Indian who, it was claimed, had a living rattlesnake in his stomach, which he could cause to appear when he wished, out of his mouth. He was considered by the Blackfeet as very strong medicine. It was a long time before I had a chance to see him, but one morning he turned up at my office with a party of Blackfeet, I being Indian agent at the time. On my promising him some tea and tobacco, he agreed to produce the snake, which he said lived in his stomach. After rubbing the pit of his stomach with his hand for a few minutes he opened his mouth. And I was startled considerably by seeing the flat head and about two inches of the neck of a good-sized rattlesnake appear. I was so close that I saw there was no deception in it. The forked tongue shot back and forth rapidly and of its liveliness there could be no doubt. After allowing me a short view, the Indian placed his hand before his mouth, and stroking his throat with the other hand, he again opened his mouth, and there was no snake visible.

"As a general rule the Blackfeet Indians are afraid of snakes and cannot be induced to touch or handle them, but one notable exception

23

I know is that of a Blood Indian named Calf Shirt, who is still living. The man carries about with him next the skin generally two and sometimes three full-sized rattlesnakes. This is during the summer, while in winter I have seen the snakes in a hole in the floor of his house in a partly torpid state. He will go down to a spot on the Belly River in the spring and capture the number of snakes he requires. This place is near old Fort Whoop Up and abounds with rattlesnakes. He has informed me that he boils the roots of a plant and washes his body with the water, and that the snakes will then allow him to catch and handle them. He has often been bitten, but he says that by drinking tea made with some herb and placing some of the masticated root over the bite he suffers no bad effects. The fangs of the snakes he carries are not extracted, and he will bet a horse with anyone who doubts that this is so, and allow any of the snakes to bite a dog, when the truth is soon seen by the death of the animal in a short time. This I have seen on several occasions.

"I have given these few instances of, to say the least, curious things done by Indian medicine men, and do not pretend to give any explanation of them; but I know that some of them are fully as wonderful and also unaccountable as anything ever done by the jugglers of India. I doubt if among the Blackfeet today, with the exception of Calf Shirt, the Blood, that tribe being a brand of the Blackfeet, anything of the kind I have mentioned is to be met with, as since the advent of the white man and the settling of the Indians on reservations all the old-time medicine men are dead, and the secret of these rites has died with them."

THE FIGURE OF A WITCH

"The Figure of a Witch" made its first appearance in the *Ottawa Journal* on August 31, 1898. It describes the outline of a rocky formation located in Rockcliffe Park, now Ottawa's exclusive residential district. Is it still there? There seem to be no contemporary references to it. No doubt it has "gone the way of the wind."

THE FIGURE OF A WITCH
Is Outlined on a Huge Rock at Rockliffe
The Figure Is Astride a Broomstick
and the Rock Is Known as the "Witches' Stone"

Ottawa has a "witches' stone" as well as a "Devil's seat."

It is one of the least known though greatest natural curiosities of this vicinity and is to be found in Rockcliffe Park. It is a figure, indelibly grained in the solid rock, of a gaunt haggard witch astride a broomstick, flying through the air, with a tangled mass of hair flowing behind her. The figure is ten feet high and is a vivid and striking likeness of a woman. It is on an immense boulder and the strange part of it is that while the boulder is of a dark brown color the figure and broomstick are of a light and marble-like substance.

This curiosity is situated within a hundred yards of the electric car track. The immense boulder through which the figure is grained, is near the edge of Pine Hill and just a few feet north of Cedar gate. For years it has been known as "the Witches' stone."

The woman is sitting astride the broomstick. One arm comes down before her and clasps the stick firmly. The other is by her side. The outline of her limbs may be plainly seen. Her body is thin and gaunt.

Her hair is formed by long tendrils of moss that have grown on the rock. The figure is blown and tattered as if it were flying through the air. Although the figure is striking and uncanny it is well deserving of the name "Witches' stone." This stone was far better known forty years ago than it is now. Trees have grown up around it and partially hidden it. In the past the mill men used to come down and shoot at the witch, using the figure as a target. That was before the days of park commissioners and park rangers.

Many interesting legends have been gathered about this strange freak of nature. The habitants along the shores of the Ottawa know it well and always speak of it with a certain amount of awe. No habitant, however brave, is said, will cross that field at night.

One of the most interesting legends that the old river men tell about the stone is the tale of how the figure came. An Indian chief of the Uttawa tribe was betrothed to a beautiful Indian maiden. Before their marriage she was bewitched and forever disappeared. Her disappearance was attributed to witchery and the medicine woman of the tribe was accused. She was bound to the same rock and burned at its base, and when the fire died down no trace of the woman was to be found; but graven in the solid rock was seen for the first time this strange figure.

Another legend tells of how the tribe used to sacrifice its victims at the foot of this stone because of the strange figure in it.

However this may be, the stone is a natural curiosity and should be better known and oftener visited than it is.

A PROFESSIONAL WIZARD

In the rural areas of Ontario and Quebec in the nineteenth century, there were to be found numerous witches and warlocks, clairvoyants and psychics, sorcerers and wizards — or at least eccentric old women and bearded men who, others said, were conversant with the so-called "black arts."

Here is the wizard Bisonette, of whom history records little more than what is recorded in this feature story and in others like it from the newspaper columns of the day. "A Canadian Wizard" appeared in the *Ponoka Herald* on January 17, 1902 (Ponoka is located between Red Deer and Edmonton, in what was yet to become the province of Alberta). Accounts like these preserved some of the lore — and recipes — that permit the casting of spells.

A CANADIAN WIZARD
Some Tales of the Dead Bisonette of Sicotte, Quebec
An Escapade of His College Days Drove Him to the Backwoods;
Credulity of Settlers Drove Him to Practice Witchcraft;
A Rival Witch — What He Did with His Large Earnings

Bisonette of Sicotte township is dead. As a professional wizard he had a large and widespread clientele, composed chiefly of the unlearned and ignorant, but comprising also some of the higher social rank. In the days before the railway, to reach his little mica-covered house in the woods, many people took the laborious drive of eighty-five miles from Ottawa. And the post-offices within a radius of thirty miles, delivered to Bisonette much mail matter, some dainty missives, and many a registered letter.

Many of the inquiries he received were concerned with matters of health. To such inquiries Bisonette was not an altogether bad adviser. He was a medical student in Montreal in his young days, but an escapade drove him from college to the backwoods. Some surprising cures of men and beast when out of pure kindness he helped his neighbors in the time before doctors settled in the locality, and the credulity of the settlers led him on to practicing witchcraft, in which he finally came himself to believe.

Much of his correspondence and most of his local business had to do with charms. These in the shape of meaningless incantations, sprigs of herbs, dried insects, bits of dried skins, ambiguous texts of Scripture, and sentences borrowed from books upon the Black Art, of which he had a curious collection, were sold to all who wanted them. His prices were always nicely graded to the customers.

Some forty miles lower down the river lived a rival of Bisonette's, a Mrs. Benham. This woman was popularly supposed to have more power on water than Bisonette, who excelled upon dry land. One day some log drivers came to her house and partook of such food as she had, but went away without paying for it. Jut as their boat pushed out into the swift current the sorceress demanded her money, when the men jeered and flatly declined to pay. The next moment their boat stopped, and, in spite of their rowing, remained stationary until they humbly besought the powerful lady to allow them to return to shore and settle their bill. At least so the story runs.

Mrs. Benham died of pneumonia one night twelve or fourteen years ago. That same night Bisonette was in attendance upon a sick horse. He knocked his head against its forehead, and then told those present to leave the stable, as he felt he was about to have a bad struggle with a rival witch, who was at work upon the suffering brute.

As the men left they declared that they saw a black cat enter the stable, and the candle in the lantern was burning low and with a blue flame. They heard the sound of a conflict between a dog and a cat, from the house, where they remained until the witch came in, his face scratched and bleeding, and exclaiming that the horse was saved at last, but Mother Benham was so badly hurt that she could not live till morning.

The doctor explained that the woman had died quite naturally from lung trouble in his presence.

A man, driving to desperation by rheumatism, made a laborious visit to Bisonette. The advice showed the wizard's acquaintance with negro voudouism. The patient was to take a two-inch augur and a two-inch plug four inches long and go at midnight into a certain bush there by moonlight to hunt up a brown ash tree. He was to bore six inches deep into this and within the hole place a lock of his hair and then breathe hard into it thirteen times. Then as quickly as possible he was to drive in the plug and let no one know where the tree was situated. The visitor received no palpable benefit, but was assured that the disease would never reach his heart unless that plug was withdrawn.

Philters are still used by the love-lorn in that region. Many a mother believes that her lad was inveigled into marriage by a love dose secretly administered, and many a young lover slyly slips the potent drops into the sought-after one's cup. One philter which a maiden bewailing the death of her lover acknowledged having administered was rather surprising. A tree toad, a black smoke, a horned pout, a bat, thirteen hairs from a black cat's tail, and a lock of the damsel's hair were put into a covered oven, and baked to a black crisp in the sand. The ashes were rubbed fine and divided into twelve parts, of which seven were left in a church, four were put in a bag and worn over the heart, and one was to be surreptitiously administered to the victim.

What became of all the money Bisonette made the local folk could not imagine. There are only three who know that all he could spare from a bare existence went by way of expiation for a crime committed against a too-confiding friend in the old days, when he was the innocent of any coquetting with the black art.

CALLING UPON A WITCH

Witches are the present-day practitioners of what was once known as the Old Religion, the pagan rites that predated the "fixed" religions that include Judaism,

Christianity and Islam. Robin Skelton, the distinguished man of letters who lived for many years in Victoria, British Columbia, identified himself as a witch. He practised the rites of wicca, and in 1988 he wrote about such practices in a modest, and even matter-of-fact, way in the last chapter of *The Memoirs of a Literary Blockhead*. He called wicca his calling — or cast of mind. In this excerpt from that volume, he tells of a cure for the lifting of a woman's curse.

Sometimes one comes across people who have been cursed. One middle-aged woman was sent to me for help by her hairdresser. She had been married several times, and her last husband had died from the consequences of alcoholism. She sat on the edge of the sofa and accepted a small glass of wine as if she thought it would bite her. She told me she hated living alone and, therefore, took rooms in people's houses, where she would share the kitchen and feel, at least a little, part of the household. Everything always went well for the first ten days and the family "turned again" her, and she became unhappy and had to move on. This kept happening. She was now so nervous she could not even contemplate getting a job and working with people. She knew they would "turn against" her too. It sounded like paranoia, but I probed a little further and discovered that her husband, shortly before his death, had given her a ring with the jovial words "I'm putting my brand on you, my girl." She always wore the ring.

I said, "Let me have it," and as I held it I could feel the energy field of the thing. It was like holding a hot coal. I said, "May I keep this for a week?" and she said I could. I cleansed the ring of the energy field and she came back a week later to get it back. This time she sat on the sofa in a relaxed manner, accepted two full glasses of wine, chatted easily, and spoke of getting an apartment for herself and maybe taking a few courses and visiting her family in Alberta. I told her that I would vet any apartment she found, as she was clearly sensitive to psychic influences, but she never came back to me, though I did make inquiries and her hairdresser told me she was doing fine. I am sure that her husband had not really intended to curse her; he had done so unwittingly. Ever since then, whenever I get a new ring myself — and I collect rings and wear one on every finger (another result of collector's disease) — I feel them out more carefully in case I am picking up something with an energy field I do not want or need.

Most people who call on the witch do so because they are at the end of their tether and know nowhere else to go. Many of them do not believe in witchcraft or magic of any kind, but can see no harm in trying this last resort.

2 Earthly Powers

IT IS FREQUENTLY forgotten that Earth itself is an immense magnet and a source of power and energy. Tiny piezoelectric effects are everyday occurrences. Nuclear fission has been known to occur naturally under extreme circumstances, wherever naturally produced radioactive substances are subjected to intense pressures. Nature has many moods, and these are reflected in violent weather conditions. In addition, psychics, mediums and people who regard themselves as sensitive to such forces and pressures talk about subtle "earth energies" that travel the Earth's "ley lines," which seem to resemble acupuncture's meridians.

The planet is not a static and inert mechanism, but a psychically or spiritually living organism. The stories in this chapter dramatize some of the powers believed to lie latent in the Earth.

AN UNUSUAL APPEARANCE

Here is a surprisingly detailed account of an atmospheric event that was observed to take place in 1837. I have this previously unpublished account through the courtesy of Allan McGillivray, curator of the Uxbridge-Scott Museum in Uxbridge, Ontario. The description is presumably that of an eclipse of the sun. The name of the observer has not been recorded, but the account has survived. In 1990, Ruth Millar of Toronto prepared a typescript from the original handwritten manuscript. Here is her description of the original manuscript:

> This paper was folded lengthwise and then crosswise, and in the lower right-hand section written thus: ★ Phenomenon / of 25 of 1st Month / 1837 / Uxbridge.
> Note: This article had been saved over the years by a cousin, and his daughter loaned it to me about two or three years ago.

For its publication here, the spelling has been regularized, but the punctuation and sentence structure have been allowed to stand. I am also grateful to Miss Millar for sharing this unusual piece of early Canadiana.

Uxbridge, January 25th, 1837

On the evening of the 25th of January between the hour of 6 or 7 the whole horizon began to wear an unusual appearance: the wind was in the west, the sky all covered with clouds and the moon not having rose darkness seemed to be established in the Dominion when suddenly the clouds became filled with brightness the earth became so bright that one could scarcely have known that it was night. Many of the inhabitants ran out of their houses as with the alarm of fire being disappointed they could find no other cause for the illumination but what appeared in the firmament at which time the clouds seemed as though they were filled with majestic brightness and casting a red reflection on the snow so one might think that a great fire was shining on upon it. This remarkable appearance of things continued about half an hour when the evening again resumed its usual appearance and remained so until half past 9 or perhaps a little more when the sky became unveiled from clouds instantaneously the moon was then risen about a ½ an hour a sudden redness shone in the windows and going immediately out we beheld the sky bearing an unusual appearance being covered with broad red streaks uniformly set in the horizon and as red as blood the appearance of which is hard to describe or to give the minds of these that did not see it a correct idea of it the whole Phenomena was still in the firmament and all drawing at one centre which was like the crown in the midst about where the sun would be its full meridian in summer time and all the streaks or rays centered around it and spread widely as they advanced until they covered the whole atmosphere from the rising of the moon south wards and westward as far as N W but in the east south east and south the colour was red as blood itself and to the W ward it was more regularly spread and the streaks not so distinct nor the colour so extra red but the crown to which all centred was no redness neither was there any unusual appearance but looked like a thin white cloud through which the stars could be perfectly seen neither was the blood any obstruction to the stars for they shone through it as bright as though it had not been there and in the north about ¼ of the horizon there was no red in it although it was less remarkable for there was a bright streak in the sky from the moon to the N as far as N W was a clear white, nearly as bright as the moon and this ray about as high in the firmament as the sun at an hour high and all below the edge of that was as dark as night and upwards from it there ran beams of light forward the centre but did not reach as high as the red neither did it mix in any way with the red but lay entirely still casting a bright reflection on the earth from the one side and from the other a redness like blood it continued for about half an hour during which time I see no variation save a regular recession of the colour until it was all gone and the sky became natural again.

RARE SENSATIONS

Random loud noises are characteristic of life in large cities, so much so that few people try to seek out their origin. But in the nineteenth century, in the towns and countryside of Canada West (today's Ontario), random loud sounds were heard less frequently; when they occurred, they were reported to local newspapermen, who wrote up short accounts of them. When they were heard, people talked about them and offered expected — and unexpected — explanations for the disturbances.

Weird noises and sounds were heard in Paris and London, Canada West, on New Year's Day, 1864. This account "Curious Phenomenon at Paris" appeared in the *Montreal Witness* on February 6 of that year.

CURIOUS PHENOMENON AT PARIS

To the Editor of the *Daily Witness*

Dear Sir,— For the interests of science, I furnish a brief notice of the rare sensations experienced by my whole family on Friday night, the 1st of the New Year. Between 9 and 10 o'clock, as my attention was diverted from an engrossing article that I was perusing, by a strange rumbling and slightly jarring vibration, which I then supposed to be caused by a heavily loaded barrow, trundled past the window on the plank walk. But on second thought that could not have been the cause, as the planks were thickly coated with ice, and the wheel on so cold a night, must have made a creaking noise, which was entirely wanting, as also any sound of foot-steps passing by.

In about an hour and a quarter after, my young folks, who had retired for the night, simultaneously called out, "What can that be?" My wife, who was up-stairs, called to me, enquiring whether I heard that strange noise. It had not made so distinct an impression on me as on them. They described it as like a very heavy log being rolled over and over, with repeated violent thumps upon the outer kitchen floor. I endeavoured to account for it as the effect of the severe frost on the roof. After a brief interval, the same violent jarrings and rumblings were repeated; but all agreed that the sound seemed to proceed from above, and I was entreated to examine the roof, and the space between it and the upper ceilings, to assure the family that the roof was not being torn away. These last sounds occurred about 20 minutes after 11.

When the report reached us of similar phenomena observed at London, C.W., I reflected more carefully on the sensations of that night, and am brought to the conclusion that they could not be explained by any ordinary superficial vibrations, and that there was no resemblance to the sharp reports occasioned by severe frost. If the cause was subterranean, doubtless others must have felt the same; and I report thus fully, with the hope that others may be led to identify the strange sensations, and furnish ampler data for scientific conclusions.

Yours very truly,
Edward Erbs
Paris, C.W., Jan. 7, 1864

P.S.— The most violent shock experienced at London, was about 2 a.m.

ON A FALL OF COLOURED HAIL AND SNOW

Everyone knows that snow is white in colour. Indeed, "as white as snow" is an idiomatic expression. But not every snowfall is white — or "as pure as the driven snow," to use another popular expression. Sometimes it is discoloured, dark black in appearance. Such an occurrence was noted in southwestern Ontario in 1868 by "Dr. A.T. MacHattie, F.C.S., &c., Lecturer in Chemistry, Glasgow." His detailed account of the phenomenon, "On the Fall of Coloured Hail and Snow in Western Canada," was published in *Chemical News*, May 4, 1877.

During my residence in Canada, nine years ago, a fall of hail and snow of peculiar character occurred, and the facts seem to me worthy of being recorded.

At London, in the province of Ontario, the fall began between 8 and 9 p.m., on February 24th, 1868, and was accompanied by a violent storm of lightning and thunder, and a strong gale from the south-east. At Sarnia, in the same province, on almost the same line of latitude and more than 50 miles distant from London, similar phenomena were observed, the fall of hail and snow did not begin till about 7 a.m., on the 25th of February. The observations in London were made by me personally; in Sarnia, by a friend.

In some places the dark-coloured shower seemed to consist of snow; in others, of hail; and my Sarnia correspondent described it as being more like "frozen rain" than either of the above.

One square yard of the dark hail or snow, when melted, deposited rather more than 5 grains of a dark grey (almost black) powder. This amount is equivalent to almost exactly 1 ton per square mile. I could not learn with certainty over what extent of district the shower fell, as a sudden thaw very soon removed all traces of its presence. Considering, however, that it was observed at two places 50 miles distant from one another, and at one of them (Sarnia) it was known to extend over 10 miles broad is not a very excessive estimate of the district covered; but of course it may have been much less or much greater, and the dark matter may not have been present in uniform quantity — most probably not. The above estimate would give no less than five hundred tons of the dark matter, and, at any rate, there is little doubt that the quantity was large considering the source.

35

On examination under the microscope I found the dark substance to consist mainly of vegetable matter far advanced in decomposition. This result has since been corroborated by Dr. James Adams, of Glasgow, who further expressed the opinion that the vegetable matter consists principally of the remains of cereals.

From the circumstance that the surface of the ground and all shallow waters in Canada were frozen for months before the shower fell, it would appear that the dark matter could hardly have come from any local source. It is more likely that it came from some distant southern district of America, where the ground was neither frozen nor covered with snow: this, however, is mere conjecture.

It will be observed, from the above remarks, that the dark matter referred to in no way resembles the siliceous-shelled microscopic organisms which have been so often observed to fall on the Atlantic Ocean and elsewhere. It is this unusual character, as well as the quantity of the above dark shower, that induces me to draw attention to it. There was no difficulty in obtaining it pure, because the shower was deposited in three distinct strata:— (1.) Pure snow. (2.) The layer containing the dark substance. And (3.) A layer of pure snow when the violence of the storm had abated.

A SUDDEN LOUD REPORT

Here is another account of a peculiar sound. Too bad it is so brief.

"A Sudden Loud Report" was contributed by an unidentified correspondent and appeared as "A Curious Phenomenon" in *Scientific American* (July 10, 1880). It is reproduced from the *Handbook of Unusual Natural Phenomena*, compiled in 1978 by William R. Corliss and published by The Sourcebook Project.

Based in Glen Arm, Maryland, The Sourcebook Project is an excellent series of books devoted to collecting, annotating and reprinting descriptions of anomalies that appeared in popular and specialist publications of the past.

The *Plaindealer*, of East Kent, Ontario, states that a curious and inexplicable phenomenon was witnessed recently by Mr. David Muckle and Mr. W.R.

McKay, two citizens of that town. The gentlemen were in a field on a farm of the former, when they heard a sudden loud report, like that of a cannon. They turned just in time to see a cloud of stones flying upward from a spot in the field. Surprised beyond measure they examined the spot, which was circular and about 16 feet across, but there was no sign of an eruption nor anything to indicate the fall of a heavy body there. The ground was simply swept clean. They were quite certain that it was not caused by a meteorite, an eruption of the earth, or a whirlwind.

DAYLIGHT DARKNESS

A phenomenon called "daylight darkness" settled over the town of Goderich, Ontario, a port on Lake Huron's eastern shore, on September 5, 1881. Such departures from the norm are exciting and frightening; they have natural causes, but not everyone automatically thinks in terms of cause and effect. This instance of darkness during the day is well described in the following account. It even refers in passing to the English prophetess Mother Shipton. "Thick Darkness" appeared in the *Winnipeg Daily Times* on September 15, 1881.

THICK DARKNESS
The Strange Occurrence of the 5th Inst.

SPECIAL CORRESPONDENT OF THE *LONDON FREE PRESS*

Goderich, Sept. 6.— Yesterday will be long remembered in Goderich. It was, in fact, the most remarkable day in its history. For several days past the atmosphere has been full of smoke, presumably from bush fires, although there have been no very large ones in the immediate vicinity; and the thermometer has mounted up among the nineties — something rather unusual in this cool lake town. Rain has been wonderfully scarce all summer, and of late the ground has become completely parched. There is no such thing as grass to be seen; pasture fields are dry and almost as dirty as the road bed. For a week or more —

"All is hot and copper sky,
The bloody sun at noon
Right above the earth did stand,
No bigger than the moon."

But yesterday afternoon it disappeared altogether, as effectually as though it had dropped out of the heavens. About noon clouds were observed gathering in the west and south. At one o'clock those who lunched at that hour found no little difficulty in distinguishing articles on the table; and shortly thereafter lamps had to be brought into requisition. From this out the gloom thickened; at two it was with great difficulty one could read large print out of doors. Three gave every appearance of midnight, and half an hour thereafter the entire town and surrounding country was veiled in inky gloom. "No sun, no moon, no stars, no noon; no proper time of day." The blackness of midnight reigned supreme. The hand held before the eyes within three inches of the face could not be seen.

To lend awe and sublimity to the scene the intense blackness was ever and anon lit up by blinding flashes of lightning; and the reverberating thunder alone broke the painful stillness. In short, the scene was one never to be forgotten by those who saw it. The weak and the ignorant were of course terrified, and thought that at last of a certainty Mother Shipton's prophecy was about to be fulfilled to the letter. And others who would be insulted, and with reason, at being termed either ignorant or weak, were beginning to ask themselves and each other what it all meant. Little groups gathered here and there about the square and watched in wonder and awe for a termination of the phenomenon, but it was a long time ere the darkness was sufficiently dissipated to see to move about outside the range of street lamps and shop windows.

At last the darkness in the east gave place to a red gleam, as though from a huge fire, and the reflection from this somewhat relieved the gloom and enabled people to see as well as upon an ordinary moonless night — but no better. And there it remained through the remainder of the afternoon and night, and not till the following morning when Old Sol put in an appearance as usual and in his usual place were apprehensions entirely removed and the alarmed ones really convinced that all was, indeed, well.

During the continuance of the darkness a small quantity of rain fell, but it was so combined with ashes, cinder and dirt that to expose one's self to it for a few minutes was to have the face and hands blackened. The next morning the whole country side was covered with a coating of dirt and filth — so much so that it was impossible to come in contact with a fence, tree, or, in fact, any exposed surface, without becoming soiled. The phenomenon is now of the past, but it is not forgotten, and is not likely to be for many a long year. And it is quite safe to say that every time the 5th of September rolls around the thought of the inhabitants of Goderich will revert back to the year eighty-one.

Lake captains say the entire shores of Superior and Huron are in a blaze. The smoke from these and other fires are no doubt brought together by the wind, and floated over in dense masses, hemming us in on every side, and as completely shutting out the sunlight as though Old Sol had dropped entirely out of the sky. This is the first time night has ever set in here shortly after noon, and lasted until next morning. May it be the last.

A MARVELLOUS MIRAGE

A mirage must be one of nature's major wonders. Not only is a mirage often breathtakingly beautiful, but it comes and goes unexpectedly. It is an ephemeral illusion, a work of art. A mirage of Niagara Falls appeared in the clouds to residents of Tonawanda, New York, and the lovely sight was recorded in "A Marvellous Mirage," in The Suspension Bridge Journal of Saturday, May 14, 1881. The account was discovered by researcher Dwight Whalen, who discussed its appearance in an article that he contributed to The Buffalo Evening News Magazine's December 5, 1982, edition. There he wrote, "It is an appreciative audience and a beautiful vision. Nature once again had fooled the eye and quickened the heart in a show that has no schedule and no repeat performances."

A strange and rare sight was seen Sunday afternoon about three o'clock by a number of persons in this village, it being no less than a beautiful mirage of Niagara Falls in the clouds just above the horizon. The reflection seemed to lie directly on the bank of fleecy clouds and was almost perfect in its details. The Suspension Bridge could be plainly seen as well as the Falls, Goat Island and some of the surrounding buildings. The wonderful spectacle, which appeared similar to a photograph on glass on an immense scale, lasted nearly if not quite half an hour, finally dissolving slowly until it had entirely disappeared.

AN EXTRAORDINARY SKY

Rare and spectacular effects in the sky have the effect of evoking fear and awe in the human race. Meteorologists may offer the last word on atmospheric phenomena, but the first word is that of members of the general public, as represented by newspaper reporters. "An Extraordinary Sky" and "The City in Darkness" appeared in adjoining columns in The (Toronto) Globe on September 6, 1881.

Instances of "midday darkness" are rare, but they are always notable and memorable. This instance occurred in Toronto the day before, on Monday, September 5. Mother Shipton, a seventeenth-century English prophetess, was something of a folk figure. Her predictions recall the Greek prophetess Cassandra, whose dire prophecies were destined never to be believed. The meaning of the words "Grimmer's terrible predictions" has been lost in the mists of time, though this might well be a reference to the prognostications of an American almanac-maker.

AN EXTRAORDINARY SKY
An Orange Dome of Rare Splendour Covers the City
The Phenomenon Lasts for Hours—
The Whole Population in the Streets—
Fears of Many that the End of the World Was Come

The one topic of conversation all over the city yesterday afternoon and evening was the wonderful appearance of the sky. Early in the forenoon the mercury had risen above 90° in the shade, and although the sky became clouded the heat was maintained long after darkness had commenced, the mercury in the city at midnight still being as high as 80°.

At half-past three in the afternoon the whole northern Heavens assumed a rich orange hue, and the rest of the sky a yellow. The orange deepened and extended as the day advanced, till at five o'clock the heavens presented the appearance of an orange dome of extraordinary beauty. The streets and buildings wore an orange tint: in fact, nearly everything looked as though viewed through an orange glass. The gas was not lit, and instead of its usual yellow, burned a brilliant white — almost as white as the electric light.

As sunset approached the orange hue deepened on city and sky alike, and the streets were filled with an interested population gazing at the strange, weird glory of the scene, and indulging in all sorts of speculations — some of them terrifying — as to the cause of the unwonted spectacle. Bush fires were held responsible by some. Others said it was a solar eclipse. Orangemen jocularly claimed it as an Orange display a little late in the season, and thousands took a more serious view, and predictions of Mother Shipton's prophecy that

> "The world to an end shall come
> In eighteen hundred and eighty-one,"

mingled strangely with Grimmer's terrible predictions, and produced a dread in the breasts of thousands that the end of the world has come.

Of course many knew that the phenomenon was simply due to the interception of the orange rays of old Sol, but between the anxious fears that the spread of bush fires throughout the Province was about to culminate in a whirlwind of flame which might destroy the city, and dread that the last trump was about to sound, a feeling of tremulousness prevailed, and the like of which has not been known in Toronto for very many years. As a matter of fact there was weeping and wailing in some homes, so great was the fear of disaster produced.

With the lightness of the sky, which was lit up as with one uniform conflagration reflected through dense clouds, was a degree of darkness which compelled the lighting of gas lamps all over the city long before the sun went down. Within half an hour after sunset the last trace of orange or red had disappeared, and the usual darkness of a cloudy, moonless night had set in.

The question most commonly asked on the street last night, as citizens and visitors groped around in the darkness, was "Where are the lights?" and many denunciations were uttered against the authorities who were responsible for the want of light. Not alone to the belated traveller did it fall to be inconvenienced from the want of gaslight. From the peculiar state of the atmosphere the streets were in utter darkness at six o'clock, and not a single lighted gas lamp was to be seen. Throughout the whole evening this state of things continued, not even a lamp having been lighted at any of the principal corners till long past midnight, and the result was that only those who were forced to do so went out at all, and that at great inconvenience and hazard to themselves.

An enquiry into the matter elicited the fact that the police authorities applied to Mr. Ashfield, Chief of the Fire Department, to have the lamps lighted, and that Mr. Ashfield applied to [Alderman] Adamson, Chairman of the Fire and Gas Committee, without any result. The authorities are well aware that at the present time the city has received a large accession to its usual number of thieves and footpads, and such an opportunity as last night afforded them of pursuing their nefarious calling would not be likely to be lost by them. To think that our city should be left in Stygian darkness on the first night of the Industrial Exhibition, when of all times the public should have the convenience and protection of lighted street lamps, is a reflection on the powers who have so ordered, and leaves them virtually responsible for whatever mishaps it may have occasioned.

NATURE'S MIRROR

"Mirage on Lake Winnipeg" was published in the Halifax *Morning Herald* on March 13, 1886. The numerous typographical errors in this account have been corrected.

MIRAGE ON LAKE WINNIPEG

In a paper read before the Young People's association of Dominion church, Ottawa, G.O. Buchanan, of Truro, gave the following curious effect of a mirage on Lake Winnipeg: "The morning proved fair. At sunrise we were off the mouth of the Broken Head river. An uncertain haze hung over the water and while looking towards the Red River some miles distant an object attracted our attention. Its resemblance to anything natural was not very striking, but as it was not very large and moving swiftly I judged it to be a vessel of some kind, and as there was not wind enough to account for its speed, I assumed it to be a steamer. I pointed out to Alex (a half-breed), that she had two smoke stacks, but I had misgivings as to whether there were any steamboats with one pipe in the bow, and another in the stern. The form of the thing was not only remarkable, but it underwent rapid transformation. A section of the figure seemed to revolve and flashed and gleamed in the rays of the rising sun. I explained to Alex that she was a side-wheeler, but I knew pretty well there were no side-wheelers on the lake.

"The situation became momentarily more interesting. The thing was coming no nearer, but it grew rapidly larger and rose up out of the water like a huge bird preparing to fly. Alex pulled in his oars. He had known from the first what the thing was. 'Windigo Boy,' he said (a 'windigo' is an evil spirit), 'see the wings.' I had nothing effectual to oppose this theory, but it collapsed of inherent weakness, for the object shot across our wake 60 yards astern. A birch bark canoe, an Indian in the stern, a squaw in the bow, paddling solemnly ashore from a visit to their nets. The magnified and distorted appearance which we had seen was due to a mirage in the atmosphere. The wisdom of the white man and the Indian alike had been turned into foolishness by a trick of nature's mirror."

METEOR MENACE

This article appeared, without a source or byline (despite a reference to "the writer") in the *Regina Leader-Post* on June 18, 1889. Some of the references (like the scholarly name Erasmus) and wording (he "entered college" rather than university) suggest that this "strange story" might have originated in an American newspaper and was simply reprinted in the columns of the *Leader-Post*. The article appears to be a cautionary tale; yet if so, it is one that lacks any moral other than the implied injunction to heed one's dreams.

KILLED BY A METEOR

Intelligent persons have ceased to believe in dreams and visions. In fact, one might say that this moribund century has been the golden age for the doubting Thomases who have successfully attacked every thing that was dear to our grandmothers and calculated to make the hair of the timid stand on end. Witches have been relegated to dismal obscurity; ghosts have been compelled to seek pastures green in the Antipodes or in the delta of the Niger, and the scions of the worthy publishers of Egyptian dream books are subsisting on the interest of the dollars paid to their fathers in years gone by credulous old women and sillier old men. Yes, it is safe to say that even Ichabod Crane, were that worthy alive to-day, would not run away from the headless specter of the Mohawk Valley. Reason, we hear on every side, has triumphed over superstition, and cold materialism had taken possession of everything and everybody.

And yet, if we look around us, with eyes and ears wide open, we can see and hear things every day which reason prompts us to doubt, but which reason can not explain. Such an occurrence the writer is about to relate for the benefit of those who believe that the Bard of Avon spoke the truth when he said to his friend,

"There are more things in Heaven and earth, Horatio,
Than are dreamt of in your philosophy."

Erasmus Johnson, the hero of the strange story about to be related, was one of the brightest and most promising students of a western college whose professors and tutors were noted for their orthodoxy and opposition to spiritualism and materialistic doctrines. Erasmus was, moreover, a son of a Presbyterian elder and had received a home training which, while narrow and unprogressive, kept his mind in healthy condition. He entered college with a clear head and a determination to acquire as much knowledge as possible. His intellectual pursuits did, however, not interfere with physical recreation, and no student displayed more energy and abandon in a game of foot-ball or a rowing match than he. Combining with his mental and physical superiority a truly altruistic disposition, he soon became a favorite with everybody.

No party in the pretty little college town was considered a success unless Erasmus Johnson contributed his presence to the occasion, and every church society was anxious to have him take a part in the various entertainments given under its auspices. He sang for the Methodists, handled the Indian clubs for the Presbyterians, recited poems for the Congregationalists and read essays for the Unitarians whenever requested to do so. He took long walks with his pedantic instructor in botany; talked philosophy with the cranky individual who taught that science in the college, and discussed German and French poetry and prose with the long-haired Teuton who presided over the destinies of modern languages and literature. He pulled an oar with his associates, acted as pitcher for the college ball nine, and was the recognized hero of the gymnasium.

That such a man should have had any faith in supernatural visions is out of the question. And yet, two weeks before the day set for the commencement exercises, Erasmus Johnson, whose face had always been a mirror of smiles and joy, appeared before his class in an almost indescribable condition. His face looked haggard and worn, black rings had formed under his eyes, his form seemed to have lost all elasticity, his hand trembled incessantly. The excitement caused by this sight was intense. In a moment he was surrounded by seven or eight of his "chums," who labored under the impression that he suffered from a sudden attack of illness.

"What is the matter?" asked his friends in chorus.

"A dream!" responded Erasmus with a sad smile.

"A dream!" repeated the students, incredulous and inclined to take the matter as a joke.

"Yes, a dream," reiterated Johnson; "a terrible dream which I can not drive out of my head, although it is as silly as it can be."

"What is it?" came from many lips.

"I dreamed that I would be killed on my wedding day in a strange and peculiar manner," explained Johnson in a hesitating way, which clearly indicated that he felt ashamed of himself for having made the confession.

The reply called forth unbounded merriment, which lasted until the professors entered the lecture hall.

Poor Johnson was made the butt of everybody's ridicule and even the young lady to whom he was engaged to be married ventured to poke fun at her lover's dream.

45

Meanwhile the commencement exercises had taken place and Johnson had been awarded the class honors as well as a gold medal for a powerful and beautiful Latin poem. He was lionized by his class, the faculty and townspeople; but never did a young man receive applause with more reserve. Ambition and hope seemed to have a dwelling place in his heart no longer. They had been superseded by melancholy, by a hideous spectre born of a dream.

A few hours before his departure from the scenes of his intellectual triumphs, he called on his most intimate college friend, who did everything in his power to revive the energy of his unfortunate visitor; going even so far as to suggest to Johnson the advisability of breaking his engagement. To this the young man would not consent, because, despite his fears and misgivings, he could not persuade himself that he had good grounds for such an action which might, moreover, break the heart of the woman he loved.

"Whatever else I have lost," he said to his friend, "my honor remains unsullied, and I would not wreck Julia's happiness on account of an uncertain something at which the world and even you laugh. No, Jack, we will be married on the 5th of August, whatever may be the consequences."

The following morning Johnson was with his parents. It is superfluous to say that they did everything in their power to overcome their son's melancholy mood. He listened to them patiently and smiled sadly when he saw his good old mother in tears. He even went so far as to simulate a cheerfulness he did not feel. He listlessly supervised the preparations for his approaching nuptials, and, accompanied by a number of relatives and friends, left for the home of his affianced on the evening of the 4th of August. The party arrived at its destination the next morning.

Johnson had passed a restless night in the sleeper, and when he arrived at the house of his future parents-in-law, looked even more careworn and haggard than usual. His friend, Jack, who also stopped at the house, was shocked, and upon inquiring for the cause of his friend's ghastly appearance, learned that the hideous dream which had wrecked his happiness had again haunted him. By dint of will power he managed to suppress his anguish, however, and succeeded in appearing before the woman he was about to marry in a seemingly happy frame of mind. The couple chatted for awhile, discussed their prospects, and dwelled at some length upon the joys that seemed to be before them.

The wedding ceremony was to be performed at 7 o'clock in the evening at the Presbyterian Church of the little city. Shortly before the hour the bridal party arrived; a half hour later the newly-wedded couple received the congratulations of their friends. The groom, sad and dejected until he had entered the church, seemed like another man. His old smile once more illuminated his face, his eyes flashed happiness, his form was erect as in the days of old. One after the other of the assembly pressed his hand and was dismissed with a pleasant word. His friend Jack was once of the last to offer his good wishes. As he approached Johnson the latter whispered:

"Thank God, Jack, the danger is over. I am married and still alive."

A few minutes before 8 o'clock the bride and groom left the church. Johnson was gay and attentive, and replied wittily to the bon-mots hurled at him by the crowd. The couple reached the sidewalk. The bride was handed into the carriage, and the groom was about to follow her. At that moment he heard a whistling noise above him, and looking up to explain the strange phenomenon, was struck on the forehead by a missile of extraordinary power. He fell heavily on the carpet-covered walk, and when his friends ran to his rescue they found — a corpse. Erasmus Johnson had certainly met his end in a strange and peculiar way. A meteorite fully two inches in diameter had crushed his skull. His dream was fulfilled. Was the vision then a coincidence or a warning? Let every reader answer the question for him or herself.

A SUBTERRANEAN STORY

Here is a lively and haunting yarn.

"A Subterranean Story" appeared in the columns of the *Manitoba Daily Free Press* (Winnipeg) on April 22, 1890. It was written by one Charles Howard Sinn and was reprinted from the *Washington Critic*. It is a lost-race story with a Canadian locale. The style is such as to convey a semblance of verisimilitude. No doubt it delighted Manitoba readers at the time of its publication. The tale bears some resemblance to James de Mille's intriguing novel *A Strange Manuscript Found in a Copper*

Cylinder. De Mille's novel appeared in 1888, two years before "A Subterranean Story," so it is possible that Sinn had read De Mille's novel when it was published in *Harper's Monthly.* At any rate, his tale is no rival for drama or imagination.

As to the locale of the account, there are possible references here to the Columbia River and to Mount Assiniboine, the highest mountain in the Rocky Mountain chain, which is situated on the Continental Divide between the present-day Trans-Canada Highway and U.S. border.

A SUBTERRANEAN STORY

Last Summer the schooner *William Haley*, of Galveston, trading among the West Indies, was becalmed near the Gulf Stream. The second day the captain's curiosity was aroused by a strange floating mass, and he ordered the mate to take a boat and examine it. The mate returned towing a log, from which the men had cut away the marine growth which had made it seem at a distance like a sea monster. The captain ordered it to be hoisted to the deck, declaring that in forty years spent at sea he had never found anything like it.

When laid on the deck it was seen to be about twenty feet long and two feet in diameter. It was of some very hard, dark colored wood, like palm, charred in places, and worn and broken, cut and torn, as if it had been whirled through torrents and maelstroms for hundreds of years. The ends were pointed, and five bands of dark metal, like bronze, were sunk in the wood, and the whole bore evidence of having passed through intense heat. On closer examination the log was seen to consist of two parts, and these bands were to bind it together. The captain had the bands cut, and in the exact center, fitted into a cavity, was a round stone eighteen inches in diameter. The rest of the wood was solid.

The captain, more disappointed at this result than he cared to confess, picked up the stone and was greatly astonished at its lightness. Examining it more closely, he remembered that when a boy on the old New Hampshire farm he used to find hollow stones with crystals in them — geodes, as he afterwards heard them called. This was probably a geode, placed in this strange receptacle for some unknown purpose. He carried it to his cabin and put it into his chest.

Two months later the old captain returned to his cottage on Galveston bay and placed among his curiosities the geode he had so strangely found in the Gulf stream. One day he studied it again, and the sunlight chanced to fall upon a narrow, irregular line.

"I declare," said the old man, "it looks like as if this stone had been patched together!"

He struck it with a hammer and it fell apart and proved to be filled with small pieces of yellowish brown wood. The shell of the stone was about an inch thick, studded over inside with thousands of garnet crystals. It had been broken into three parts and fastened together again with some sort of cement which showed plainly on the inside.

The old captain poured the pieces of wood on the table. They were perfectly dry and hard. They seemed like strips of bamboo and were numbered and covered with writing, made by pricking marks with some sharp instrument like an awl. He found the first piece of wood and began to read, for it was in English. The work of deciphering the tiny dents on the bits of wood soon became the captain's chief occupation. He copied each sentence off in his old log book as fast as it was made out. Five or six sentences were about all his eyes would stand without a rest, so that it was a long time before the narrative was at all complete. The narrative runs as follows:

Hearts of the Rockies,
About Sept. 17, 1886.

I am an American, Timothy Parsons, of Machias, Me. I have no living relatives. I write this in a vast vaulted chamber, hewn from the solid granite by some prehistoric race. I have been for months a wanderer in these subterranean spaces, and now I have contrived a way to send my message out to the world that I shall probably never see again. If some miner, tunneling in the Rockies, comes upon a vaulted chamber, with heaps of ancient weapons of bronze, bars of gold and precious stones that no man may number, let him give Christian burial to the poor human bones that lie in this horrible treasure house. He will find all that is left of my mortal frame near the great ever burning lamp, under the dome of the central hall. That lamp is fed from some reservoir of natural gas. It was lighted when I came, months ago. For all I know otherwise, it has burned there for thousands of years.

The entrance to this sub-montane river is in the Assinnaboine mountains, north of the United States lines. I was a prospector there for several years, and I heard stories among the older Indians that a river greater than the Columbus had once flown where the Rocky mountains now are; that the Great Spirit had piled the mountains over it and buried it deep underground. At last a medicine man, whose life I had once saved, told me that he knew how to get to the river, and he took me into a cavern in a deep gorge. Here we lived for a week, exploring by means of pine torches, and at last found a passage which ran steadily downward. This, the Indian told me, was the path by which his ancestors, who once lived in the middle of the earth, had found their way to the light of day.

I think we were about three thousand feet below the entrance of the cave, when we began to hear the sound of roaring waters. The sound increased until we stood by an underground river, of whose width and depth we could form no ideas. The light of our torches did not even reveal the height of the roof overhead. My guide told me that this was the mother of all the rivers of the world. No other person except himself knew of its existence. It flowed from the end of the north to the extreme south. It grew even warmer and warmer. There was a time when the people lived along its channel, and there were houses and cities of the dead there and many strange things. It was full of fish without eyes and they were good to eat. If I could help him build a raft he would float with me down this river. The old, old stories said that no one could go upon it for many miles. It ran down a hollow under the mountains.

We built and equipped our raft and launched it on the most foolhardy adventure, I do believe, that ever occupied the attention of men. We lit torches and set them in sockets on the raft, and we were well armed. For two weeks we moved down the high archway at a steady rate of only about three miles an hour. The average width of the stream was about 500 feet, but at times it widened out to almost twice that. It swarmed with many kinds of fish, and they were very easy to secure. The rock walls and roof seemed to be of solid granite. We were below the latter formations.

As nearly as I can calculate we were about a thousand miles from where our voyage began, and nothing had yet happened to disturb its monotony, when we began to find traces of ancient work and workers. An angle in the wall was hewn into a Titanic figure; at another point there seemed to be regular windows, and a dwelling was perched far up in the granite dome.

The Indian told me more of the traditions of his race as we drifted past these things. "They were very great people who lived here. They had many things; they knew more than the white men. They are all dead now." And I gathered from his chance remarks that he thought they had left secrets in their cave dwellings which would make him the biggest Indian on the continent if he could discover them.

Suddenly we found that the river was flowing much faster, and we failed to check our raft. We went over a waterfall, perhaps seventy feet high, and were thrown on a shelf of rock at the side of the river below. I was unhurt, but my companion was so badly injured that he died in a few hours. I repaired the raft after a fashion and continued the voyage, finding it impossible to contrive any way to scale the sides of the waterfall and attempt a return. All our torches were lost, and the attempt to proceed further seemed but the last act of despair. A few hours later I saw a light gleam over the river in a very remarkable way, shining clear across, as if from the headlight of a locomotive high up on the wall. This aroused me somewhat from my stupor and misery. I sat up on the raft and steered it close to the edge of the river to see what wonderful thing had happened.

As I came nearer I saw that an irregular hole was in the wall a thousand feet above the water, and the light shone out through it. It was a cheerful thing to look at, and I hung to the granite and shouted, but to no effect. Then I saw a broken place in the wall a little further down, and let the raft drift along to the base of a broad though much worn and broken flight of steps winding up the cliff. That brought me at last to the place of the light, a domed hall overlooking the river, hewn out of the rock and having in its centre a metal basin with a jet of natural gas. I have had to cut off a part of this metal basin since, but I have not harmed the inscriptions. There are many gas jets, but in the other chambers I have had to light them.

I have lived here for months, and I have explored all the chambers of the place. There is no escape, so far as I can see. The river, twenty miles below, plunges down vaster descents, and the water gets so hot that I should be boiled alive if I tried the voyage. I have discovered a log of tropic wood like palm and a geode in which I can send a message to the world of sunlight. Perhaps this will get through the fires and float to the surface somewhere. I am convinced that the river which brought me here flows on into the Gulf of Mexico, and that sooner or later my log will be picked up. Perhaps this river is really the source of the Gulf stream.

I will not write down my discoveries, not in their order, but as a whole. My story must be brief, or this scant means of record will fail me.

This place seems to have been approached only by the river. It consists of six large, domed halls, connected with a seventh, in which the light burns. There are swords of bronze, spearheads and other weapons stored in one chamber. There have been costly fabrics also, but they have perished, and only a few fragments are left. In another hall are many treasures accumulated.

One hall is especially the hall of pictures and of writing. I spend many hours there. I see the history of this race — their wars, their heroes, their mythology.

The most wonderful chamber of all is the hall to the north. That is the chamber of death and silence. When first I entered this hall I lighted all the gas jets. Around the walls were high cases of drawers and on the front of each was a portrait. I examined them for hours before I felt any desire to do more. Among them I observed a very beautiful face — that of a young girl just entering womanhood. This wonderful race possessed the highest artistic skill and delicacy of expression. The face of this girl, except that the colors had faded, might have been the admired masterpiece of the Paris Salon. I felt a sudden interest in the face and caught the drawer handles and pulled it out. In the wide, deep space into which I looked lay, robed in white, her hands folded, the form of the girl whose picture was outside. How beautiful she was. She lay as if only asleep. Then slowly, as I looked, the whole figure melted down and faded away to a pile of dust. I closed the shrine and touched no more of them, but I often go and look at the faded painting and think how lovely the girl was.

The paintings on the walls of this mural chamber show that the people had two systems of disposing of their dead. The great mass were consigned to the river, but the bodies of all those who were famous for beauty, wisdom or any good quality were preserved by a process of embalming, which they evidently thought would make them endure for ages. There are probably 12,000 separate bodies here, and they represent more than twenty successive generations, if I rightly understand the system of family grouping. If people lived as long as they do now, there was an average of about fifteen additions each year to this great Westminster Abbey of the past. From a sort of map painted on one of the walls I obtain the idea of many and thickly populated communities which used this place as the sepulcher of their chosen few.

Evidently that was before volcanic outbursts made the channel of the river like a cauldron boiling over endless fires. All along the course are towns marked, groups of rock-hewn rooms on the cliffs, populated lands on the river, promontories from whose sides fountains of light seemed to spring. Did thousands of people once live and find happiness in these vast vaults of death? Things must have been very different then from now. They must have had many reservoirs of natural gas. The animal life in the river must have been much more varied. Indeed, there are pictures in the Hall of War, as I have named it, that show two things plainly — that there were thousands of caverns extending over hundreds of miles, and peopled by animals with which the heroes fought, and that the river was swarming with existence.

Moreover, I find everywhere, chief of the symbols of life, in the most sacred places, a food root like a water nut, from which grew white leaves and seeds. There must have been some electric principle evolved here, by the vast warm lakes of the river, lit with soft light everywhere at certain seasons. For now I come to the strangest fact of all that I gather from the records of the race; these people had two kinds of light; one they found and lit — that they knew as the lesser God of Life; the other, coming from north to south, twice each year, filled for many weeks the whole channel of the river, from depth to dome, making the very water translucent. The water root and its grain ripened and were harvested in the last days of the light. Two crops a year they gathered, and held their days of the feasts of the great God of Life.

I have tried to put together all I can of their picture writings and their paintings, so as to understand what sort of men and women they were. I confess that I have learned to admire them greatly. They were a strong, brave, loving and beautiful people. I am sorry they are all gone. I never cared half as much about the dead Etruscans or Carthaginians. The earliest chapter in their history, so far as I discover, is a picture of a line of men and women descending into a cave and a dragon pursuing them. This seems to point to a former residence on the face of the earth, and to some disaster — war, flood, pestilence or some fierce monster — which drove the survivors into the depths of the earth for shelter.

But all these thoughts are vain and foolish. I have explored the cliffs of the river and the walls of the mighty halls which shelter me. I have attempted to cut a tunnel upward past the waterfall, using the ancient weapons which lie in such numbers on the floor. The bronze wears out fast, but if I live long enough something may be done. I will close my record and launch it down the river. Then I may try to cut my way out to the sunlight.

Here the story closed. Some day, perhaps, an old man, white-haired and pale as one from the lowest dungeon of a bastile, will climb slowly out of some canyon of the Rockies to tell the world more about his discovery of a lost race.

UPSIDE DOWN IN THE SKY

"Upside Down in the Sky" appeared as "Not the Snake Kind, Mac" in the *Lethbridge News* on November 21, 1894. The account is reprinted from the *Vancouver World*. Inverted aerial mirages like the ones described here were commonly reported in the nineteenth century, especially in the northern regions of the world.

Just what the reason is has not yet been ascertained, but it is a fact that the citizens of several towns in Manitoba and the Northwest have recently seen mirages. Winnipeg recently saw Stonewall, penitentiary and all, upside down in the sky. The warning is obvious. Calgary saw the Rockies inverted in the blue heavens above the city. The particular brands most popular in the prairie towns at present may have something to do with the case. Both mirages occurred or appeared shortly after Hallowe'en.

THE POLAR WORLD

Lost races abound in the globe's polar zones, at least in traveller's tales and novels of fantasy and science fiction. Here is a traveller's tale — in part a survivor's tale as well — of a journey made to an inaccessible place where once there were wonders to behold.

"Saw North Pole" appeared in the *Saint John* (New Brunswick) *Daily Sun* on March 28, 1900. The subject's name is spelled "Le Joie" in the subheading and "La Joie" in the news story itself. The story presumably originally appeared in the *New York Herald*, a newspaper noted for publishing bizarre or highly imaginative stories. At the time of publication, the North Pole was much in the news, as it was about to be claimed — or "attained," as the expression has it — by rival claimants.

SAW NORTH POLE
Strange Story of a Trapper
Joseph Z. Le Joie, a French Canadian,
Excites Interest of Scientists by Claim that He Visited
"Farthest North" and Found New Race

New York, March 18.— Joseph Zotique La Joie says that he discovered the north pole and a new race of people. He is a French-Canadian hunter and trapper, who has spent many years in the Arctic regions. His story is a marvellous one. By the request of the *New York Herald*, and accompanied by one of the *New York Herald*'s reporters, he went on Wednesday last to Washington. He courted scientific investigation of his stories, and they are now being scientifically investigated.

At the Hotel Raleigh in Washington on Wednesday last Mr. La Joie met General A.W. Greely, chief of the signal service and an Arctic explorer of great fame; Admiral George W. Melville of the United States navy (retired), of whom Melville Island is named and who is recognized as one of the greatest living authorities on Arctic matters. Professor J.W. McGee of the Smithsonian Institution, of world wide celebrity as an ethnologist, and other great scientists. Not one of these scientists is willing to unqualifiedly endorse the statements made by M. La Joie. All have found in his explanations some apparent inconsistencies, but all have also found in them much accuracy concerning matters with which they are well acquainted.

On the whole, it seems that there is probably considerable truth in the strange stories told by M. La Joie. That the man penetrated far into the Arctic is certain. He claims to be able to substantiate all of his amazing statements by producing relics of the new race of people which he found in the "farthest north," and even by showing the bodies of two natives of this strange tribe, which he says are cached within comparatively easy access.

In December, 1886, according to his narrative, La Joie and his father started from Montreal for Battleford, Northwest Territory. After three years' hunting through British Columbia and Alaska he arrived at Great Bear Lake in the fall of 1889. Game having grown scarce, he determined to push further north with a partner, a man named George White. Toward the spring of 1892 they found themselves near Cape Brianard. Hunting in this vicinity, they learned from the natives of an iron post left by some explorer. On this they found the following marks: "82 degrees latitude north, 83 degrees longitude west."

To the north of this a few miles they made their camp in May, 1892. This camp was established at the junction of two immense icebergs, and White proposed that they separate and each take a ten days' journey on three diverging points of ice to find the best hunting ground. La Joie, while returning, felt on the seventh day a tremendous shock like an earthquake. It meant that the ice had parted and that he was adrift. Admiral Melville, the other day in Washington, agreed that La Joie's description of the phenomenon was accurate. The berg drifted to the north. For three days he lived on fish, hoping against hope that a wind that had sprung up from the south would drive him back to the main land. For a period of thirty-six days he was adrift, he says, amid terrible storms of snow, hail and sleet. Land was sighted on several occasions, but he was unable to get ashore. On the morning of the thirty-seventh day, having eaten six of his dogs and suffered many torments, La Joie found that the berg on which he had drifted had touched land. He got ashore with his remaining dogs. He says that the farther north the berg drifted the milder became the climate.

That night La Joie was awakened by the barking of his dogs. He jumped to his feet and found that he was surrounded by a tribe of copper colored natives, who were shooting at him with bows and arrows. La Joie was armed only with a knife and a club, but his double suit of skin protected him from the arrows. The next day they were willing to treat for peace.

He describes the men whom he joined as belonging to a strange race, speaking a tongue entirely unlike that of the other natives whom he had met in his travels. Their complexion, he states, was of a reddish-brown hue, and their eyes and hair were either black or brown. The men were very large, averaging more than 6 feet in height. Their clothes were made of skins and shaped after a strange fashion. He remained in the camp five months. The party, having concluded the hunt in which they were engaged, took La Joie with them to their principal settlement, a five days' journey across a rocky country. They came finally to the entrance to a great cave. The sub-chief in charge of the party summoned to the mouth of the cave the great chief of all the tribes which inhabit that country. The leader scrutinized the stranger for a period of five minutes, and then said something to his people in their native language. The stranger, thinking that they were about to kill him, turned and ran until out of the range of arrows, then, stopping, he took from his pocket a flint a steel. With these he struck fire. La Joie gathered some swigs and built a fire. For a few minutes the natives watched him, and then approached, threw down their bows and arrows, and indicated that they wished to be friends. They had known nothing of fire previously.

La Joie states that he soon came to live with the natives on terms of the most friendly intercourse. Owing to the reverence in which he was held, they made him, he says, the chief and ruler of the tribe, a position he held for two years. Since his arrival on the island La Joie's attention had been repeatedly attracted by a strange and apparently volcanic light. This shone forth steadily at all times, casting an effulgent glowing over the surrounding country. La Joie determined to investigate. He finally set forth with a party of natives and came within full view of the great mountain from which the light seemed to come. Here he discovered what he firmly believes to be the north pole.

MIRAGE

Naturalists and readers who enjoy the great outdoors will find the following passage paints a lovely picture. "Mirage" appeared in the *Rocky Mountain Echo* of Rocky Mountain House, Alberta, on July 21, 1903.

Those who drove home from Gillingham at 4:00 o'clock on Saturday morning witnessed one of the finest mirages that has been seen for many years. One old-timer here declares it to be the most beautiful mirage he has ever seen. At first it had the appearance of clouds of the conformation of a range of mountains. Little by little, as in the development of a negative, it distinctly unfolded its beauties until a replica of the Kootenay Lakes, and the range of mountains from Chief Mountain a hundred miles or more to the north, was plainly to be seen in the sky above the eastern rim of the world. Looking over the Porcupines, the towering reflections of the main range of the Rockies were distinctly visible. The line of snow and the contour of each mountain could be clearly seen, and in comparison to their vast height, the Porcupines seemed a very low range of foothills. The mirage commenced to fade when our party reached the South Fork bridge and when we got to the top of the hill like a slowly dissolving view, the vision slowly melted away. It was an impressive sight, and will not soon be forgotten. Sceptics say such visions are common after Gillingham cricket matches, but the three men who saw this one are teetotalers (or nearly so) and can vouch for each other's sobriety and veracity.

MENACE OF LIGHTNING

The weather is always newsworthy and sometimes noteworthy. Here is a noteworthy account. "Remarkable Phenomenon" appeared in the *Calgary Herald* on April 21, 1903. The bolt of lightning appeared in the town of Lebret, District of Assiniboia (later the Province of Alberta).

REMARKABLE PHENOMENON

A most remarkable phenomenon occurred near Lebret, Assa., on Good Friday. Old residents know of nothing to equal it in the history of lightning and thunderstorms in this district.

On Friday, April 10, at 7:00 p.m., three sons and a daughter of Mr. Paquin, who reside on and work their farm north of here, and E. Thomas, their guest, were sitting about the parlour after supper, chatting and smoking, enjoying the warmth inside in contrast to the first thunderstorm of the season that raged without, when in a moment, in the wink of an eye, the following happened:

Each had a slightly different version, though all heard a deafening crash, and saw a blinding glare of light, and the lamp flame apparently reached the ceiling. They felt a sharp contraction of the muscles and were then in bewildering darkness, with the furniture overturned and a very offensive smell in the room.

A second flash of lightning revealed the position of the window and showed the demolished wall, and as bricks and mortar were still falling from the chimney, all able to do so made a rush for the door. When safely outside they spoke to one another, and though one brother, Adelard, came out later than the others and seemed dazed, the only person missing was Mr. Thomas.

Having lit a lantern they re-entered the house and found Mr. Thomas prostrate, with arms stretched out at right angles to his body. He was perfectly rigid, one boot had been torn off his foot, and near him lay two dogs that had been killed and badly singed.

They thought Mr. Thomas dead, but he presently spoke and said he had been conscious all the time, knew that Adelard Paquin had been hurled across him, and lay there for a minute, though he could not feel him.

As Mr. Thomas showed no signs of recovery, after putting out the fires, the whole family drove to the house of their father, four miles away, in the village of Lebret. Mr. Thomas's limbs were still rigid when they arrived there. He was undressed and put to bed. The course of the lightning was plainly traced. After striking and demolishing the chimney and part of the side of the house, it crossed to Mr. Thomas and ripped the back of his waistcoat and shirt and burned his underclothing and skin from the back of his right shoulder blade in a narrow streak down to his belt, following the belt half round the body to the front of the left leg, which it traversed straight down to his toes, ripping his trousers at the bottom, and tearing the front part of his boot to pieces and burning the sole through where three iron nails had been driven.

The lightning must then have jumped to two dogs, which it killed, and partly roasted, and then crossed to the wall of the building, following the sill, and ripping the plaster a short distance. Before making its exit through a hole it burned into the porch, which it threw from the house, and in which it killed another grown dog and one of four puppies.

This latter was only discovered on visiting the house Saturday morning, April 11, when the interior of the house presented a wild scene, plaster, brick, broken glass, jagged boards, smashed crockery, clothing, pictures, and overturned furniture being scattered promiscuously.

Mr. Thomas recovered the use of his limbs gradually, and was able to be out next day, feeling no more inconvenience after his wonderful experience than the dressing on his burns and a swelling on his left instep would have caused, and which might have been received under very ordinary circumstances.

ARK IN ARCTIC?

What begins as an intriguing news story about the sighting of the remains of Noah's Ark on the shore of the Arctic Ocean digresses into hearsay about an abandoned Russian ship with Cyrillic inscriptions — and then into gossip about playing tricks on the native population of the Yukon Territory. "Sees Ark in Arctic" was published in the *Dawson Daily News* on May 9, 1908.

SEES ARK IN ARCTIC
Musher Arrives from Near Chandlar and Tells of Craft
Details Are Told
May Have Been Floating Russian Fort — Unique Letters

The story of the existence of a vast craft on a high hill overlooking a string of lakes, 30 to 40 miles from the head of the Chandlar river, is brought by N.J. Brown, a recent arrival from that district, an old time friend of Dave Shindler.

The story is vouched for by Brown, and is the first authenticated report ever brought here which may be taken as a corroboration of the remarkable report made five years ago by Casey Moran of the existence of a huge craft near the Arctic coast which was supposed by some to be Noah's ark.

The big structure, as described by Brown, may have been a Russian fort. He believes it may have been a sort of floating fort in some of the lakes of that vicinity, built and used by the early Russians, and later abandoned then stranded by the water falling.

The structure is one story high, reaching from 12 to 14 feet to the eaves, is 100 yards long, is made with copper nails, bolts and washers, has doors and windows in the upper works, and bears peculiar letters, said to be unknown to any traveler yet in that vicinity. Some Russian words, he says, also are lettered on the craft.

The Indians in the vicinity are in the habit of going to the nearby lakes to fish, and they have used the craft, says Brown, as a place in which to dry fish and to rendezvous.

The natives of the district, says Brown, are very superstitious, and he had them going by making imitation bear tracks, each 36 inches long, in the sand on the lake shore. He took the Indians to the lake, ostensibly to fish, and when they saw the tracks they were greatly alarmed, and hiked back to camp, refusing to go again to the lake, and now are full of the story of the great bear which is prowling in the vicinity.

Gat Campbell, a trader of the district, made up a twenty-four-foot man of himself, and added to the alarm of the natives. Campbell is an old circus man, and did the stunt to perfection. He put imitation trousers the full length of a pair of stilts, and mounted them himself. Taking a gun and a megaphone, and striding through the woods in sight of the Indians, he caused a panic. The simple-minded folk fairly tumbled over each other in the wild endeavor to escape the giant. They immediately moved to another locality, and since then have been camping far from the abode of the mammoth bear and the wonderful man, and have not allowed the children to stray out of sight of the tents.

Brown also recalls the story of the big moose of Mayo. Some white hunters made several imitation three-foot tracks on the river sands there, and rowed across the river and made others. Then they took the Indians to see the tracks.

The tracks were so large, and naturally so far apart that the aborigines imagined the moose stepped across the river. They thought that such a moose was better avoided than sought, and they took to another district, where they still talk about the "Big Moose," always with apologies to Alex McDonald.

WONDERFUL MIRAGES IN THE SKY

From the tongues of travellers in northern latitudes come remarkable accounts of strange sights, including "cities in the sky." Actual cities are seen from an aerial perspective to be floating or shimmering in the atmosphere. These are optical illusions, to be sure, but they are fascinating to behold. The cities come complete with "moving parts," so to speak. In a handful of instances, the cities have been identified. Quite often the cities are ones located in the north of England. How is this possible? The effect may be explained by a range of optical, visual and meteorological causes. Reflected light is transported in the upper atmosphere halfway around the world, to the astonishment of homesick travellers.

William Parker was an officer with the North-West Mounted Police. He enlisted as a sub-constable in 1874 and retired as an inspector in 1912. He kept a record of his experiences and observations. One of these experiences was the sight of this remarkable mirage. He saw it in 1876, while on a march approaching the South Saskatchewan River on his way to Fort Carleton. The passage is reprinted from *William Parker: Mounted Policeman*, edited by Hugh A. Dempsey and published in 1973 by the Glenbow-Alberta Institute in Calgary.

The next day, September 27th, the prairie was black with herds of buffalo and numerous bands of antelope. In the evening we camped at Egg Lake which was covered with ducks and geese; we shot over fifty of them. When travelling across this vast plain we would see a ridge ahead of us and wondered what we would see on the other side of it. On arrival, there was nothing but another similar ridge ahead, and this went on day after day.

We did see some wonderful mirages in the sky. One especially was like a large city upside down, showing houses, large buildings and churches, even to the spires. Another showed beautiful trees. Then there was a ground mirage showing lovely lakes of water in the distance; these have fooled many a traveller who, in driving to the place, discovered there was no lake or water to be seen.

NATURE'S MYSTERY

Mirages exert an almost magnetic fascination. They were more commonly reported in the past than they are today; one of the factors in their decline is quite possibly the pollution of the air. "Nature's Mystery" appeared in the *Calgary Herald* on February 10, 1905.

NATURE'S MYSTERY

Monday the 6th instant the settlers at Shepard were treated to one of those curious spectacles, a mirage. An image of the town of Macleod, which lies about one hundred miles to the south, suddenly became clearly visible apparently over the south side of Shepard Lake. Not only was the town visible but a large circle of surrounding country dotted with ranches and other features of the landscape. People could be seen walking or driving in the streets. The Old Man's River, with the Canadian Pacific railway bridge crossing it, the railway station itself, and the cars standing on the track were all plainly pictured. The mirage lasted a little over ten minutes and then vanished as quietly as it came.

THE BLUISH LIGHT

Rochelle M. Wallis lives in retirement in Ridgeway, Ontario. She read in the *Fort Erie Review* that I was collecting accounts of odd and unusual experiences for one of my publications. She mislaid the notice, but a year or so later she came across the clipping and resolved to prepare an account of an experience that had occurred to her many years earlier.

On November 1, 1991, she sent me the following account. It is interesting how the incident of the "bluish light" has remained so vivid in her memory — for close to eight decades! It is also intriguing that the memory of an event or experience that occurred to an eight-year-old child way back in 1913 should be independently confirmed to the satisfaction of an adult in 1965.

I remember well when I was eight years old. We lived in a log house by Georgian Bay, at Pine Point, or Pointe aux Pins as the place was then called. My two brothers and I slept upstairs and our parents downstairs. The stairway was behind a pantry, and there was a door one step up. Also, the stovepipe went through the floor and up, so we could get some warmth. One side of the house had no windows, as there was a long shed located there.

During the night, I woke thinking someone was coming up the stairs. I heard the sound of shoe packs or moccasins, yet no sound approached the bed. I heard this sound again. I was scared and woke one of my brothers. He said, "Just pull the covers over your head and go to sleep. It will soon be morning."

A short time later I heard my mother say to my father, "Ed, wake up! There's something or someone here."

He got up and answered, "It looks like a lantern. Someone is going past on the road."

She said, "No! Take a look. There's a light with a bluish colour and flame over the rocking chair."

There was a light above the trivet on the stove, where the teapot stood. Then it played over the baby's cradle in the corner. My father could see it, too.

Then it appeared at the foot of their bed. I heard my mother say there was a heavy weight on her legs. Dad said, "Whoever you are, speak, and say what you want, or get out!" His actual words were, "Get the hell out!" I remember well. This bluish light hovered, then moved toward the window by the stove, and finally disappeared.

My brothers slept through it all. But I was awake.

When we were called to get up and to go to school, Dad had already gone out. In those days, children were seen but not heard. But instead of going to work, Dad had gone to the post office to send money for a Mass for the Dead to be said. This was at my mother's request. She had lost a sister a short while before, and being Catholic, my mother thought she needed prayers to be said for the spirit to be at rest.

My parents never spoke of this incident to us. My mother died two years later, in 1915. A week before my father died in 1965, he related this incident to me. He likely never knew that I had heard it, and that I had been scared nearly out of my wits.

I'm now in my eighty-sixth year. The past is vivid in my memory.

3 Wild Things

IN THIS CHAPTER will be found an assortment of "wild things"; we'll rub shoulders with mammoths of antiquity, beasts that roam the land, demons that haunt the woods, and serpents that sport in the waters of lakes and rivers.

Here are descriptions of appearances of living, or once-living, beings and creatures, and they should inspire fear in the hearts of right-thinking Canadians! Since time immemorial, men and women have been claiming encounters with strange creatures like these on the land, in the sea and in the air. Myths, legends, lore, journals and literature are replete with narratives of living horrors and terrors. Some of the accounts are, at core, deeply psychological, whereas others seem to be based on actual observation and study.

These "wild things" have haunted Canadians in the past, and the descendants of these "creatures" or "critters" will probably continue to do so in the future.

THE LOUP-GAROU

Cryptozoology is the name given to the study of strange or secret animals such as the Yeti (the wild mountain man of Nepal) and Nessie (the fabulous aquatic creature said to make its home in Scotland's Loch Ness). The Canadian equivalents of these creatures are the Sasquatch and Ogopogo — respectively, a land creature and a lake monster that are frequently sighted in the wooded interior and in the coastal waters of British Columbia. There is no shortage of such creatures to be found in Canada and in the extensive and exciting literature of cryptozoology.

There are references to the werewolf in the lore and literature of Quebec, where the creature is called the *loup-garou*. Indeed, there are intriguing references to the werewolf in the history and literature of the *ancien régime*. Here is one reference that is mentioned from time to time in books prepared by writers who have yet to see a *loup-garou* or even the original printed reference to it! The reference, but one paragraph in length, appeared under the heading "Intelligence Extraordinaire" in a general column in the newspaper *La Gazette de Québec* (Quebec City) dated July 16, 1767.

Apparently this *loup-garou*, seen in October and November of 1766 in the vicinity of Kamouraska on the south shore of the St. Lawrence River, was some wild creature or other, a rather weak and retiring one. In this way it bore no resemblance to that champion shape-shifter: the half-man, half-wolf played by Lon Chaney Jr. in the Republic movies of the 1940s. The passage here is translated from the French.

EXTRAORDINARY INTELLIGENCE

From Kamouraska, 2 December. We learn that a certain Werewolf, that has lurked in this province for several years, and that has done much damage in the district of Quebec, has suffered several considerable assaults in the month of October last, on various animals who have been unleashed against this monster, and notably the following 3rd of November, that he received such a furious blow from a little lean animal, that the people believed that they were entirely delivered from that fatal animal in view of the fact that it remained for some time having withdrawn to its lair, to the great pleasure of the public. But they came to learn, by the most mournful of misfortunes, that, to the contrary, it had reappeared, more violent than ever, and it created terrible carnage wherever it went.

Distrust, then, all the tricks of this evil beast, and be very careful not to get caught between its paws.

WILD MEN OF THE WOODS

"An Indian Tradition" appeared in the Victoria *Daily Colonist* on October 6, 1860. The correspondent is identified only by his (or her) initials: J.D. It seems the Sim-moqui are "wild men of the woods." It is interesting to note that the Sasquatch reported in western Canada is a hairy, manlike being, whereas Bigfoot, his American cousin, is not manlike at all but a hairy, apelike creature.

AN INDIAN TRADITION
The Sim-moqui

Having a little leisure time, one fine evening in the spring of 1853, I started out for a few hours' ramble on the banks of the Camas-sau (the Indian name for the Victoria arm or slough). As I walked along, I met a Cowichan Indian, and understanding the language perfectly, I entered into conversation with him. He commenced telling a heap of stories about hob-goblins, ghosts, etc., and after I had listened some time, he asked if I had ever heard of the Sim-moquis? I replied I never had. "Well," said he, "sit down a bit, and I'll tell you a story about them."

I obeyed and, sitting down, listened to his tale, which ran very much as follows:

"By the side of a lake amongst the highest mountains of this Island, where the crack of a rifle has never yet been heard and the deer and bears roam all unacquainted with the smell of the deadly gunpowder, lives the terrible Sim-moquis. From these mountains the daring hunter, who ventures to pursue the game to their fastnesses, seldom returns to tell the tale of his wanderings. No berries in the whole world are so large, or so sweet, or so nourishing, as the berries in the Sim-moquis country; yet who dare gather them besides their terrible owners?

"The Sim-moquis are a tall, strong, athletic race, with heavy black whiskers and matted hair. They are totally without knee or elbow-joints, and depend upon staffs to assist them in rising from recumbent attitudes, or in sitting down. They never rise but leap with the aid of their staffs to a great distance. Like the deer, whose wide-spread antlers would seem to be a hindrance to its rapid progress through the forests and thickets, the Sim-moqui never miscalculates the distance he has to spring, or the space allowed him in which to leap. His eyes are large and red, and shine like a torch; his teeth are black; his hands and feet are webbed like a water-fowl. They have canoes and hunt with bows and arrows made from the bones of dead Sim-moquis.

"The unfortunates, who chance to visit their country, are immediately seized upon and led into captivity. If they happen to be men, they perform all the drudgery; if women, they take them to wife, to try if they cannot introduce the fashion of knee and elbow-joints into the race."

"Did you ever see any of those strange people?" I asked my companion.

"No," he replied; "but my father did. It was one time when some of the Nanimooch (Nanaimo) Indian women went out berrying, and wandered far up the side of a very high mountain. The farther they went, the larger and the better the berries became, and as they gathered them into their baskets, they wondered at their size and excellence. Higher and higher they went, alternately filling their baskets and pouring them out upon the ground, only to fill them again with still finer olallies. At last they reached the top of the mountain, and there their wondering eyes gazed upon a sight which caused them to cry aloud. Berries grew everywhere as large as their baskets; the air was filled with the fragrance from the many-coloured flowers that adorned the green carpet at their feet. The trees, too, were mighty, and their tops were lost to view among a few fleecy clouds that were wafted by a gentle breeze through the air high above them.

"As they stood and wondered at the strange sights above and around them, the sun suddenly sank to rest behind a still higher mountain in the west, and then they felt their danger. 'The Sim-moquis!' burst from their pallid lips, and they seized their baskets and swiftly prepared to descend. But, alas! they had not bent the twigs of the saplings as they came along, and they had no mark by which to guide them back to their homes. They sought for a Sim-moquis trail; but those people leave no trail. As I said before, they leap, by aid of their staffs, over the closest thickets and through the densest forests. After searching for a long, long time in vain for the way down, the poor women threw themselves upon the ground and wept bitterly. Tears dropped like rain, and the ground at their feet was moistened by the crystal drops that fell from their eyes. They thought of their homes and of their little ones, and bemoaned their sad lots in accents of grief and despair.

"Suddenly, while they were seated thus, they saw two lights in the distance, and heard a rushing sound through the air (as of a limb of a tree falling to the ground). The poor creatures started to their feet and essayed to run; but, too late! A Sim-moqui leaped with the swiftness of an arrow shot from a bow into their midst, and motioned them to stay. The affrighted maidens obeyed, and examined the stranger critically. He was tall and straight; his hair was blacker than the features of the blackest raven, and it was neatly combed too. His features were regular and handsome, and half concealed by the flowing whiskers and moustaches that adorned his face; but his colour was much darker than that of any Indian ever before seen. His limbs — who shall describe them? — were straight and appeared strong, but were thin as that sapling" (our friend here pointed to a young fir-tree about six inches in circumference).

"His arms, too, were straight like sticks, and as he extended his hand as a token of friendship towards the unfortunate girls, they saw that the stories which their grandparents had often told them of the absence of knee and elbow-joints among the Sim-moquis were indeed true. His red eyes glistened and shone in the dark like a lantern, and were the lights which had first attracted the women's attention. After they had sat some little time in silence — for the Sim-moqui language was strange to them — their visitor rose, by means of his staff, and placing his hand to his chin, opened his mouth, and uttered a loud, piercing cry. In an instant a commotion was heard in the bushes, and in a few seconds lights glanced in all directions, and soon huge, unwashed, unjointed Sim-moquis leaped into the open space in which the captives stood. The light from their flaming eyes fell upon the maidens, and objects in the immediate vicinity became as clear as noon-day. No need for torches where the Sim-moquis live," continued the narrator. "Every Sim-moqui is provided with two torches — that is, his eyes. If a fire be needed, dry sticks of matches are not required — his eyes start the wood into a blaze; if his hands be cold, he raises them to a level with his natural torches and warms them.

"The newcomers held a short consultation with the Sim-moqui who had first joined the unhappy women, and then, at the word of command, six stalwart youths approached, and each seizing a woman threw her over his shoulder and commenced leaping through the air, on their way up the mountain. The rest of the party followed, singing a war-song, and so they went on during the night, toiling up the mountainside, until the first dawn of day. Then they sat down by the side of a running brook, prepared a hasty meal of dried venison, and coiling themselves up like hedgehogs, went to sleep, after binding their captives securely. I might here remark that the Sim-moqui never travels in the daytime, as he is as blind as a bat while the sun is shining.

"When the night came, and the women did not return, the lodges of the Nanimooches were in a state of excitement, and a solemn council was held. The unanimous opinion was that the Sim-moquis had carried their females off. For some time, no one ventured to go forth and attempt their rescue, such was the dread in which the mountain savages were held by the coast Indians. At last my father, who was a chief, addressed them in tones of eloquence — pictured the distress which the poor creatures must feel, and the horrible treatment they would receive. At the conclusion of his speech a dozen braves started up, seized their rifles, and prepared to follow my father in search of the lost ones. It was midnight when they commenced to travel up the mountain side, but they walked briskly, and by daylight reached the top of the mountain, the beauties of which had so charmed their countrywomen the evening before. They were so astonished, and wished to remain a short time to feast their eyes upon the wonders of nature. But my father urged them to continue their search, and after a brief rest, they commenced to climb another high mountain — the same over which the Sim-moquis had passed with their captives a few hours before. Night was coming on apace when the pursuers reached the summit, and throwing themselves upon the ground, after a hasty meal, sought repose.

"My father, however, could not sleep, but lay wrapped in his blankets for a short time musing upon the lost ones and the probabilities of rescuing them. At last, he rose from his couch, and was walking up and down in front of the camp, when his eyes suddenly detected the glimmer of a light at some distance to the north. Awakening his companions, they stole, gun in hand, towards the light, and soon came upon the band of Sim-moquis, who had encamped for the night on a grassy knoll. They were all asleep; and to the utter amazement of my father, he discovered that the light he had seen came from the eye of a sentry, perched upon a high rock. Levelling his gun at this sentinel, my father directed his followers each to pick his man. This having been done, a dozen rifles cracked at once, and a dozen Sim-moquis bit the dust. The rest, owing to the absence of joints, were slaughtered before they could rise to their feet. The captives were unloosened, and they threw themselves sobbing upon the breasts of their rescuers. My father, before he left the spot, examined the body of the sentry, and discovered that one of his red eyes was still open; the other was closed tightly. The party, after securing all the valuables they could find, started down the mountain and reached home the next day."

"And are there any Sim-moquis now-a-days?" I asked the narrator, as he turned to leave.

"Oh, yes," said he as he walked away; "lots of them. They live by the side of a lake on a big mountain, and the shores of the lake are covered with gold."

I walked home in the dark, Mr. Editor, musing on what I had heard, and after seven years' lapse have committed it to paper for your especial benefit. If you believe it, publish it; but if you are at all sceptical on the subject, commit the document to the flames.

THE LAKE UTOPIA MONSTER

The lakes and rivers of the Maritimes are the domains of innumerable monsters, and the Lake Utopia Monster is among the best known of these menacing aquatic creatures. (Perhaps this is so because of the sound of those words: Who would ever think to link a "monster" with a reference to Lake Utopia? Come to think of it, who would ever name a lake in New Brunswick after Utopia, the fictional ideal society?)

"The Monster of Lake Utopia" first appeared in the *Summerside* (P.E.I.) *Progress* on August 19, 1867. It was contributed by the correspondent of the *Saint John* (New Brunswick) *Globe*.

THE MONSTER OF LAKE UTOPIA

A correspondent of the Saint John, N.B., *Globe*, writing from "St. George, Aug. 6," gives the following account of a monster in Utopia

Lake, in addition to that which he contributed some time ago to the same paper, and which we then transferred to our columns:

Agreeably to my promise that, should any further be developed respecting the strange monster in Lake Utopia I would write you, I now beg to say that it has been seen by a number of persons since, in different parts of the lake, and on Wednesday, July 24th, by thirteen persons, some of whom are of the most reliable character. I would have written you sooner, but being rather sceptical about it myself, I waited to get the correct accounts from the lips of the individuals themselves; and I now have no hesitation in saying that some huge animal of fearful aspect exists in the waters of Utopia. To the north and east of lake Utopia, there is a small lake well known to the sporting fraternity, which connects with the larger waters by a stream, perhaps 400 yards in length. About midway on this stream, between the two lakes, Messrs. H. & J. Ludgate have a saw mill in operation. The deals when sawn are floated down the stream to the deep water in Utopia, where they are made into rafts to float down to St. George. On the day before alluded to, a number of men engaged in rafting, had their attention drawn to a violent agitation of the water, about 100 yards distant out in the lake, which continued for a time, and then, there appeared distinctly above the water a huge bulky object, variously estimated from 20 to 40 feet in length, and from 4 to 10 feet across the widest part. The men describe the skin as presenting a shaggy appearance, not unlike a buffalo robe, and of a reddish brown color. It created a great quantity of foam which drifted up to the shore in huge flakes. At no time could they see the head of it; but at a distance of 20 or 25 feet in rear of the large mass, could be seen what they supposed to be a tail from the movements. The man called H. Ludgate, Esq., who was at the mill, and he and his son, together with others, ran down and witnessed the evolutions of this strange creature. Mr. Ludgate told me himself that it agitated the water to a perfect boiling, seething state, and threw up in its course edgings and mud from the bottom, occasionally rising itself to the top; a dark cumbrous body — not unlike a large stick of timber — disappearing again almost instantly. It finally moved off, and they could trace its course down the lake by the foam it created long after it went below the surface. Later in the day Mr. Thomas White, his two sons, and a hired man haying in the field, saw it seven different times, and Mr. White says it came up at the outer end of the raft, quite close to it; the men at work at the inner end being turned away did not observe their acquaintance of the morning.

Mr. White's description of it is about the same. He, being farther off, could not describe the skin of the animal, but says that when most exposed it resembled a large rock left bare of the tide, 10 feet across; and he further states that he can safely swear he saw 30 feet in length of it. His statement is corroborated by his sons, and by all of the thirteen persons who saw it the same day. Now, Mr. Editor, heretofore I could scarcely believe in the existence of such an animal and unprecedent inhabitant of our lake; but when I heard men of the character of H. Ludgate, Esq., Charles Ludgate, Charles Mealy, Thomas White, Robert White and many others say positively that they saw it as described, and when I take into consideration the destruction of fish which must take place in Utopia every year — otherwise it would teem with splendid trout, perch, cusk and smelt, and together with these the tradition of forty years,— I must say that in common with the majority of our citizens, I firmly believe that a monster of vast dimensions and formidable appearance is located in the lake. Two of our most enterprising citizens, Mr. H.A. Smith, and W.W. Shaw, have had hooks made and attached to lines buoyed in the lake for some time, but so far without any satisfactory result. It is the opinion of many that a large net will be required to capture the creature, and I understand that a movement is on foot quietly, to make the attempt, which I hope will succeed. The people living in the vicinity of the lake are really afraid to cross it in boats; and if you could only hear some of the oldest settlers who saw this "thing" tell the story with fear and trembling, you would be fully impressed with the truth of their assertions, and consider them justified in their fears.

THE GREAT SEA-SERPENT

The article headed "The Great Sea-Serpent" appeared in the *Huron Expositor* (Seaforth, Ontario) of May 21, 1869. Neither the name of the author nor that of the Nova Scotian fishing village is given. Unfortunately, the author's "two rough sketches," although mentioned here, were not reproduced in the columns of the newspaper.

THE GREAT SEA-SERPENT

In the year 1855 I had occasion to visit the neighbouring province of Nova Scotia, and was compelled, from the nature of my business, to remain there several months. I heard, while there, many curious stories related by persons well educated and intelligent, as well as by ignorant fishermen, which were so remarkable that I took the trouble of marking the circumstances in the hope that time might give me an opportunity to unravel the mystery, and among these was the report of repeated appearance in the harbours of the Province, of the veritable sea-serpent.

The shores of the peninsula, both in the Atlantic and the Bay of Fundy coast, are deeply indented with numerous capacious harbours, which on the western side, are subject to remarkable tides, or periodical currents, so powerful as to divert vessels crossing the mouth of the Bay from their course to the extent of many miles.

It was on the afternoon of a warm quiet day in the month of August, when I arrived. I drove up the one single street of the village and inquired for the house of Tom Larkin, whose acquaintance I had made on my trip from Boston. I found it without difficulty, a one-story cottage of wood, unpainted, and protected with an embankment of rock wood or kelp that reached almost to the windowsill. Great heaps of wood, in lengths of from eight and twenty feet, rose behind the cottage almost to the ridge pole, and a barn of modest dimensions stood at the edge of the hill at the foot of which the cottage was built. In front, across the rarely used road, stretched a slope of grass and gray rock, while beyond was the smooth waters of the harbour and the boundless sea, whose restless surges beat upon the beach across the narrow strip which separated the cove from the Atlantic.

Larkin, I ascertained, was not at home. He and his two boys were outside the harbour in their little sloop, making a catch. His daughter, a stout, rosy maid of fourteen, led my horse to the barn and fed him. At her invitation, I partook of some cold salmon and barley bread and we walked over to the "Pint," where half the women and children of the village were gathered. As we ascended the slope, which overhung the mouth of the harbour, I noticed a great agitation among the women, some throwing up their hands, some running towards the village, giving

utterance to the screams of terror. "Something's happened to the boats,"
said Jenny, "or one of the children has fell in." We sped up the hill,
inquiring of the screaming fugitives what was the matter. The only reply
I understood was, "The snake! The snake!" Jenny uttered an exclamation
of alarm but we went on. A fleet of fishing boats were pulling rapidly in
for the mouth of the harbour with every appearance of apprehension.
The men, we could see, were straining every muscle to gain shelter.

It was an improvised race, each boat seemingly determined to out-
strip the others. They did not appear to be a musket-shot from us as we
looked down upon them from the cliff. I could see the agonized exertions
of the men, and hear plainly the swift and regular strokes of their oars.
But nothing to cause the alarm was visible.

"It is a sheer panic," said I, aloud.

"It's the snake, and that's what it is," answered Jenny.

"Can you see it?"

"No. He's sounded, may hap." Then with a shriek, she exclaimed,
"There he comes! My God!" and she covered her eyes with her apron
and pointed with her hand at the last lagging boat.

I looked, and sure enough, there was a monster apparently within a
stone's throw of the two-masted white boat, whose crew of one man and
two boys was making every effort to escape. Ah, never can I forget that
sight! It was terrible! Slowly and majestically moved that hideous length
of undulating terror, but fast enough to keep pace with the boats. Near
what might be a head, rose a hump of crest, crowded with a waving mass
of long, pendulous hair like a mane, while behind, for forty or fifty feet,
slowly moved, or rolled, the spirals of his immense snakelike body. The
movement was in vertical curves, the contortions of the back alternately
rising and falling from the head to the tail, leaving behind a wake, like
that of a screw-steamer upon the glassy surface of the ocean.

The noise of the yells on the shore and the rattle of the oars in the
row locks did not seem to disturb him, but on he came and was now so
near, as he followed the boats through the channel into the harbour, that
I believe I could have shot him from where I stood. In a moment he
raised his head, from which the water poured in showers, and opening
the horrid jaws he gave utterance to a noise resembling nothing so
much as the hissing sound of steam from the escape-pipe of a boiler. In

spite of the knowledge of the security of my position, I shuddered as I gazed and heard.

He turned his head and displayed the inside of the jaws, armed with rows of glistening teeth, while from the lower section depended a long tuft of hair like a goat's beard. The deep-sunk evil eye was defended by a projectile that gave it a most sinister expression. The head and upper portion of the body was of a dark, dingy blue, fading to yellowish white on the belly. Under the mane as it floated about the neck, I could see the scales which defended the hide glistening in the sun. The head appeared to be of a smooth, horny texture and perhaps five or six feet long from the muzzle to the neck. I could see nothing like a fin or gills. I am thus particular in describing the monster, as I had a remarkably good opportunity to observe his appearance at a very moderate distance.

After the boats arrived at the shore, the monster turned slowly around and moved towards the sea, remaining at least ten minutes in full view, so that I had ample time to make two rough sketches of him. Before reaching the open sea, and while abreast of the cliff on which I stood, he slowly sunk while he moved ocean ward, and I supposed I had seen the last of him. But I was mistaken, as will be seen.

The little village was in a state of unusual excitement that night. Knots of men gathered about the two little stores, and in hoarse whispers talked of the cause of their panic. The great regret seemed to be that for a while, at least, their fishing operations must be suspended, none having the hardihood to venture out while the presence of the snake was suspected. I was anxious, notwithstanding the alarming indications, to have a day's fishing on the morrow, but could not find anyone to go with me. Larkin told me he "wouldn't go for the best catch of the season." One of the boys, however, a fine manly fellow of seventeen, offered to go if he could prevail on Sam Hethcote to accompany us. Sam was found and promised.

Next morning was foggy, so that it was near noon before we had a clear sky. Then the fog dissipated, and we started down the harbour, two at the oars, amid the warnings of old, grave-looking fishermen, and the evil prophecies of the women. Just outside the harbour we anchored and prepared to fish. The water was of that transparent hue which, at times, allows the eye to pierce twenty or thirty feet below the surface. For more than an hour we enjoyed excellent success when the fish refused to bite. After long silence in the hope of a nibbler, Hethcote remarked that "the snake must have come again, or we'd do better," and proposing baiting for him. I, tired of the dullness, stretched myself athwart, and with my head over the gunwale, gazed down into the clear green depths. By using my hands as a tube to concentrate my sight, it seemed as though I could pierce at least fifty feet. Thus silently musing on the wonders of the unknown depths of Neptune's dark empire, and particularly of that monstrous denizen who yesterday showed his huge proportions, I became aware of some immense, moving mass in the line of my sight. First it was confused and indistinct, but presently, as it assumed form and I became aware of its character, the cold perspiration of fear started out from my face. It was the snake.

Fear paralyzed my voice. I dared not speak. I gazed in entranced horror at the object of terror. There he lay directly under my face. It seemed that I could touch him with an oar. Supposing, seeing the shadow of the boat, he should rise and crush it with his powerful jaws?

The thought was agony [but] still I gazed silently. The tide was "making," and the serpent lay head to the current, which was flowing into the harbour, keeping up an undulatory movement just sufficient to retain his position. The shell-like head was just abaft the stern of the boat, and the immense mane flowing wavingly, either by the motion of the current or the convulsions of the body. To my affrighted sight, that portion of the body in the line of my clearest vision appeared to be six or seven feet in diameter. It may have been, yet I think not.

The instinct of self-preservation nerved me at last. I turned to my companions who were as listless as I had been, and placing my fingers on my lips, motioned them to look over the side. As they did so, one after the other, the ghastly appearance of terror struck their faces [and] showed that they comprehended the situation.

Hethcote moved silently to the stern and cut the rope that held the killick, and we drifted quietly with the tide into the harbour. At what was deemed a safe distance, we put out the oars and pulled steadily forward. I watched the spot we left as I pulled the after oar, when I was startled by a "breach," and the convulsions of the snake could be seen sculling his huge carcass seaward.

MUST HAVE BEEN A SEA-SERPENT

Here is a splendid account of the sighting of a "sea-serpent" off the Grand Banks of Newfoundland. The account originally appeared under the heading "The Sea-Serpent Shows Himself" in *The New York Times*, November 11, 1879.

THE SEA-SERPENT SHOWS HIMSELF
Mr. Rowell's Story
A Water-Snake 400 Feet Long, with a Bed Head

Fourth Officer F.G. Rowell, of the steam-ship *Anchoria*, of the Anchor Line, which arrived at this port from Glasgow late Sunday evening, says that on Thursday last, while on the Newfoundland Banks, he saw a sea-serpent which he estimates to have been fully as long as the steam-ship. According to "Lloyd's Shipping Record," the *Anchoria* is 408 feet long. Mr. Rowell was walking the bridge at four bells in the afternoon watch, when he noticed a disturbance in the water about a mile distant on the port beam. At first he thought the commotion was caused by a school of porpoises, but, on closer observation, he changed his mind. When he looked through a pair of strong glasses he saw the head and a portion of the body of the sea-serpent rising above the water. Portions of the back of the creature could be seen rising out of the sea at intervals as it propelled itself along on the top of the water. Its motions were similar to those of the land-snake as it moves along on the ground. The water in the wake of the creature had been lashed into foam by its tail. Its head was large and contained an enormous mouth, which opened frequently and spat out large quantities of water. Its tongue, which was extremely long, could be seen at times, but no teeth or fangs were observed. The body of the serpent was round, and its color was black. It was moving in the same direction as the steam-ship, and at a greater rate of speed. When the creature had got a little ahead of the vessel it sank down into the water and disappeared.

Several passengers were on deck at the time. Observing the commotion on the sea, they asked Mr. Baxter, the second officer, what the thing moving in the water could be. He was able to take only a hurried glance, before he was called to the other side of the vessel in the performance of his duties. When he returned with his glasses the creature was not in sight. Mr. Baxter says he thinks that it must have been a sea-serpent, and he places implicit reliance on the fourth officer's statement. Mr. Rowell has made marine animals the subject of study, and has always believed in the existence of sea-serpents; but his desire to see one of these animals had never before been gratified.

THE BEAR-MAN

The Maritime woods are — or at least were — home to a great variety of animals... and a few beings that were feared to be half-animal and half-human. "A New 'What Is It'" appeared in the Saint John, New Brunswick, *Daily Sun* on October 7, 1882. It was credited to the "New York *Correspondence*."

A NEW "WHAT IS IT"
From the Woods of Northern New Brunswick

The transition may be somewhat sudden, but I saw the "Bear-Man" at Brighton the same day. He reminded me of Quilp, only he was less intelligent and consequently not as capable of being a villain. A sort of a lair is partitioned off in one corner of the museum for him, where he is concealed from view except when the spectators are allowed to pass through and look at him. When we went in he was sitting quietly on a raised platform which was carpeted and railed in. This was a special privilege given by his keeper, a weak-looking man with a long brown beard.

On seeing us the wild man sprang forward and snapped his jaws like a dog. His head is abnormally large, and is covered with long, curly brown hair. His eyes are gray, very small and shaped something like those of the Japanese. From his broad forehead his face tapers to a pointed chin, on which there is a tuft of fine hair. There is a suggestion of the pig in his lips, when they are extended as they are when he snaps. The neck is thick and strong; the chest and shoulders broad in proportion to his height, (or rather length, as he does not walk erect), and his arms are

81

thick and muscular between the shoulder and elbow. The muscles of his arms are at the back instead of on the anterior surface. His forearms are smaller in proportion than the upper arms, but his hands are large and fat. Each hand has a double thumb and six fingers. They are stubby and callous on the palm, like the paws of an animal. His knees have the appearance of being double-jointed, and his legs below the knees are without the usual muscular development. There are six toes to each foot, which is broad and flat like the hands.

While he was being inspected, "Heddy," as his keeper called him, sat with his legs drawn up, much as a tailor sits when at work on his bench, playing with a string of beads. Occasionally he picked a few loose beads from a box and added them to the string.

"He is always doing something," said the keeper, "just like a bear. He can't keep still."

"I must do something," said Heddy, looking up.

This remark was a revelation to us, as we had been informed that the bear-man could understand a few words, but could not talk.

One of the doors swung part way open.

"Shut that door, Jack," said the man-bear, addressing the giant.

The monster kept up his snapping at intervals. Once he snapped at me and made me jump back involuntarily, striking my elbow against the iron railing. When he perceived that I suffered pain he appeared to be very sorry for me.

"You made me do that," said I sharply.

"No, I didn't," he replied, as if he meant he didn't intend anything of the kind.

When several spectators came into the small enclosure, Heddy jumped down upon the floor and made at them. He hopped along upon his hands and feet after the manner of a toad. The crowd retreated perceptibly. A man whom he seized by the leg shook him off and slammed the door shut.

The keeper said that he captured the bear-man in the woods in the northern part of New Brunswick. He was in the nude state then, and lived on what he could pick up around lumber camps. His mother was an intelligent woman, but the monster was supposed to have received the physical formation of the bear from the fact that the mother was frightened by a bear before his birth. The man-bear, he said, had a tail, which was not a prolongation of the spinal column, but a tail like that of an animal. This was his story, and he looked like a man who was lying. Of course he was.

When the time came to admit the crowd, a wisp of rope was tied around Heddy's belt loosely. A chain, which was fastened to the wall, was snapped into this, and the wild man was fast. As each person passed before him, he jumped at them as a chained bull-dog would, grinding his teeth and growling. Women screamed and shrank from him, and almost went into hysterics. The very nervous persons were warned against going in. The man-bear knew enough not to jump too hard. If he had he would have broken the rope. This creature, divested of all humbug, is a queer animal and makes one feel a trifle uncertain about one's ancestry.

A HUMAN BEAR

"A Human Bear" appeared in the Victoria *Daily Colonist* on September 21, 1887. A reference to a Seattle newspaper appears in the first sentence of this account.

A HUMAN BEAR
It Looks like a Bear, Crawls like a Bear, and Acts like a Bear

A large party of Clayoquot Indians, says the *Seattle [Post-Intelligencer]*, from British Columbia, appeared in this city yesterday on their way to the hop fields. Accompanying them is probably as curious a specimen of unfortunate humanity as ever was born. It is neither a man nor a brute, but appears to be on the line dividing the one from the other. Considered as a human being, the being is a man; considered as a brute, it is a bear. It looks but little more like a man than a monkey does, except that the features are a little more distinct and there is not a coat of hair on his body. It cannot talk or walk upright. It crawls along on its hands and feet with the peculiar swinging motion of the bear. Its feet are at a very acute angle with the front of the leg, and when crawling the hands move with an inward swing like the front feet of a bear. The expression is almost that of a bear. There is a peculiarly wild look about it, and the eyes are restless and sharp. Everybody instinctively called it an "Indian Bear."

The Indians said they seldom take it along with them anywhere, but this time there was no one to stay with it. They say it is 20 years old. But little attention appears to be paid to it by the Indians, and it wobbles around with about the aimlessness of an old dog, seeking a warm place, and eyeing suspiciously the approach of anyone not familiar with it. The Indians say that a short time before it was born, its mother was frightened by a bear.

CHASED BY A WILD MAN

The motif of the Wild Man of the Woods is a staple of folklore. The legend is encountered in many, if not all, of the world's cultures. It was more familiar in the past, but even today "wild children" turn up, and there is debate as to how many characteristics (such as the power of speech) are inherently human and how many of them (for example, the ability to count) are acquired. In Europe, the motif took the form of the Feral Child who was denied the benefits of civilization. Much ink was spilt on the attempt to determine the language spoken by "the natural man" or "the child of nature." The Hebrew language was preferred as the "original language of man" or "the mother tongue of the world," but linguists could never come to an agreement about such matters. In the summer camp tales of Ontario, the motif of the Feral Child took the form of the Hermit in the Bush. In western Canada, watch out for the hairy wild man, the Sasquatch.

"Chased by a Wild Man" appeared in the *Winnipeg Free Press* on October 8, 1887. The account is apparently reprinted from the *Brandon* (Manitoba) *Sun*.

CHASED BY A WILD MAN
The Weird Adventure of Two Manitoba College Students

About a week since two young gentlemen, Messrs. McEwen and Mulvey, who are teaching school some distance southwest of this city, were on their way to Brandon to attend the convention of teachers. They left the place at which they were staying very late in the evening, and were accompanied part of the distance by some young friends, who had a dog with them. Taking leave of their friends they started northward. They had not gone far before they entered a wheat field, and were somewhat surprised to see an apparition in the shape of a man spring from behind the shocks, and run towards them. They were not frightened at first, thinking it was one of the party they had left playing pranks upon them. The figure approaching nearer, though, gave them a close and better view, and they discovered that it was a man with nothing upon him but a breech cloth, his hair, long and dishevelled, flying in the wind, and was foaming at the mouth. The man was coming towards them at a rapid gait, and they ordered him to stand back. At this he commenced to bark, and the young men to run.

It was a test of fleetness. There is no question that the wild man, for there is no doubt that the man was fairly wild, would have caught them. His bounds are described as being leaps such as they had never seen a man take. His barking caused the dog that was with the young men to bark, and hearing this, he immediately turned and ran in the direction of the noise. In a few minutes he caught up to them; but the dog giving him chase he ran, and ran so swiftly that he soon outfooted the dog, and was soon lost in the distance. The time was about one o'clock in the morning, and the night well lighted by the moon. The neighbours turned out to follow, but he had either hidden himself or got far away before they turned out. No one else in the district has ever seen him that we have heard of, and his appearance is shrouded in the mysterious.

A WONDERFUL COW

"A Wonderful Cow" appeared in *The* (Toronto) *Globe* on May 25, 1889. In the account, the name of the township appears both as Tecumseh and Tecumseth. The modern spelling of the village's name is Bond Head. The account locates the Carter farm on Lot 4, the affidavit on Lot 20. Approaching the farm from Toronto, the unnamed newspaperman, no doubt a city man, was more impressed with the beauty and utility of the farmland than with the "miraculous" birth on the farm. The tale is quite amusing.

GIVES BIRTH TO TWO LAMBS AND A CALF
The Family Thriving Township of Tecumseh
Made Famous by the Event
A Talk with the Owner—
No Doubt about the Authenticity of the Affair—
Mr. Carter's Affidavit—
A Splendid Farming District—
Fall Wheat Doing Well— Stock Raising—
The County School House.

The farmers of the Township of Tecumseh, in South Simcoe, are greatly interested at present in a strange freak of nature which has taken place in their midst, being nothing less than a cow giving birth to two lambs and a calf.

The interesting event occurred at the farm of John Henry Carter, lot 4, 8th concession line, on Sunday, April 14, and, when the news spread abroad, so many people wanted to see the curiosities that Mr. Carter finally decided to get rid of them and disposed of the cow and her progeny to Isaac M. Cross, an enterprising young farmer of Bondhead.

The animals were removed to Tottenham and a few days ago *The Globe* was invited to send up a man to see the stock and investigate independently the correctness of the story.

Starting out on Saturday a reporter reached Tottenham in the evening and immediately proceeded to the barn where the wonderful cow and her family were located.

At first glance the reporter was rather disappointed in the lambs, having entertained some vague ideas on the subject, and hoping to see a fully developed calf with the face of a lamb or vice versa. But they appeared to his uneducated eye to be ordinary lambs and nothing more. This was at a first glance. A subsequent careful examination and comparison with other lambs of the same age showed a marked difference.

Those of the unnatural parentage are larger and coarser, the wool is darker and in towards the pelt it is like the hair on a maltese cat; there is a tuft of hair on the breast between the forelegs similar to that of a calf. The legs are hairy and the wool is slightly streaked with hair. The mouth is dark inside and larger and firmer looking than that of a lamb, and the tail is frequently thrown over the back after the manner of a calf.

They are both ewe lambs. These indications, to an experienced breeder, are of themselves sufficient to prove the authenticity of the story regarding their strange birth.

If the lambs continue to thrive and develop more like calves, they will be worth thousands of dollars for exhibition purposes. There is a strong likelihood of their growing to a large size, and on both their heads there are dark spots, indicating a possibility of horns. They are at present as large as ordinary year-old lambs.

The cow is an ordinary, common-grade, red cow, without any pretensions to pedigree.

It is kept in the next stall to the lambs, and munches away quite contentedly.

The calf, which was born shortly after the lambs as stated in Mr. Carter's affidavit given below, is also in the group, but it has not the slightest claim to distinction, further than the fact that it is brother to the lambs. All four are healthy and vigorous-looking and will probably live to be the centre of attraction for many agricultural eyes.

Having seen the lambs the reporter decided to drive out and see Mr. Carter, the original owner of the curiosities, and in the interval something was learned of the flourishing Village of Tottenham. It has almost 800 population, is situated on the Northern & Northwestern Railway in South Simcoe and depends for its trade on the surrounding farming district.

There was a boom there some time ago, but at present things are quiet.

Land is stationary at $40 per foot and downwards, and the reporter was surprised to find some of the residents up there are putting their spare cash into Toronto real estate and have the fever just as bad as any in the city. Whether the Junction had played out, or the boom like to be worth much east of the Don were all-important questions.

Many of the residents had seen the lambs, but they appeared to be more interested in the movements of the owners than in the animals, and speculated freely as to what money could be made out of the enterprise.

It would be astonishing, were it not so common, to notice how quickly the most private matters become public property in a village.

The reporter was not half an hour in Tottenham before he had been told several times by perfect strangers that Mr. C. had paid so much for the cow and lambs; that Mr. S. gave so much for a half interest; that Mr. S. then sold out to Mr. N. for so much, and that Mr. C. was holding out for something big. This, with numerous stories about the neighbourhood, helped to while away the night.

A pleasant drive was enjoyed to Mr. Carter's farm. The weather was all that could be desired, and on either side stretched magnificent landscape. Mr. Carter's place was reached about noon, and on driving up that gentleman came out and very hospitably received his visitors. He is an honest, sturdy-looking farmer of about 55 years, and one look in his face convinced the reporter that there was good grounds for the respect and esteem in which he is held by neighbours and farmers for miles around. His farm comprises one hundred acres with another hundred lying some distance back, and he willingly, though in a quiet matter-of-fact way, talked of the event that had brought him a certain amount of notoriety. He repeated circumstantially the story as given on the affidavit, and stated that he would not have sold the cow and lambs only for the annoyance caused by curious people wanting to see them. He did not wish to make money out of the freak, and intended to have watched how they would develop. He pointed out several lambs of the same age frisking about, and they appeared to be kittens in comparison with the phenomenated ones. The reporter saw on this farm a splendid specimen of a peacock. It raised its beautiful tail and strutted about with all the proverbial pride of its race and seemed to be almost out of place in the homely backyard.

Mr. Carter's story, given in the form of an affidavit, is as follows:—

County of Simcoe, I, John Henry Carter,

To wit, of the Township of Tecumseth, in the County of Simcoe, Farmer, make oath and say:

That I am the owner of, and have owned for some time past, the cow described in the annexed bill of sale, the same being red in colour, with white stripe on the face, seven years old, and called Perkin.

That some time ago I noticed the said cow was with calf, and on Sunday, the 14th day of April, 1889, after returning from church, I drove my horse into my farmyard upon lot No. 20 in the eighth concession of the said Township of Tecumseth. This was a few minutes after one o'clock in the afternoon. As I drove into the farmyard, the said cow came towards the yard, having left the rest of the cattle. I knew it was near the time that the said cow ought to drop her calf, and I observed then that she appeared restless. I put my horse into the stable and then drove the cow into another barnyard and closed the gate. There was not another animal in the yard with the cow when I closed the gate and fastened it. I then went away from the yard and returned again in a few minutes, and seeing that the cow was all right, I went to my house and ate my dinner.

Immediately after dinner I returned to the yard where the said cow was, and as I was passing a shed I saw the said cow lying down under the shed, and hearing the said cow making a peculiar grunting sound, I stopped a few seconds to see what was the matter with her. As I stood there the cow jumped up and gave a mew sound and commenced to lick with her tongue what I then supposed to be a calf. While still watching the cow and what I supposed to be a calf the cow was licking, a head was raised that I saw at once was a lamb's head, and that there were two lambs the cow was licking and not a calf. I then took the lambs in my hands.

The cow commenced to bellow and appeared upon the point of attacking me. I placed the lambs upon some long manure straw in the sun to dry. The cow followed me and again licked the lambs until she had got them to stand up. As soon as the lambs were able to stand up the cow again laid down beside the lambs. I then saw that the said cow was in the act of having or dropping another, what on closer examination appeared to be a calf.

I immediately went to my house to inform my family of what had occurred and returned at once to the said cow, and upon my return to the yard the said cow had the calf also by her side, licking it also. All this time there was no other animal in the yard. I then went for my neighbour, Mr. Alexander Sutherland, and brought him over to my place to see the lambs and the calf. I then explained to Mr. Sutherland that the said cow was the mother of the two lambs and the calf. As I was showing the lambs to Mr. Sutherland one of them jumped out of the sleigh-box and went towards the cow. The cow turned round towards the lamb and commenced licking it. The lamb then got up upon its hind legs and, reaching to one of the teats of the cow, commenced sucking it. We then took the other lamb in our hands and I held it up to the cow's teat, and that lamb also sucked at the teat as long as I held it there. The calf also sucked at one of teats of the cow. Since that time we have fed the said lambs by milking the said cow and giving the milk to the said lambs to drink.

The said lambs commenced eating hay when they were two days old. The said lambs and calf are in good health and strength. I say positively that the said cow is the mother of the said lambs and the said calf, and that the said lambs are not the progeny of any ewe, and that there was not a ewe in the said yard with the cow, or any place near it, at the time the said lambs were born or dropped.

The sale herein made is upon the faith that the said lambs and calf are the progeny of the said cow.

Sworn before me at Bradford, in the Co. of Simcoe, on the 8th day of May, 1889.

(Signed) Geo. Mount

A Commissioner, etc.

(Signed) John H. Carter

Parting with Mr. Carter, the drive was continued to Bondhead, a village about three miles south-east, to the farm of Mr. Cross, sen., where the reporter had been kindly invited to spend the night. Here a hearty country reception was met with, and after dinner a long and instructive conversation on subjects sacred and secular was enjoyed with Mr. Cross.

As a result of this, the reporter came away with highly respectful feelings towards farmers as a class, especially those whose judgment has been mellowed by years. On Sunday evening service was attended at the Methodist Church, where Rev. Mr. Edwards preached to a small congregation on Mary's gratitude to the Saviour, as shown in her offering of precious ointment. Returning to the homestead, the remainder of the evening was spent in conversation and singing gospel hymns.

To reach Toronto on Monday morning it was necessary to take an early drive of six miles from Bondhead to Bradford, where the Northern train leaves at 8:10. The drive through this district (along the seventh concession line), revealed a finer class of farms than had heretofore been seen. Every house along the road was of solid brick and wore an appearance of affluence and comfort. About sixty years ago the first settlers found this district an almost impenetrable forest, but since that time an entire change has been effected; the timber has been cut down — save here and there, a grove left to beautify the country — stumps have been removed, and every year the soil yields abundant crops of wheat, peas, clover, or whatever may be sown. The present owners are nearly all descendants of the original settlers, and have kept on improving their holdings until they have to-day as fine a farm district as could be found anywhere in Ontario, or, for that matter, in Canada. There are several families of Stoddarts on this line, working together about 1,400 acres of land, and Col. Tyrwhitt, M.P. for South Simcoe, has a fine farm near Bradford.

After driving extensively through the Townships of Tecumseth and West Gwillimbury, one could hardly come away with anything but an exalted opinion of Ontario's agricultural resources. A better time of the year could not have been selected for such a visit. The grass and foliage were in full bloom, and recent showers had freshened up the face of nature. The air carried to the senses a sweet fragrance of apple-blossom and lilac; robins, wild canaries, greybirds, blackbirds and crows flitted from tree to tree. Young colts careened through the fields, while lowing kine and bleating lambs added their attractions to the scene.

The crops gave promise of a good harvest and a number of farmers spoke to state that fall wheat throughout the district was well up and other crops would be satisfactory. To the west of Tecumseh a good deal of attention is given to the raising of stock. In many of the fields along the Northern & Northwestern three or four colts were to be seen, and in one field as many as six were observed. In cattle breeding very little is done in the line of quality and as a consequence the stock raised is inferior.

A noticeable feature, and one deserving of credit, was the wisdom of setting apart small groves of trees when clearing the timber land. Nearly every farmer has at least four of the five acres of maple, cedar, spruce or hemlock that would be invaluable in thickly populated cities and that are no less valuable where they are. The difficulty is that timber becoming scarce may induce farmers to cut down these very desirable and useful groves.

If asked what was the most cheerless sight in these fertile districts one would be compelled to answer, the country school house. Several of them were passed on the way and they looked more dispiriting than a graveyard. In nearly every case they were situated on a piece of high ground without any trees in the vicinity — a severely plain wooden building in the centre of a barren piece of ground, enclosed with a dilapidated fence, and an unsightly outhouse in one corner. Probably the building had once been painted, but successive rains had washed the boards to a dull grey colour, and left it like a stranded Noah's ark.

THE SWAMP HORROR

"The Swamp Horror" appeared in the *Calgary Herald* on January 18, 1890. Its editors reprinted it from the pages of the *Winnipeg Free Press*. The reminiscence was apparently written by one Luke Sharp for the Detroit *Free Press*. As it happens, "Luke Sharpe" is the pseudonym adopted by the Toronto-raised novelist Robert Barr (1850–1912), who at this time was employed by the Detroit paper. Perhaps this explains the "writerly" quality of the gruesome account.

THE SWAMP HORROR

I spoke in the previous article of the dismal swamp that stood on the eastern limits of the village of Bruceville. Some time or other, probably before the village had been settled, there had come through the forest a tornado, and it had lashed the trees down in all sorts of shapes over the partly submerged land. Then at some other period a fire had swept through this, and had left it one of the most desolate, forlorn-looking, tangled mazes of half-burnt wood that could be imagined. Years had passed since that time, and repeated rains had washed most of the black off the wood and left the white, gaunt limbs sticking up in the air, like spectral arms, and made the ghostly place to us boys a region of terror and a first-rate place to avoid. Nobody, as far as I have been able to learn, had penetrated into the innermost recesses of that swamp. No boy that I ever knew dared to enter the swamp even in the brightest sunlight, while the thought of that swamp at night! — whew — it makes me shudder even now.

Nobody was more afraid of that swamp than I was, yet I think I may claim to have been the first boy that ever explored it, and that is the reason that my hair today is gray. I may say that about this time a great mystery shook the village from its circumference to its centre. The mystery was the strange disappearance of three cows that belonged to three of our villagers. Nearly every one of the villagers kept a cow, and these cows grazed on the commons that adjoined the village.

One day three of the most valuable cows were missing, and a search all over the country for them was unsuccessful. This mysterious disappearance caused more talk and gossip in that village than the murder of three men would have done in a larger town. Everybody had a theory as to how the cows had disappeared. I remember that a lot of wandering gypsies came along at that time, and one of the owners of the cows consulted a gypsy as to their whereabouts. After paying the fee the gypsy told him, somewhat vaguely, that he would hear of the cow, but that she feared he would not take as much interest in the animal after she was found as he had done before. This turned out, however, to be strictly accurate.

About this time someone introduced in the village a strange contrivance which was known as a kite. Improbable as it may seem, this invention would sail in the upper skies without the aid of gas, which is used to elevate a balloon. The way it was made was thus:

A hoop of a barrel was taken and was cut so that it made a semi-circle; then a piece of lath was fastened to the centre of that semi-circular hoop, and a piece of string was tied to the end of the hoop and down to the bottom of the lath. A cross piece of lath was also made to strengthen the affair, and then we cut a newspaper into shape and pasted it over the string and lath and hoop ends. A long tail was attached to the end of the lath, made of string, to which was tied little bits of paper, somewhat after the forms of curl papers used by ladies in those days to keep their hair in curl. Then a long string was attached to this kite, and if the breeze was good and you held on one end of the string, the affair rose gracefully in the heavens.

There was great competition among us boys in kite flying, and the wild desire to own the kite that would fly the highest caused bitter rivalry. I succeeded in getting a very good kite, and bankrupted myself in buying a lot of string as an attachment. After purchasing that ball of twine, I was poor in this world's goods, with the exception of that kite, which proudly floated away above its fellows. We used to tie our kite string to the fences, and leave the kites floating up all day, and I have seen as many as ten or fifteen kites hovering away above the village.

One day, when the wind was blowing from the village over the swamp, some envious villain, whose identity I have not been able to discover to this day, cut the string of my kite at the fence. If I had found out who the boy was at the time, I venture to say that there would have been the biggest fight that the village of Bruceville ever saw. I was in another part of the village when the disaster happened, and I saw with horror that my kite, which floated so high above the rest, suddenly began to waver and then floated off towards the east, wobbling to one side and then to the other in a drunken, stupid sort of fashion, and finally fluttered down to the ground somewhere on the other side of the swamp. In doing this it trailed the long line of valuable string clear across the dismal swamp.

It was hard to believe that there could exist in the world such desperate villainy as would prompt a boy to the awful deed. I passed through the village weeping loudly over the disaster, but this attracted very little attention; it was merely thought that I had got one of my usual thrashings, and there seemed to be a belief in the village that whenever that interesting episode occurred, it was richly deserved. I found the end of the string near the edge of the swamp, and I got a stick and began to wind it and save as much as possible of the string. I don't suppose any less consideration would have induced me to brave the terrors of that swamp, but through the wild entanglement I went, winding up the string, which was stretched over bush and bramble, and now and then stuck on the gaunt branches of some of the dead trees.

When I got about half way through the swamp, I began to realize that I was going to present a very picturesque sight when I got to the other side of it. My clothes were all in rags. I had fallen into the mud three or four times and my face and hands were scratched and bleeding with the brambles, but I saw that if I kept on I was going to save all the string and ultimately get the kite.

Just beyond the middle of the swamp there appeared to be an open place, and when I broke through the bushes I found there a little lake and in the centre a dry and grassy island. The dead stillness of the spot, although it was so near the village, began to make an impression on my sensitive nerves, and I wondered whether, after all, the string was worth the fearful price I was paying for it. I began to fear ghosts, spooks, bears, lions, tigers and one thing and another, when a sight more horrible than all of those together burst upon me as I cleared the brambles and stood in this green place. There, huddled together, lay the three cows. Their bulging, sightless eyeballs stared at me. Their throats were cut so that their heads were nearly half off. Their bodies were bloated and swollen out of all semblance to the original cows.

Thousands of years of life could not bring to me a moment of greater horror than that was. It would not have been so bad if I had been on the road, where I could have run at the top of my speed for the village. But here I was, hemmed in by an almost impassable swamp, that had taken me already an hour of hard wear and tear to get through. With a yell that pierced the heavens and must have startled the villagers, if any of them had been listening, I dropped the coveted string and dashed madly through the wilderness. How I ever got out to dry land again I never knew. It was a fearful struggle of unprecedented horror. I dared not look around. The hot breath of the cows was on the back of my neck. I felt that their ghosts were following. Those awful eyeballs peered from every dark recess of the swamp.

When I tore through the outer edge of the swamp, I had still strength enough to rush across the commons and dash madly down the main street of the village, all tattered and torn and bleeding, the light of insanity in my eye and the strength of insanity in my limbs, yelling at the top of my voice, calling: "The cows! The cows! They are in the middle of the big swamp with their throats cut!" and when I reached my own door, stumbled and fell into the entrance, to the consternation of my relatives, and, either from the excitement of the fearful episode or the fall, lay there insensible.

A body of men, although they seemed to doubt my story, penetrated in to the green island of the swamp, where they found the cows and buried them, but no one ever knew how the animals got in there or who committed the dastardly deed that led to their death.

WHAT I SAW IN THE REARVIEW MIRROR

Memphré is the name given to the lake monster that is said to make its habitat in the waters of Lake Memphremagog in Quebec's Eastern Townships. Leo Gervais is one of the four hundred or so residents and visitors who, since 1813 (and presumably earlier), have reported seeing "something strange" in this beautiful lake. The ever-elusive creature acquired the catchy name Memphré in the 1960s.

Gervais has contributed a remarkably clear, level-headed account of a sighting. When he is not vacationing in the area, he is the editor of *The Monitor*, a weekly paper that serves Montreal's West End. I received Gervais's account from Jacques Boisvert, a longtime resident of the city of Magog, which is located on the shore of Lake Memphremagog. Boisvert is one of the founders of La Société de dracontologie/International Dracontology Society, which celebrated its tenth anniversary at the newly dedicated Place Memphré — *"Site d'observation de créatures lacustres non identifiées"* — on June 19, 1996. On that occasion, speeches referred playfully to Memphré as the lake's "oldest resident." Here is a glimpse of him ... or her... or it.

It was the summer of 1987. I was twenty-one, in my second year of university, and enjoying what was a wonderfully sunny July day. I had driven the 140 kilometres or so from Montreal to my friend Andy Matthew's cottage on Lake Memphremagog, on the Knowlton side of the lake, near Knowlton's landing.

His cottage was on the lot right next to the Glenbrooke, a longtime bed and breakfast which, although not as fashionable as in its heyday back in the '40s and '50s, was still frequented by summer vacationers.

I rounded the last curve on the twisty gravel road approaching Andy's place. This turn dipped, then hairpinned to the left. On the right, as you turned, the lake was about fifty metres down a sloping hill. On this sunny, windless day the lake looked like it was covered with diamonds, reflecting the brightness on its watery surface like so many scattered jewels.

After making the hairpin, I looked in my rearview mirror — a reflex, I suppose. I could see the road behind me and part of the lake in reflection, still shimmering in the bright of the day. In that brief moment that I looked in the mirror, I saw something else.

A dark, serpentine form moved in the lake about twenty metres from shore. I cannot say I saw a head, but the body had to be at least twenty feet long, since I watched it for a few seconds as it came above the surface and then disappeared, leaving a large ripple effect in the otherwise still lake.

I stopped the car and got out, surveying the spot where I had seen the snakelike form. The ripple was not caused by a fish — it was much too big for that.

I saw nothing else. After several anxious moments of hoping to get another look at which I'd seen, I continued on the last quarter-mile to Andy's cottage. Upon arrival, I told him what I'd seen and he, of course, laughed. But after detailing my sighting, he grudgingly acknowledged it may have been Memphré.

4 Hardly Human

IN THIS SECTION, we will encounter an array of land and sea creatures, some of which are half-human, while others are "hardly human." In the former category are the beguiling creatures known as mermaids. Perhaps it is not surprising that descriptions of these doleful creatures — sirens, really, lolling in the waves within the sight, but beyond the reach, of goggle-eyed sailors — are plentiful in the logbooks maintained by sea captains and merchant mariners. At the same time, there are reports aplenty of mummies and petrified creatures, "men of stone." Needless to add, merfolk have nothing at all in common with these preserved bodies of the long dead, but they share space in this chapter because the annals of early Canada seem to be full of references to them. They seem to bear little or no resemblance at all to the mummified pharaohs of ancient Egypt — except for the fascination that follows their discovery and the threat of their "re-animation"! To keep the reader of this section on his or her toes, there is also the surprising appearance of the Devil himself!

THAT MONSTER OF A MERMAN

Nicolas Denys (1598–1688), a colonist and promoter of the fisheries and the fur trade throughout Acadia, was born in Tours, France. He worked as a merchant at La Rochelle from 1632, and died at his trading post at Nepisiguit, Acadia. He is the narrator of the account of the sighting of "a Merman" that follows.

Denys's account appears in his book *The Description and Natural History of the Coasts of North America (Acadia)*, which was originally published in Paris in 1672 and was translated into English and edited for the Champlain Society by W.F. Ganong in 1908. A passage of cryptozoological interest appears in the "Collateral Documents" section of Ganong's edition; it first appeared, not in the original French edition of Denys's, but as an interpolation into the Dutch translation, first published in 1688. The illustration also derives from that translation.

Did the mariners of the Acadia of the 1650s believe in the existence of a race of mer-beings, creatures that are half-human and half-fish? Whether or not they did, they reported seeing at least one such creature.

I must here make a little digression in order to relate a matter which deserves special notice and of which there have been eye-witnesses enough so as not to bring the truth of the same into doubt. While in the year 1656 three ships were lying on this coast for the sake of catching cod, the men of Captain Pierre Rouleau, lying farthest away from the shore, noticed some distance away in the sea a peculiar commotion that was not caused by anything which had the form of any known fish. They stared at it for some time without knowing what to make of it. Since the opinions about it were very much divided, as it usually is among men who have little knowledge, they rowed in the boats to the ship to get a telescope. Then they saw clearly that this fish, or to say better, this monster, which still retained the same appearance, seemed to take pleasure in the beams of the sun (for it was about 2 p.m. and very clear and fine weather); it seemed to play in the gently undulating water, and looked somewhat like a human being. This caused general astonishment and likewise great curiosity to see this strange creature near by, and, if possible, to catch it.

Upon the order of the Captain they therefore kept very quiet, in order not to drive it away by any noise, and descended quickly into the boats with ropes and other things, by means of which they thought they could most easily get the monster alive into their hands. But while the men of the Captain named were thus engaged, those also of the other two ships, although they had lain farther away, had caught sight of the same object, and being extremely curious to get a nearer acquaintance, had betaken themselves to their boats and had taken the oars in hand. Captain Rouleau, who was himself in one of his boats, rightly understanding that in this way they would by no means attain their end, but, on the contrary, would by untimely noise drive away the monster, beckoned all these vessels together and gave command to row out a long way on both sides, in order thus unforeseen to fall upon it from behind. This was done in all quietness, but it came to pass that one of the sailors, or the fishermen, throwing out overboard away from the boat, cast a rope over the head of the Merman (for it was in fact a Merman), but since he did not quickly enough draw it shut, he shot down through the loop and away under water, presenting in his lowest part, which became of the quick movement could not well be made out, the appearance of a great beast.

At once all the boats gathered round in order to catch him in case he should come up once more, each one holding himself ready for that purpose with ropes and cords. But instead of showing himself there again above water, he came to view farther out to sea, and with his hands, whereof the fingers (if indeed the things were fingers that stood in the place of fingers) were firmly bound to each other with membranes just as those of swans' feet or geese feet, he brushed out of his eyes his mossy hair, and which he also seemed to be covered over the whole body as far as it was seen above water, in some places more, in others less. The fishermen distributed themselves again, and went a long way around, in order to make another attempt; but the Merman, apparently noticing that they had designs on him, shot under water, and after that did not show himself again, to the great dejection of the fishermen, who many a time went there to be on the lookout, and incessantly racked their brains to invent stratagems to catch him.

I am sure this digression has not been unpleasant to the reader, yet one might have wished that the trouble of the fishers had had better success, and that they might have gotten that monster of a Merman into their power. Now let us take up again the broken thread of our story.

ACCOUNT OF A MERMAID

"Account of a Mermaid" appeared in the Halifax *Gazette* on December 5, 1765. The description is seemingly set in the days of the Dutch occupancy of Manhattan Island.

Some Years ago, as the Milk maids of Campen (a Port-Town in the United Provinces) were crossing a Lake in order to come at their Flocks, they espied a human Head above Water, but believed their eyes deceived them, till the repeated Sight confirmed their Assurance, whereupon they resolved one Night, to watch her, and saw that she repaired to a slaggy Place, where it was Ebb, and near the Side; whereupon, early in the Morning they got a great many Boats, and invironed the Place in the form of a half Moon, and disturbed her, but she attempting to get under the Boats, and finding her Way stopt up by Staves and other Things on purpose flattened, began to flounce and make an hideous deafening Noise, and with her Hands and Tail sunk a Boat or two, but at last was tired out and taken; the Maids used her kindly, and cleansed the Sea Mess and Shells from off her, and offered her Water, Fish, Milk, Bread, &c. which she refused, but with good Usage in a Day or two, they got her to eat and drink, though she endeavoured to make her Escape again to Sea; her Hair was long and black, her Face human, her Teeth very strong, her Breasts and Belly to her Navel were perfect; the lower Parts of her Body ended in a strong Fish Tail; the Magistrates of Harlem, commanded her to be sent to them, for that the Place where she was caught, was in their Jurisdiction: When she was bro't thither, she was put into the Town-house, and had a Dame to attend on her and to teach her. She learnt to Spin and show Devotion at Prayer, she would laugh, and when Women came into the Town-house to spin with her for Diversion, she would signify by Signs she knew their Meaning, though she could never be taught to speak. She would wear no Cloaths in Summer; Part of her Hair was filleted up in a Dutch Dress, and Part hang'd long naturally. She would have her Tail in Water, and accordingly had a Tub of Water under her Chair made on purpose for her. She eat Milk, Water, Bread, Butter and Fish; she lived thus out of her Element (except her Tail) fifteen Years: Her Picture was painted on a Board with Oil, and hangs now in the Town-house of Harlem. When she died the Magistrates suffered a Place in the Church-yard for her Interment.

EXTRAORDINARY, IF TRUE

Here is another mermaid sighting. "Extraordinary, If True" comes from the *Novascotian*, November 26, 1860.

A correspondent of the Miramichi *Colonial Times* writing from Youghal, [New Brunswick] Oct. 28, relates the following extraordinary circumstance. He says that one night last spring he had a peculiar dream, repeated several times during the night, of digging up a large quantity of money at a certain locality called Tinker Point. On visiting the spot in the morning, he was so impressed with the accuracy with which the locality had been described in his dream, that he resolved to test the truth of the nocturnal revelation still further, and, furnishing himself with pick and spade, commenced digging. He says:—

> "After working for a time, and almost going to give it up for a bad job, my spade struck upon some wooden substance which proved to be a coffin, in which was the remains of a human body, of extraordinary length and size, measuring 8 feet 6 inches, which apparently has been buried some years ago. There was no appearance of flesh or clothing, and when the coffin was opened there was no difficulty in discerning the outlines of a huge well-developed body, but immediately after the air coming in contact with it, the body seemed to dissolve leaving nothing but the immense skeleton and a quantity of dust. In the coffin was found some old rusted implements of warfare. In a small earthenware vessel singularly sealed, I found an old manuscript written on parchment in some foreign language, but not being able to decipher or translate the contents of the same, I some time ago deposited it with Mr. End of this place, but having not since had any conversation with that gentleman on the subject.
>
> "The skeleton I have had conveyed to Dr. Nicholson's office, where the curious have an opportunity of feasting their eyes on this giant!"

CONSIDERABLE ALARM

This news story is reprinted from the columns of the Victoria *Daily Colonist* on July 1, 1863. Sailors have been seeing mermaids and sirens since time immemorial. Now and then, landlubbers also report the unexpected sight of these creatures. The beings themselves are usually as astonished to see humans as humans are to see them. Neither the newspaperman who wrote this story nor Mr. Graham, who reported seeing this "mythological marine animal," tried to relate it to a known species of marine animal. Instead, the creature is related to previous sightings by Natives and to their beliefs.

A MERMAID IN THE GULF

Mr. Graham, who is erecting a saw mill on Burrard Inlet, has just given us an interesting description of one of these mythological marine animals which he saw on Monday week in the Gulf of Georgia, about midway between the Inlet and the mouth of the Fraser. It was about 6 o'clock p.m., when he saw it gradually rise above the surface of the water within about 30 yards of where he was, showing the entire bust, in which position it remained for the space of five minutes looking in the direction of the boat in which he and two Indians were sitting, when it slowly sank into its native element. The Indians evinced considerable alarm at the strange phenomenon. Mr. Graham describes it as having the appearance of a female with long hair of a yellowish-brown tinge drooping over its shoulders, the color of the skin being a dark olive. The Indians have a legend that if this animal is seen and not killed, those by whom it is seen will pine away and die, and relate an instance of the kind as having occurred amongst the Squamish tribe. Hence the alarm of these Indians at the sight of the one alluded to. They also state that many years ago one was killed on Squamish river by an aged Indian.

A CASE OF PETRIFACTION

"Remarkable Transformation" appeared in the Brandon, Manitoba, *Mail* on July 8, 1886. The account is apparently reprinted from another newspaper, the *Argus* of St. Marys, Ontario.

REMARKABLE TRANSFORMATION
Details of an Interesting Case of Petrification
A Resurrected Body that Weighed over Half a Ton

The St. Mary's *Argus* says:— A well-developed case of petrification has recently been discovered at Sault Ste. Marie, in the following interesting manner:— Several years ago there dwelt on Sugar Island a family by the name of Chappel. Mrs. Chappel who, though rather a corpulent person, weighing up to the time of her death, over 200 pounds, was, nevertheless, very handsome, energetic, intelligent, and beautiful, and, though still possessed of many beautiful traits of Christian character, also retained some very peculiar notions. Amongst these latter might be recorded her earnest desire to be buried in a lovely, sequestered nook on the farm; that her coffin be made of tamarack and her shroud of black satin. It is needless to say that these wishes, with many other minor details, were faithfully and affectionately fulfilled by her sorrowing husband and children.

Two years later the husband was laid beside his beloved consort, P.M. Chappel, merchant, Sault Ste. Marie, and W.W. Chappel, proprietor of the Summer Resort, Horse Shoe Harbor, Drummond Island, sons of the deceased, resolved to have the family burying ground, in the beautiful cemetery at Sault Ste. Marie. Having given directions to have the remains conveyed up the river, they, in company with a number of friends, proceeded to the wharf, where a great surprise awaited them. As it required the united efforts of half-a-dozen men to remove the coffins from the boat, it was thought advisable to remove the lids, and an examination of the contents revealed a more than ordinary transformation, for instead of earth and ashes, two stone bodies lay before them, that of Mrs. Chappel being pronounced perfectly petrified, and weighing bout eleven hundred pounds. The grave clothes had not changed, and even the tints of the artificial flowers that composed the wreath and motto, "Safe in the arms of Jesus," which lay on her breast, were as fresh and beautiful as when placed there ten years before by loving hands.

For three days previous to their reinterment, the bodies lay at the grave's mouth, and were inspected by hundreds of people, including the resident doctors and army surgeon of that place.

THE BODY OF A PETRIFIED MAN

This story of a body-snatching, and of the exhibition of human remains, appeared as "A Curious Case" in the *Macleod Gazette* (based in present-day Alberta) on June 31, 1896. The reader cannot help but wonder about the resolution of this case, which was before the Winnipeg court, to say nothing of the nature of the process of petrification.

A CURIOUS CASE

A curious case is now occupying the attention of the police court in Winnipeg, two men being charged with stealing the body of a petrified man from a farm in Minnesota. The story in connection with this petrified man is decidedly romantic. The body was discovered on June 8th last by two farm laborers who were putting in a culvert, buried in a bed of white alkali clay, three feet below the surface. The body was then sold to a third party for $1,000. In the meantime the owner of the farm where the body was discovered heard of the incident, claimed the body and retrieved it. A compromise was effected by a company being formed and the body was taken on exhibition through several towns. New claimants then appeared on the scene in the persons of two old gentlemen named Lecount, who state that the petrified remains were those of their father. The company, however, got the body by furnishing a bond, and took it to the Winnipeg fair, where the Lecounts followed them and swore out warrants against them. The Lecounts claim their father, Antoine Lecount, a French half-breed guide, was conducting a party of English tourists from Fort Garry to Fort Snelling. He was accompanied by his wife and two sons — the prosecutors — who were then 10 and 11 years of age. This was 58 years ago. One of the English gentlemen was insane and one morning seized a rifle and shot their father in the breast. The mother and her two sons buried the body in the spot in which the petrified corpse was found. Their only desire, they state, is to give their father's remains Christian burial.

THE DEVIL HIMSELF

Where else would the Devil appear but in the sanctuary of a church, where members of the congregation — who believe in his existence as they do in the existence of angels — have gathered? There are people who regard the Devil as a real power or personality, rather like an inverted version of God. There are other people who see him, like the angels, as a folk figure, the personifications of bad or good inclinations or influences. However bizarre they are, people's beliefs are not to be tampered with.

"The Devil in Church" appeared in the *Ottawa Free Press* on December 6, 1897. The Hornerites were followers of R.C. Horner, the Ontario-born Methodist evangelical preacher who in 1895 led the members of his congregations out of mainstream Methodism and into the aura of the Holiness movement. He never wore a dress tie after the Devil tried to use one to strangle him.

THE DEVIL IN CHURCH
Hornerite Congregation Gets a Scare at Madoc
Boys Say It Is a Joke

A very strange thing occurred recently at a Hornerite meeting held at the meeting house of that sect, situated seven miles north of Madoc, known as "McCoy's," says the Tweed *News*. The people came as usual to their place of meeting, an old wooden building, through the cracks and crevices of which the wind blew with many a ghostly and weird sound. As the meeting progressed, and as the preacher arrived at that part of his discourse in which he had occasion to speak of the devil, there arose immediately in their midst, through and from beneath the floor, a spectre so awful in appearance that the audience and preacher alike were wholly paralyzed with fear. The latter had hardly ceased speaking when there rang out a voice terrible to hear:

"I am the devil; I'll have you. Ha, ha, ha."

Fire issued from his mouth and nostrils. He needed not this to proclaim himself, as from his appearance his identification was an easy matter. He is described as having two horns, one protruding from either side of the head, a cloven foot and a clanking chain, two flaming eyes like balls of fire and a large appendage at the rear. His ears were perpendicular and pointed at the top, and a fiery blaze encircled his whole body and head. His figure was tall and slim and his position erect, and when he spoke the building shook as if by an earthquake.

He had not yet ceased his sardonic "Ha, ha," when the terrified people and preacher alike rushed pell-mell for the door over seats and one another in their frantic endeavors to rid themselves of so awful a presence. Following them closely, this fiery fiend's sardonic voice was again heard and seemed more terrible than before. "I am the devil; I'll have you. Ha, ha, ha."

No further warning was needed. The terrified people fled in all directions, leaving "His Satanic Majesty" in full possession of their meeting house.

A few days after the occurrence some of the sports of the neighborhood whispered about that it was a practical joke, conceived by them, but the Hornerites refuse to believe them.

THE MUMMY

"The Mummy of Harrison Lake" appeared in the Victoria *Daily Colonist* on September 16, 1899. The writer makes a number of extreme observations that no archaeologist, anthropologist or ethnologist would dare make today!

HARLAN SMITH'S CONTRIBUTION TO ARCHAEOLOGICAL LORE OF THIS PROVINCE
His Ancient [Mummy]
Sent to New York Museum
as Ruler of Northwest Indians

FROM OUR OWN CORRESPONDENT

Vancouver, Sept. 14.— Prof. Harlan L. Smith, of New York, who recently made the discovery of an Indian mummy near Harrison Lake a few days ago, shipped it to New York. Professor Smith thinks, and local archaeologists agree with him, that the mummy is probably hundreds of years old.

107

It is the most remarkable find of a two years' search for native relics, pursued by Professor Smith on this Coast.

A couple of years ago a well-known New York millionaire, whose interests were, particularly at that time, in the Klondike, subscribed a large amount of money to the National Museum of New York, as an endowment for the purpose of carrying on anthropological research on the Pacific Coast.

Professor Smith and his staff are now about finishing their work here, and the find that they made the other day is by far the most interesting of any discoveries ever made west of the Rockies.

Professor Smith had been scouring the district around Harrison Lake for two months. The section is a well-known mining district, and the formation of a limestone character, in which relics of soft material have been easily preserved. The mummy was found in a cave immediately alongside a trail leading up the mountain. Smith and his men had passed the place dozens of times, without ever thinking of the possibility of the existence of a cave in the vicinity. A great mass of white limestone and granite formed the "hog's back" of the mountainside, and where the cave was found was somewhat moss grown and weather beaten. Big boulders, which scores of years ago had fallen from the mountain, were piled up several feet in front of the cave. One day in passing by Professor Smith noticed the smooth stones which blockaded the entrance to the cave, and he immediately proceeded to investigate.

The face of the rock was covered with strange hieroglyphics, much defaced. Professor Smith says:

"After using a pick a short time we had practically to blast the face of the rock away, as the cave had been hermetically sealed. The reason for this was apparent from what we found later. We lighted ourselves into the cave, which was perhaps 20 feet square, and high enough for convenient standing room. I do not think that there had ever been any mineral found in the cave, but as the sunlight streamed in at the newly made opening, the walls fairly blazed with crystal reflections. Around the sides of the cave were shelves hewn out of the rock, and in one of these we found the sarcophagus which contained the mummy which has been shipped to New York. The other shelves had evidently been intended for like receptacles, but for some reason the cave had been sealed up with only one body in the vault.

"The sarcophagus was simply a stone coffin, and without any top covering. Anyone who has ever opened an Egyptian mummy case, no matter how many thousand years the subject has been disposed of in this way, will always afterward recognize the peculiar odour, which was the same which emanated from the sarcophagus we found.

"The wrappings were of peculiar texture. From the neck downwards there was fully a dozen folds of a thick cloth composed half of hair and half of stringy bark. I have seen the same sort of matting used by the Indians in Alaska. The face looks very similar to the ordinary Egyptian mummy, and was preserved as well as any of the mummies I have seen. The particular feature of the ancient's head was his high forehead, which makes me think that he was of the tribes who must have lived before the flat-faced, squat-headed Siwash Indians of the present day.

"We unwrapped one hand, which was shrivelled up to mere skin and bone, some of the nails having already disappeared. The mummy had been a tall man of large proportions, another indication of his being of a race different from the Pacific Coast Indians, who are short, and do not average 5 feet. The mummy, by actual measurement, was over 6 feet tall.

"Around the ankles and wrists were bands of silver, alloyed with some other metal, which went to show, with the other trappings and the sarcophagus, that the man must have been a ruler of his people.

"I think he must have been a member of the tribes living in the Northwest before the forbears of the present race arrived — as is generally conceded — from the Eastern Asiatic coast.

"The texture of the wrappings, as I have already mentioned, bore some evidences of a civilization at least a few degrees above the standard of savages."

Professor Smith's statements are verified by parties living in the district, who have examined the cave and have seen the mummy.

Professor Smith is now in Secum, Ore., looking up the particulars of some important discoveries there. He will return to New York in October.

MERMAID?

Comic relief might be the best way to describe the following item. It was published in the *Saint John* (New Brunswick) *Daily Sun* on December 20, 1902, and it appeared in the guise of a news item. But patently it is an early instance of an "infomercial" or "advertorial."

WHAT THE MERMAID SAW IN THE CANADIAN LAKES
A Message to Canadian Women

Being a Mermaid of the Canadian Lakes, I only know Canadian women as they can be seen from my watery bed in the vast depths. I often wonder if up there in the sunlight you have pretty dells, mountains, and sandy wastes, such as we have in dear old water-land. I don't know about your mountains and your dells, but I do know you must have wastes; for every day, and particularly on one day of the week, you send down to us more waste than you know of. When your soap suds flow into our pure water, we have the power of sight to divide in the water the true from the false; and we find that in your soap suds there is a mixture that you cannot see, a mixture of silicates, ground glass, and adulterations that never dissolve in water, and consequently must be useless for washing purposes. You must waste money in buying such concoctions, you waste time in using them, you waste your clothes in rubbing them in. Alas! there is a lot of waste up there in the sunlight; but there is no waste in Sunlight Soap. Where Sunlight Soap is used by any of you, I find no leading refuse, no adulterations coming down to me in my home in the deep. Sunlight Soap reduces expense in the wear of clothes, and you don't waste money on loading mixtures, such as I have seen in common soap suds.

Please, dear Canadian women, don't send down any soap suds but those of Sunlight Soap. Have respect for your dear Canadian waters, and your purses, is the message of the Mermaid of the Canadian Lakes.

CREATURES THAT ARE PROBABLY UNIQUE

Today, mermaids are held to be creatures of the imagination, delightful beings that belong in the pages of children's books and in fairy tales like Hans Christian Andersen's "The Little Mermaid." It was not always so in the past. Perhaps they once existed in the real world. Perhaps at one time they inhabited the world's seas. After all, they have been described by practical-minded Canadian sailors and seamen. Here is one such description of a sighting. This intriguing item, "Real Mermaids in Hamilton," comes from the August 31, 1917, edition of the *Delbourne* (Alberta) *Progress*.

REAL MERMAIDS IN HAMILTON
Spaniard Possesses Two Most Curious Creatures, Half Human, Half Fish

J.E. Smith, a Spaniard residing in Hamilton, Ont., possesses two creatures that are probably unique. He considers them to be mermaids. Though these are described as "fabled" or "fictitious" creatures in the dictionaries, the creatures in Mr. Smith's hands have heads shaped like those of human beings and bodies that are distinctively fish-like. One is much larger than the other, and is considered to be the mother, and reckoned to be 300 years old. Both have fine hair like a human being, and a small moustache and beard. The head is attached to a human-like neck which merges into the fish-like body, and the arms are something like those of a monkey, only that the fingers are webbed. He has been offered $700 for his curios. It is said that the creatures were found in the wreck of a ship in the Arabian Sea.

AN ANCIENT MAMMOTH

Mammoths, elephant-like creatures that roamed the polar world, are part of the fossil record. They lived during the Pleistocene Epoch, which lasted from 2.5 million years ago to 10,000 years ago. In modern times there are reliable reports of the carcasses of woolly mammoths being accidently exposed, thawed and consumed by dogs and men. For instance, the Russian writer Alexander Solzhenitsyn described the "good luck" of prisoners in a Siberian gulag who accidentally came upon the once-frozen flesh of a mammoth and gobbled it up.

"Dawson Prospector Says He Has Found Ancient Mammoth" appeared in the *Dawson Daily News* on July 22, 1915. R.A. Fox's tale may very well be a tall tale. In this instance the "mammoth steak" might be a portion of indigestible asbestos fibre.

DAWSON PROSPECTOR SAYS HE HAS FOUND ANCIENT MAMMOTH

"Waitah, bring me a mammoth steak!"

Such may be the cry in Dawson within a few days if R.A. Fox has just what he thinks he has. Fox blew into town today from up the Yukon with a gunnysack filled with what he declares is the steak of a prehistoric mammoth.

"Have I got it? Well, I should say I have," declared Fox today.

"Just wait a few minutes," continued Fox, "and I will bring you some of the mammoth with the fat clinging to the sides of the meat."

Fox was gone a short while, and returned to the *News* office with several slabs wrapped in a gunnysack. Unwrapping it in the presence of several who had not been informed what the material was supposed to be, Fox said:

"Now, see here, what is it?"

A sourdough miner stepped up and looked through his glasses carefully as he turned over the strange substance.

"Why," exclaimed the sourdough, "that's asbestos. Sure thing. I've seen it in the raw state, and I've seen the finished product."

A veteran "print" who had called on the *News* dropped in and asked what it was.

Feeling the material carefully, he declared, "Why asbestos, of course. Wish I had plenty of that for future use."

In ambled a third man, who was shown a piece, and asked his verdict. "Well, it looks like wood fibre," declared he cautiously.

A cheechaco from Tacoma walked in and was shown the samples.

"What does she look like, Mr. Cheechaco?" said the discoverer.

"You don't get me on that," said the cheechaco. "I've visited Seattle in my day, and I have nothing to say."

"Well, now just let me tell you fellows what it is you are looking at," said Fox. "That long, white, stringy, slabby stuff is nothing more or less than the flesh of a prehistoric mammoth reduced to fibre. That whiter portion, which is less marked by strings, is the residue of the fat. The real grease evaporated."

"Where did you shoot that mammoth?" piped a fellow in the crowd.

"Well, may be you boys think you have it on me," rejoined Fox, "but let me tell you I did shoot him, and I shot him on the Yukon river bank above Dawson, and the carcass is now there."

All the fellows opened their mouths with astonishment. Everyone was from Missouri.

"But it's the way," said Fox. "I shot him while he was lying compressed under a million tons of rock, and where he had been resting for two hundred million years.

"As I was coming down the Yukon river in the canoe the other day, I put over to the right limit of the river below the mouth of the Sixty-mile river.

"In a secluded bend in the river, where it was almost a cove, I observed in a cliff about thirty feet high a singular whitish object projecting a foot or so from the regular face of the rock. I got closer to it, and on inspection found it was the end of a mammoth tusk. I took a shot at it with my rifle and brought down a part of the ivory. That confirmed my first suspicions. I had done ivory carving in Dawson for years, and I know mammoth ivory from mastodon ivory quite well. The mastodon ivory is checked like a crocodile hide, and yellowish, while that of the mammoth is whitish and has a long grain.

"After securing the sample of the tusk, I got several sticks of dynamite, and placed them in the face of the bluff just beneath the point where the tusk protruded. There is where I shot the mammoth. Those several shots of dynamite disturbed enough of his prehistoric majesty to afford me these samples. The dynamite explosions freed a cap of rock along the face of the bluff so that the mammoth remains were exposed. The strata is two feet thick and twenty feet along the exposed edge. I did not have time to drift in on the proposition, but I feel assured the bones are there unless absorbed or done away by leaching of the water and the chemical action in the rocks.

"Now, it is only a matter of recovering the rest of the fibre. I believe that the mammoth was caught under the heavy rock from above, which crushed him against the other rock beneath, and, being encased hermetically, the fibre was preserved. I threw some of the white fibre to my cats, and they gnawed on it. Since it did not hurt them, I have eaten some, and I think mammoth steak is all right. Of course it is a little drier than jerked beef, and lacks the salt, but we can get plenty of salt.

"Dr. Alfred Brooks, the American geologist, will be here tomorrow on the Dawson, and I shall call the mammoth discovery to his attention, and get his views on the matter. When Dr. Cairnes, the Canadian geologist, arrives here later this season, I shall ask him to go up and examine the find, and he may tell me just how to remove the big fellow."

Mr. Fox has samples of the mammoth at Nick's place, on Queen street. Mr. Fox has been prospecting and following other pursuits in Yukon several years.

Several years ago he had a thrilling experience in a cabin on Quartz creek, where a miner who had been killed by an accident, reappeared at night in the corner of the cabin and operated a rocker and held a conversation with Fox. At the end of the conversation the phantom form disappeared suddenly.

THE PETRIFIED WOMAN OF MUD ISLAND

"The Petrified Woman of Mud Island" was written by Bonnycastle Dale and it appeared in the *Calgary Herald* on November 23, 1929. In a florid style more characteristic of the latter half of the nineteenth century than it is of the first half of the twentieth, the writer records the details of a Maritime tradition. Sable Island lies in the Gulf of St. Lawrence.

While we call Sable Island, 150 miles seaward, "The Graveyard of the Atlantic," we call the reefs and submerged islands — past the "Devil's Limb" and "Limb's Limb" westward to the "Noddy," twenty miles out —

"The Hospital." On the jagged spears of these foam-streaked rocks, many's the stout bark, the tall creaking ship, the wallowing, smoke-spurting tug and collier have crashed — all now rusted, sea-wracked, torn and riven hulls, some that we ourselves saw wrecked, others for half a century back, others like the unknown bottom that struck on Mud Island (Big Mud) sometimes in the dim past, so long ago that only this odd story survives it for three-score years and ten.

As you go westward around Cape Sable, Nova Scotia, past "Seal" and "Noddy," you come to the far outlying Mud Island. It is in the twenty-five-fathom line and subject to the mighty tides that sweep and scour the Bay of Fundy. (Imagine, my mid-continental readers, the great Lake Ontario — twice — filled and twice emptied every twenty-four hours, and then you can glimpse the power and fury of the fifty-six-foot tide which sweeps on and up to the end of "The Bay.")

The distressed vessel with its human burden was swept thus far up the great bay and struck on "Big Mud," and the next tides the pitiful bodies of Negroes and whites were swept ashore on the flood. The great bay was not girdled by lighthouses as it is today, and the story spread but slowly. We know that the boat was a packet — steam and sail — and that not all the bodies which came ashore were dead; in one, a white girl, life still lingered. But, notwithstanding all the few lobster-fishermen gathered there could do (so my informant, the lighthouse-keeper, told me), she died, and was given Christian burial.

Big Mud Island was then used mainly for summer shanties for the lobstermen of the Mud Island Lobster Company, and soon the wreck and the few lonely graves lay unnoticed, a nine-days' wonder passed by. The lobster pots were set, drawn, the season passed, and the island lay almost deserted. Year after year, every March, these lobstermen, and at times their families, too, returned for the short spring season, and one day, in an idle moment, a visitor with that fiendish lust for curiosities dug down into the shallow grave of the shipwrecked girl. The spot where it had been buried was right in the seepage run of a tiny creek, full only in the early spring melting time.

Soon the rude shelf which enclosed the body was reached and torn asunder and the digging tool struck something which sounded like stone. The visitor sent out a call for assistance, and soon the petrified body of the poor drowned girl was exposed to the glare of the spring sun. It was as hard and as unyielding as marble. The lime contents of the underground seepage had thoroughly filled each cavity and vein and artery, soaking in and replacing its natural contents with the filmy deposits which, once they dried out as the summers advanced, were stone-like in their formation.

This story, sent abroad by word of mouth in the early seventies, spread like wildfire, and the result was that visitors poured in daily to see the strange sight of a body marble-like in its consistency but faithful still to its human form in every line, shrunken though some of the once fuller parts were. Merciful people reburied the poor body, but the next few hours saw fresh visitors feverishly digging up what should by all our precepts be hallowed ground. Nor were the ghoulish excavators careful.

The fingers of the petrified body were especially brittle and were broken off and some were carried away to the great scandal of this most peaceful people, for, though the waters of Fundy writhe and tear along, sixty feet deep of continual ebb and flow, and the winds thrash the seas, and these Acadians and Nova Scotians, French and British, all good neighbours now, daily snatch a living from this confused sea, they are a most simple hospitable people.

The priests and the clergy and the councils took up the tale, and orders were sent to Big Mud Island to bury the body deeply and put up a headboard. This, too, was thrown over and the body again exhumed. Now the real governors of the island, the Mud Island Lobster Company, took a hand, and they wrote to the man who lived there all the year, shepherding the half-wild sheep (which also snatched a living from the sea, a precarious living on dulce and laver and kelp), ordering him to take the poor abused body and secretly and at night convey it into the woods and hide it and to bury it deeply.

They also bade him make a sketch of the exact spot where the body lay. So at last the harried remains rested securely hidden from the clutching fingers of the ghouls. So well did the island shepherd do his work that not a trace of the body can be found today.

You can get this tale from the mouths of the older people all along that shore. Go by motor-boat, from Wedgeport via Calf Island, Bald and Inner Bald direct to Mud Island. See Gannet Rock, if you pass outside

Spectacle Island. If ever the body comes to light again, I trust that a fund will be raised for cement block interment and a suitable headstone erected.

I thoroughly believe the story, as it was told to me by a man so faithful in his work, so trustworthy, so hospitable to us during the two years when we dwelt in the little cabin by "The Light," and we also heard it repeated by many mouths for miles along Fundy's rude shores.

5 Omens and Prophecies

AN OMEN OR premonition may take the form of a vague feeling, sign, warning, forerunner, harbinger or vision. A prophecy may be rooted in revelation, soothsaying, prediction, forecasting, statistical modelling or probability analysis. Palmists, crystal-ball readers and fortune-tellers work from their parlours or storefronts, whereas their more sophisticated and business-oriented cousins, futurologists or futuristists, address business groups in boardrooms, hotels and universities. Everyone wants to know the future, or at least to have "an edge" on it. But is any such knowledge possible? Readers may come to their own conclusions after reading about some of these omens and prophecies from the Canadian past that were seemingly fulfilled.

THE QUEBEC EARTHQUAKE

Marie de l'Incarnation was one of the most remarkable women ever to live in this country. Marie Guyart (1599–1672) was born in Tours, France, and from her earliest years she seemed concerned with matters both material and mystical. As a child she had a dream in which she saw the Lord and heard him ask her, "Do you want to be mine?" She immediately replied, "Yes." She did not enter a convent right away, but entered into the state of marriage and bore a son. Then her husband died.

Not long after she was widowed, she experienced what she called her "conversation." This occurred on March 24, 1620, in her twenty-first year. She felt herself immersed in the blood of the Son of God. The experience left her with "a clearness more certain than any certitude." In later years she described it as "an inner paradise." There are further details in Marie-Emmanuel Chabot's entry on Marie de l'Incarnation in Volume I of the *Dictionary of Canadian Biography*.

Marie Guyart entered the Ursuline order at Tours, taking her vows in 1633 and assuming the name of Marie de l'Incarnation. She dreamed of a vast country full of mountains, valleys and heavy fogs. In another dream or vision, she beheld the Lord speaking to her and saying, "It was Canada that I showed you; you must go there to build a house for Jesus and Mary." In 1639, she set sail for Quebec.

There is no need to go into detail concerning her life in New France, but it is important to realize that she regarded her actions as guided by God, so certain was she of her apostolic vocation. It gave her strength to establish the Ursuline order in New France, to found a convent school to educate young French and Indian girls, to master the Algonkian language and compile word lists, and to write an immense number of letters. From the time of her death in Quebec in 1672, she was venerated as a saint. Bishop Laval wrote that "she was dead to herself ... and Jesus Christ possessed her so completely." She was subsequently sanctified by the Vatican.

Of the estimated 13,000 letters that Marie de l'Incarnation wrote in New France, only a couple of hundred have been preserved. They are rich in descriptions of the spiritual and secular life. Joyce Marshall translated and edited *Word from New France: The Selected Letters of Marie de l'Incarnation*, which was published by the Oxford University Press in 1967.

After having a strange experience, Marie de l'Incarnation wrote the following letter in confidence to her son. "My very dear son," she wrote on August 20, 1663, continuing:

I have waited to give you an account separately of the earthquake this year in our New France, which was so prodigious, so violent, and so terrifying that I have no words strong enough to describe it and even fear lest what I shall say be deemed incredible and fabulous.

On the 3rd day of February of this year 1663 a woman Savage, but a very good and very excellent Christian, wakened in her cabin while all the others slept, heard a distinct and articulated voice that said to her, "In two days, very astonishing and marvellous things will come to pass." And the next day, while she was in the forest with her sister, cutting her daily provision of wood, she distinctly heard the same voice, which said, "Tomorrow, between five and six o'clock in the evening, the earth will be shaken and will tremble in an astonishing way."

She reported what she had heard to the others in her cabin, who received it with indifference as being a dream or the work of her imagination. The weather was meanwhile quite calm that day, and even more so the day following.

On the fifth day, the feast of St. Agatha, Virgin and Martyr, at about half past five in the evening, a person of proven virtue [Mother Marie-Catherine de Saint-Augustin], who has frequent communication with God, saw that he was extremely provoked against the sins committed in this country and felt at the same time disposed to ask him to deal with these sinners as they deserved. While she was offering her prayers for this to divine Majesty, and also for souls in mortal sin, that his justice be not without mercy, also beseeching the martyrs of Japan, whose feast was being held that day, to consent to make application for this as would be most suitable to God's glory, she had a presentiment — or rather an infallible conviction — that God was ready to punish the country for the sins committed here, especially the contempt for the ordinances of the Church.

She heard the voices of these demons saying, "Now many people are frightened. There will be many conversions, we know, but that will last but a little time. We will find ways to get the world back for ourselves. Meanwhile let us continue to shake it and do our best to turn everything over."

The weather was very calm and serene and the vision still had not passed when a sound of terrifying rumbling was heard in the distance, as if a great many carriages were speeding wildly over the cobble-stones. This noise had scarcely caught the attention than there was heard under the earth on the earth and from all sides what seemed a horrifying confusion of waves and billows. There was a sound like hail on the roofs, in the granaries, and in the rooms. It seemed as if the marble of which the foundation of this country is almost entirely composed and our houses are built were about to open and break into pieces to gulf us down.

Thick dust flew from all sides. Doors opened of themselves. Others, which were open, closed. The bells of all our churches and the chimes of our clocks pealed quite alone, and steeples and houses shook like trees in the wind — all this in a horrible confusion of overturning furniture, falling stones, parting floors, and splitting walls. Amidst all this the domestic animals were heard howling. Some ran out of their houses; others ran in. In a word, we were all so frightened we believed it was the eve of Judgement, since all the portents were to be seen.

★

I close this account of the 20th of the same month, not knowing where all this commotion will end, for the earthquakes still continue. But the wondrous thing is that amidst so great and universal a wreckage, no-one has perished or even been injured. This is a quite visible sign of God's protection of his people, which gives us just cause to believe that he is angry with us only to save us. And we hope he will take his glory from our fears, by conversion of so many souls that had slept in their sins and could not waken from their sleep by the movements of interior grace alone.

SECOND SIGHT

The notion of "second sight" is centuries, if not millennia, old. It is a form of knowing, analogous to "seeing" in the sense of "viewing" or "imagining." It is done (if it is done) without the use of the five senses. Perhaps there is a sixth sense, like intuition or imagination, that may account for its operation. The following account of extrasensory communication appeared under the title "A Ghost Story" in the November 7, 1859, edition of the *Novascotian*.

A GHOST STORY

Mr. Hector M'Donald, of Canada, was recently on a visit to Boston. When he left home his family were enjoying good health, and he anticipated a pleasant journey. The second morning after his arrival in Boston, when leaving his bed to dress for breakfast, he saw reflected in a mirror the corpse of a woman lying in the bed from which he had just risen. Spell-bound, he gazed with intense feeling, and tried to recognize the features of the corpse, but in vain; he could not even move his eyelids; he felt deprived of action, for how long he knew not. He was at least startled by the ringing of the bell for breakfast, and sprang to the bed to satisfy himself if what he had seen reflected in the mirror was real or an illusion. He found the bed as he left it, he looked again into the mirror, but only saw the bed truly reflected. During the day he thought much upon the illusion, and determined next morning to rub his eyes and feel perfectly sure that he was wide awake before he left bed. But, notwithstanding these precautions, the vision was repeated with this addition, that he thought he recognized in the corpse some resemblance to the features of his wife.

In the course of the second day he received a letter from his wife, in which she stated that she was quite well, and hoped he was enjoying himself among his friends. As he was devotedly attached to her, and always anxious for her safety, he supposed that his morbid fears had conjured up the vision he had seen reflected in the glass; and went about his business as cheerfully as usual.— On the morning of the third day, after he had dressed, he found himself in thought in his own house, leaning over the coffin of his wife. His friends were assembled, the minister was performing the funeral services, his children wept — he was in the house of death. He followed the corpse to the grave; he heard the earth rumble upon the coffin, he saw the grave filled and the green sods covered over it; yet, by some strange power, he could see through the ground the entire form of his wife as she lay in her coffin.

He looked in the face of those around him, but no one seemed to notice him; he tried to weep, but the tears refused to flow, his very heart felt as hard as a rock. Enraged at his own want of feeling, he determined to throw himself upon the grave and lie there till his heart should break, when he was recalled to consciousness by a friend, who entered the room to inform him that breakfast was ready. He started as if awoke from a profound sleep, though he was standing before the mirror with a hairbrush in his hand.

After composing himself, he related to his friend what he had seen, and both concluded that a good breakfast only was wanting to dissipate his unpleasant impressions. A few days afterwards, however, he received the melancholy intelligence that his wife had died suddenly, and the time corresponded with the day he had been startled by the first vision in the mirror. When he returned home he described minutely all the details of the funeral he had seen in his vision, and they corresponded with the facts. This is probably one of the most vivid instances of clairvoyance on record. Mr. M'Donald knows nothing of modern spiritualism or clairvoyance, as most of his life has been passed upon a farm and among forests. It may not be amiss to state that his father, who was a Scotch Highlander, had the gift of "second sight."

A PROBLEMATIC DREAM

The only information I have on Cromwell F. Varley, the writer of the account that appears below, or on the "problematic dream" that he experienced at Harbour Grace, Newfoundland, in 1860, is derived from the interesting and important book titled *Noted Witnesses for Psychic Occurrences*. It was compiled by Walter Franklin Prince, a noted psychologist and psychical researcher, and the publication is an annotated anthology of more than 170 experiences of psychic experiences of a spontaneous or sporadic nature, as distinct from accounts of experiences that resulted from planned experiments. His book was published by the Boston Society for Psychical Research in 1928. Gardner Murphy contributed a new introduction to the 1963 edition issued by University Books of New Hyde Park, New York.

"This incident was told by Mr. Varley, a prominent English electrician, to the London Dialectical Society," wrote Prince, who cited as his source the 1873 *Report on Spiritualism of the Committee of the London Dialectical Society*. Prince went on to discuss the curious characteristics of this dream, which he considered to be "problematic."

This is one of the most interesting dreams for study with which I am acquainted. On the one hand it is easy to form a theory of normal explanation. While dreaming he heard the sound, correctly guessed that it was caused by a falling plank, inferred that therefore there was probably a yard near the house containing timber, also inferred from the sound that the plank must be too heavy to be lifted by one man, and correctly guessed that there were two. All this, although a happy combination of accurate inferences and guesses, might be possible. But Mr. Varley testifies that he dreamed he saw the stack of timber and two men approach, ascend the stack and lift the plank, and that he dreamed a device to make himself

123

wake, before he had the sensation of noise in the dream. An ordinary person might during the time which had elapsed since the dream, nine years, have misplaced the order of its details, but it is less likely that a man of science strongly impressed and bound to study his recollections on waking, should have done so. But there is some evidence tending to show that dreams affected by real sensory impressions do sometimes rearrange the time order so as to present on waking the illusion that the cause of the sensory impression was imaged before the impression itself was received. But it is at least exceedingly rare that a dream should present imagery corresponding to the real facts, as though by inferences, and yet not connect that imagery at all with the sensory impression as its cause, but attribute the cause to something entirely different. Mr. Varley's dream correctly pictured the real external facts, yard, stack of timber, two men, plank and fall of the plank, but ascribed the sound to a bomb! If "clairvoyance," whatever process that term really covers, is deemed established by a mass of other evidence, it is perhaps simpler to ascribe this particular case to it.

Prince was not the only researcher intrigued with Varley's vision. A number of Varley's experiences were reproduced in shortened form by Leslie Shepard in the first volume of his monumental 1979 work *Encyclopedia of Occultism and Parapsychology*. Shepard noted that Varley seemed able to bring about "the liberation of the double in the state of sleep."

I have had another case in 1860; I went to find the first Atlantic Cable; when I arrived at Halifax my name was telegraphed to New York. Mr. Cyrus Field telegraphed the fact to St. John's and then to Harbour Grace; so that when I arrived I was very cordially received at each place, and at Harbour Grace found there was a supper prepared. Some speeches followed and we sat up late. I had to catch the steamer that went early the next morning and was fearful of not waking in time, but I employed a plan which had often proved successful before, *viz.*, that of willing strongly that I should wake at the proper time. Morning came and I saw myself in bed fast asleep; I tried to wake myself, but could not. After a while I found myself hunting about for some means of more power, when I saw a yard in which was a large stack of timber and two men approaching; they ascended the stack of timber and lifted a heavy plank. It occurred to me to make my body dream that there was a bombshell thrown in front of me which was fizzing at the touch-hole, and when the men threw the plank down I made my body dream that the bomb had burst and cut open my face. It woke me, but with a clear recollection of the two actions — one, the intelligent mind acting upon the brain in the body, which could be made to believe any ridiculous impression that the former produced by will power.

I did not allow a second to elapse before I leapt out of bed, opened the window, and there were the yard, the timber, and the two men, just as my spirit had seen them. I had no previous knowledge at all of the locality; it was dark the previous evening when I entered the town, and I did not even know there was a yard there at all. It was evident I had seen these things while my body lay asleep. I could not see the timber until the window had been opened.

INDIAN PROPHECY

It is often argued that the indigenous peoples of the world enjoy a special relationship with the world of nature and a special insight into the nature of man. One ethnologist referred to this traditional way of knowledge as "a participation mystique." It is held to embrace knowledge, insight and wisdom concerning nature's remedies, spirits of plants and animals, and the power of prophecy.

"A Remarkable Indian Prophecy" is reprinted from the January 9, 1880, edition of the Fort Benton, Montana, *Daily Record*.

A REMARKABLE INDIAN PROPHECY
The Coming of the Mounted Police Foretold by a Medicine Man
The People Who Part Their Hair in the Middle
Woeful Times for the Bloods Predicted
A Pipe-Stem Chief Warns His Tribe to Beware of the Whites
The White Squaw Chief
No Use for a Grandmother

Late advices from Fort Macleod, in regard to Indian matters, state that but few Indians remain in that country.

The Stonies and Sarcees, who have never yet left the Northern Territories, are endeavouring to gain a scanty subsistence from such small game as may be found, and a few Blackfeet also remain; but it is the intention of all to emigrate from a country which to them seems to hold out no other inducement but starvation. They begin to realize that the predictions of their prophets and medicine men have come to pass. Those intelligent reds some years ago, after many preparatory ceremonies, made an ascent to the summit of Chief Mountain and there, smoking to the direction of the North, the South, the East and the West, invoked the Great Spirit to grant them a sight into the future and show them the extent and duration of the buffalo herds, the dependence of their people.

Having remained several days in the vicinity of Min-as-to-co, or Chief Mountain, they returned to their lodges, and calling a grand council of their various bands, they imparted to them their visions in words to the effect that the wrath of the Great Spirit was about to descend upon them in punishment for their past misdeeds. They told their astonished and frightened listeners that a white woman would be Chief over them all, and that she would send many of her children, all dressed in red cloth, to teach the young men how to live without hunting or going to war, and invite them to work with their hands instead; and that those people dressed in red would after a while compel all the men who had more than one wife to send the remainder away; that they would not allow them to buy fire-water, steal horses, or even go on the warpath against their enemies.

"Some of you old married men," said they, "will like the great change for a short time, because you will not be compelled to tie up your horses at night to guard against the thief or enemy, nor will you be obliged to pile up logs and dried meat around the outside and inside of your lodges to stop a bullet. This change will seem like a rest after all the excitements you have passed through in your days of drunkenness; but another change will come over you. We have looked over all the buffalo herds in our country and over their future feeding grounds and I tell you not many snows will come and go before we will have to leave the land where we were born and where our fathers died.

"Our new grandmother, that white woman chief I told you about, will find it impossible to keep us here and furnish us with all we want. We will have to take our lodges and move far away to the land of the stranger and camp among our enemies, they will attack us and kill our women and children or lead them into slavery and leave us afoot to mourn our losses. The Great Spirit will send us sickness and hunger and keep the buffalo going from one place to another so that we will not be able to follow them, and deep snows and many strange people will come between us and our meat. After a while we will smoke with all our enemies that live like us on the prairie, and whose hearts are bad toward the white man. We will then be strong and drive the whites away so that the buffalo may return to our country and we will be happy."

The Blood tribe arose and said to his followers:

"I had a dream and I saw a large camp of strange people. They were tall and good looking for people who live on the prairie and their hair was parted in the middle like a woman's. They had many lodges, horses and mules, better and larger ones than ours. They also had strong guns, which they claimed to have taken from the whites. I approached this camp of over one hundred lodges, and being discovered, one of the medicine men came out to meet me, and asked:

"'Who are you? and whence do you come?'

"I told him that I was a Pipe-stem, Chief of the Bloods, and that I was in search of a new country for my people, that the hearts of the white men who had come to us were getting bad and that we could no longer live where we were born.

"The stranger took me by the hand and said, 'I belong to the great Dacotah and there are not a great many of us. I pity you and your people because we once were like you. But now, look at us, we feel strong, we have good horses, good mules and guns which we have taken from the white dogs that were driving us towards the mountains of the setting sun. Look at me — my medicine is strong and while I wear this medicine robe my enemies cannot do me harm.' And to prove his medicine he called his soldiers and ordered them to load their guns. Then, wrapping his medicine robe around him he stood and received the fire of the whole party unharmed. I looked on in astonishment and walking up to him I examined the robe and found that it was whole — but that all the bullets had fallen at his feet.

"My dream ended and I was awakened by the cries of my children for meat. Now, my children, I feel that in a short time I shall die, for what I saw in my dream must have been in the 'Happy Hunting Grounds.' But I advise you to remember my words: Be suspicious of the whites, watch them, and be careful of your land for which the dogs will want to pay you with paper. Should you ever meet any people like those I have described from my dream, smoke with them. I think they must be a great people, with great hearts, and the colour of their skin is the same as our own. I would not advise you to make war with the whites until compelled by hunger or other causes. The Bloods have many friends among the whites, but it is best for you to keep away from all those white chiefs that are sent from afar to take care of you. By going to see them you will lose your time, and the few things you receive would be much cheaper bought from a trader than taken for nothing in that way. You will lose the flesh from your horses and return starving from the agencies.

"You have seen the great many foolish men the Great Father has sent to talk with us. Their tongues are long, but their eyes are bleared. They cannot see far, and they make their tongues do that which their eyes should first learn. They will tell you that the Great Father is sending plenty of everything to feed his hungry children, and that it will be here in so many days, and invite you all to be there. Don't believe them; don't go there; their talk is paper talk, and the paper has a crooked tongue, and when no goods are there at the appointed time, the white man says some one has lied to himself. He should have guarded his tongue till his eyes told him the time to tell the truth. Some of you think it is bad to quarrel with the whites, because they furnish you with powder, knives, blankets, tobacco, sugar, tea and flour. I say to you, my children, that you can have the same as our people did before the white dogs came.

"You young people, now growing up, would soon learn how to chase the game over cut banks and into many places where you might easily kill it with the bow and arrow, which all of you know how to use and how to make. You would learn to skin and cut up the buffalo with a stone, and the hide is all the clothing you require. Only tobacco you cannot get like our fathers, and you can do without that if necessary.

"You don't want any traders among you, and your women will not have to work so hard dressing skins and furs, all they should do would be to prepare sufficient clothing to cover the nakedness and keep warm the bodies of their own people. Look at your women, they look old and weary before they are young; their hearts are sad and all from the hard work to gladden the trader. You are children, when the white man shows you his goods. Don't look at those things and you will not want them. I have been a fool when I was young or I would have listened to the medicine men and followed their advice. But now I will die, and I hope to meet those strange people I have told you about. I will die with a strong heart if my people think I have spoken well."

MRS. COO

Mrs. Coo was a respected fortune-teller in New Glasgow, Nova Scotia. In folk memory it is recalled that she predicted the explosion in the Foord mine. The clairvoyant was subsequently interviewed by a reporter from Halifax, who published his story about her and her abilities in the *Halifax Chronicle*. "The Stellarton Fortune-Teller" was reprinted in the Toronto *Mail* on November 20, 1880. Yet to be located is the original report of the Foord mine disaster, as well as any independent confirmation that Mrs. Coo's prophecy was uttered and recorded before the event. But what *was* found is another newspaper account of her prophetic abilities, which is reprinted later in this chapter.

THE STELLARTON FORTUNE-TELLER
Interview with the Woman Who Predicted the Colliery Disaster

The Stellarton correspondent of the *Halifax Chronicle* has the following:—
Enquiry among the miners showed that it was quite true that this and the other disaster had been foretold by this Mrs. Coo before spoken of. Most of the miners regarded it as a good joke, and even still are sensible enough

129

to say the woman only made a lucky guess. But some of the more super-stitious did put faith in it, and the day before the explosion it was the subject of conversation in many of the shanties. One woman, it is said, was so impressed with a belief in the prediction that she hid her husband's boots the next day and delayed him so long in hunting for them that the explosion occurred before he went down the shaft. It seems, however, that her warnings of danger in the mine were not always the same. To some men who consulted her she said working in the pit would be safe up to a certain day after the second breaking in of water, but to others this day was different, thus showing, she said, that some would be in danger before others; but in the majority of cases the 12th was regarded as the day.

This evening I went over to consult this oracle in the outskirts of New Glasgow. I was shown her house, a little one-story building. We knocked at the door, which was opened by a rather pretty young woman, and, in response to our enquiry for Mrs. Coo, were at once shown into the parlour, a comfortably furnished room in which a cheerful fire was burning. The black cat was not there, nor were there any notice-able sulphurous fumes, which was reassuring. On the table was a church hymn-book, a couple of fashionable novels from Mudie's Library, London, and one or two school books. We now waited anxiously for the appearance of the soothsayer — expecting, of course, to see an old hag with a crutch and sinister eye, such being the general idea of the sooth-sayer, but she turned out to be a by no means ill-looking woman of great size, with a brawny arm bared to the elbow which might have levelled a man with one blow. She is about forty years of age, and the wife of a foundry workman, now absent in the States. Not being in very good circumstances, and having other mouths to feed as well as her own, she read destiny in a tea-cup at a dollar a read.

I inquired if she had really predicted the disasters to the Foord pit. She replied in the affirmative, and, moreover, said she had predicted the destructions of the Drummond colliery weeks before it occurred, nam-ing several persons who had consulted her in reference thereto. Could she tell anything further about the Foord pit? She could, "but business was business." This meant coin, and the difficulty having been smoothed over she raised the book of fate in the shape of a white tea-cup with powdered tea grounds in the bottom. She began to read out whole sentences, the most of which were nothing but the talk peculiar to all similar humbugs, made up of words the meaning of which the reader herself evidently did not know. Here and there she would look up and explain the meaning of what she saw. There will be another breaking in of the water, but not loss of life, which may mean the pouring in of water now going on. There would be two more men killed very shortly by something falling on them, or in some sudden and violent manner. One of these was a large and handsome man, and had a loud voice; the other was shorter. She could see that no fire was yet near the shafts, and none would go into the North side of the cage pit or the old Bye pit. She could see six bodies near together and not far from the main shaft bottom. She described them. The Foord Pit was not lost, and much money would be made from it by one who now had great anxiety. One number from now, whether month or year she could not tell, the men might take their picks and enter the mines once more with safety. Nearly all the bodies would be recovered. These and many more prophecies did the woman get out.

Much more did she tell, and all with an evidence of deepest earnestness, which would certainly lead one to suppose that the woman really believed what she was getting off. When asked if she thought she was doing right in thus pretending to read the future, she denied the pretense, said it was a gift she had, and that she would be no man if, when she saw danger in the path of mankind, she did not warn them, for a price of course. It seems the woman has been pursuing this business for many years, and I am told in many instances her prophecies turned out correct, and these were heralded forth, but nothing is said of the hundreds of other instances where her guessing was as wide of the mark as it is to be hoped the present prediction of further loss of life about the Foord pit soon may prove to be.

BY MEANS OF A DREAM

It is often held that dreams may do any one of or all of the following: predict the future, recall the past, expose our fears, express our hopes, reveal unconscious concerns, limn destiny or fate or communicate between the living and the dead. "A Strange Story" originally appeared in the *Toronto News* on October 12, 1882. Here, a dream communicates beyond the grave.

131

A STRANGE STORY
A Lost Man Found by Means of a Dream
A Speedy Answer to Prayer

FROM THE MAIL

Kingston, Oct. 11.— A most marvellous occurrence transpired at Inverary a few days ago, the most interesting facts of which arrived here to-day. Lawrence Carey, an old man 70 years of age, got lost in the woods on Thursday morning, and a vigilant search of three days failed to find him. On Sunday morning about 100 men took part in the search, but they all met at Carey's house with the same story — no trace of him. An open-air prayer-meeting was held, and the Rev. B. Young engaged in prayer for the safe deliverance of the lost one to his friends. While he was enumerating Carey's many virtues as a friend and a neighbour, there was scarce a dry eye in the whole assemblage; Mrs. Hogan, a relation of Carey's, overcome by her emotion, was carried off the ground in a fainting fit. Before the meeting had broken up, as if in answer to Rev. Mr. Young's affecting appeal, joyous shouts were heard, and Mr. Magee, of Inverary, came up in hot haste with the glad tidings that the lost was found.

Magee, it appears, had been engaged in the search all day Saturday, having always taken a very warm interest in Carey. On Saturday night he had a startling dream, in which he avers the Holy Virgin appeared to him, and described to him the exact spot where Carey was to be found. In the morning he related his dream to a number of neighbours, and told them that he thought he knew such a place as the one described in his dream about two miles north of Hart's dwelling. They hooted at the absurdity of the thing. As night approached, however, and no trace of Carey had been found, his strange dream made such a deep impression on his mind that he started to go in quest of the place resembling the one described to him. He found it without much difficulty, a large opening in the earth between two hills, some six or eight feet in depth, apparently formed by some convulsion of nature. The walls are rocky and precipitous, and there at the bottom, strange to say, lay Carey, the object of all their search, buried in a deep sleep. Mr.

Magee lost no time in arousing the unconscious sleeper, who, through exposure and want of proper sustenance, was unable to stand upon his feet. He could give no satisfactory account of how he had got there, nor how long he had remained in what would have assuredly been his living tomb had it not been for Magee's discovery. It appears that he left home on Thursday evening to look for the cattle, but lost his way, and wandered about in the darkness until he fell into the pit in which he was found, and was through physical infirmities unable to get out.

A PLANET READER

Here is an amusing interview conducted by a journalist with a fortune-teller. The journalist calls the fortune-teller a "planet reader" or a "planet writer." The journalist has in mind someone who consults the stars in order to make predictions. This teller of fortunes is an astrologer, rather than a palmist or a crystal-ball gazer. In this instance the woman's predictions go awry. "Revealing the Future" appeared in the *Victoria Daily Colonist* on September 4, 1886. The author identifies himself in the text as William Winterbottom.

REVEALING THE FUTURE
Mr. Winterbottom's Interview with a Planet Reader

A young man whose present circumstances are such as to convince him that they will have to radically change if he is to enjoy prosperity in the near future, and wishing to be prepared for any sudden transition that might be awaiting him called yesterday upon a planet writer who is doing a land-office business in this city. Upon arriving, in response to a light and rather nervous tap, he was ushered into a darkened room with a certain solemnity. Worked up to a state in which he was ready to believe anything it is small wonder that, during the few moments in which he was unable to discern anything, his imagination fully supplied him with conjectures. As his gaze became accustomed to the comparative gloom he noticed, uneasily, a number of skulls placed on the mantle shelf, on a bookcase, and in various parts of the room, where, also, appeared musty-looking charts,

133

an orrery, a collection of old teeth that looked as though a raid had been made on the business accumulations of an industrious dentist, and various other dainties in the shape of dried frogs, a small alligator's skin, etc. These the visitor noticed more intuitively than particularly, for his attention was quickly concentrated upon the figure of a woman seated at a table. She was erect of mien, and, apparently unheeding the black cat upon her shoulder, looked straight before her, which happened to be at the visitor.

"Aha!" she said at last in a sepulchral tone; "and so you've come."

It never entered the mind of the young man that this was a self-evident fact; and, attributing the knowledge to her supernatural powers, he stammered out, "Yes;— I—."

"Enough," said the madam, "I know already," and relapsed into silence. After a minute's pause, during which the young man's uneasiness increased, the planet-reader resumed: "I know your name; but just to see if you are telling the truth let me hear you utter it. It is—."

"William Winterbottom," almost gasped the young man, astounded at her wonderful prescience. "You have told truly," said the seeress, who could see by his face that he had; "and now tell me the hour and day on which you were born. One dollar, please!" The young man having complied with this dual request, the seeress knocked the cat from her shoulder, looked at a chart, made several mystic signs in the air, snapped her fingers (not defiantly) — pirouetted three times on her right heel — stopped directly in front of the amazed Winterbottom, and said: "You came to see me about getting married!"

Pausing a moment to regain his self-possession, Mr. Winterbottom answered, "I think there is some mistake. I came to see if the Cormorant street ghost was any relation to a maiden aunt of mine named Greenway, who ran away with a bootblack in Pennsylvania several years ago, and has not since—."

"Silence, scoffer!" responded the planet-reader, who, after having made a mistake could stick to it as well as anybody; "you are going to get married to a tall girl with red hair—."

"No! no!" protested Winterbottom.

"—with turned-up nose and freckled face," proceeded the seeress with deliberate cruelty; "and she's going to boss you too! The fates decreed it a thousand years ago."

Desperate at the thought of such a fearful fate William Winterbottom rose to his feet. "They did, did they?" he queried; "well, let me tell you I regard it as a horrible conspiracy on their part and look upon you as concerned in it. Now let me tell you your fortune. If you are in Victoria twenty-four hours from now it will be your fate to appear in the police court. You are exactly described in the vagrancy act, and it is already decreed that you shall be punished under it. And I don't charge you a cent for the information, either."

And with a "Ha! ha!" fully as sepulchral as that with which he had been greeted by the planet reader, Mr. Winterbottom departed.

PLANETARY VOYAGE

Many detailed accounts of visits to fortune-tellers, especially those who employ astrological charts rather than tea leaves in their "readings," make for enjoyable reading. This account is no exception. "Sailing 'Round the Stars" appeared in the *Victoria Daily Colonist* on September 24, 1886. It would be interesting to know the name of the reporter who contributed this account, so as to read other work of his (or hers). But the reporter left the piece unsigned.

"SAILING 'ROUND THE STARS"
A Trip to the Planets
Fortune-Telling by Consultation with the Heavenly Bodies

There is a rare pathos and beauty in the mythological stories of the planets, although it is a branch of literature overlooked by a vast majority of people. The attraction has not been wanting, however, to many superstitious persons both in the United States and England who are to-day turning their limited knowledge to good account pecuniarily. It is estimated that there are a thousand fortune-tellers who use the planets as a means of plying their calling. From a source so exalted the subjects expect to hear marvellous things about themselves, and despite the seeming absurdity of it, hundreds of people seek these supposed planetary agents for advice and a peep into the future.

135

Hearing that a fortune-teller received visitors here in Victoria a gentleman lately from the east called to test her powers, and, according to his own story, the experience was a novel one. Being ushered into a cozy sitting room he met a pleasant lady, who hearing his errand became enthusiastic on the subject at once. Producing a pencil and a slip of paper she said:

"Write your name, date of birth, and the hour, if you are positive of it, on this slip of paper. That will do. So you were born on the third of January at 2 o'clock in the afternoon. I don't believe you are right about being born in the afternoon, it was in the morning about the time Jupiter first appeared above the horizon."

"Why? Were you present when I made my bow to the world, madam!"

"No, I was not."

"Well, I was, and ought to know when I first wrestled with life."

The planet reader paused, then continued: "It may be so, yet your planet is Jupiter, if my calculations are correct."

"Hardly Jupiter, madam, for had I been descendant from the ancient God of war Zeus my natural instinct would have guided me to a more heroic life than that of a plumber, which I don't mind telling you is my occupation."

"A plumber! and with such soft hands," she exclaimed: I saw I was cornered.

"Madam!" I replied quickly, "I am a boss plumber; I plan the work, my men execute it."

"Ah! yes, I see; I thought you might be one of those abominable newspaper reporters. Well, Mr.—"

"Smooth is my name, Eph. Smooth," I interrupted.

"Well, Mr. Smooth," she continued, "you are born under a lucky planet. According to the belief of the Romans, Jupiter determined the course of all earthly affairs, and revealed the future through signs in the heavens and the flight of birds. I refer to Jupiter Capitolinus, the mythological God known as Optimus Maximus."

"Excuse me, Madam, but the God Jupiter of mythology has very little connection with the planet Jupiter."

"Yes, he has, but antiquity is not to be viewed and explained according to the ideas and customs of modern times. Has it never occurred to you that from the first matter containing the seeds of all future being a race was created through God able to comprehend the source from which the various forms of the material world were produced; and in contemplating these forms as they were distributed into abiding places they perceived that the same energy of emanation gave existence to living beings as well as the God who inhabit the heavenly bodies and various other parts. These first people looked upon every planet and star as a living, breathing thing. To them the vast space in which they floated was not too great for comprehension, and they moved about in familiar contact with the inhabitants of these various parts thrown off from the same matter and distributed throughout the universe. Would it be reasonable to believe that of all the bodies formed form chaos, that the earth, the smallest should be the only one inhabited by human beings? Would it bespeak the infinite wisdom of the creature to suppose that from his effort only the minor part of matter was turned to account, and the major part left a worthless mass? If he had desired to produce the earth, from chaos, without creating other worlds, could he not have done so, without forming six other bodies of twice the magnitude and importance in the planetary world? Therefore I contend that as every planet emanated from the same matter, was formed by the same creator, they are all inhabited by a race of living rational beings.

"That is all very well, madam; but how could a race of beings exist on Mercury, or even Jupiter with their proximity to the sun?"

"I do not say people of the earth temperament could exist on these planets,— they are endowed with temperaments suited to the planet upon which they live. I believe there is a constant interchange of souls or life sparks between the planets. To die is but to live again. Death is a change necessary to fit a soul for the climate of another planet. It is the reformation of matter and conducted by the same agency that first produced the planetary bodies and then caused them to be inhabited. Can you reasonably say that Jupiter, revolving around the sun at a mean distance of 475,000,000 miles is uninhabitable? Here we have a planet 88,000 miles in diameter, or one-tenth of the sun, its volume 1,400 times that of the earth, revolving at the rate of 500 miles per minute, to the earth's 17 miles per minute. Was all this created for naught? I tell you there are living beings on that planet, and, young man, they are souls from this world prepared for existence

137

there. They are transformed by death into beings who can live in a ten hour day and years that are equal to travel of ours,— comprising nearly 10,000 of our days."

"Then you believe in the immortality of the soul, madam?"

"Most assuredly I do; it seems to me any one of ordinary sense ought to be convinced on this point. As birds migrate from one zone to another, so I believe human souls migrate, through intervention of the supreme power that rules the universe, from one planet to another. Nothing dies but life is formed from that death, and the great work of progression goes steadily on. A horse dies, soon worms are created, they in turn are transformed into moths and thence into beautiful butterflies. Every tree and plant of nature is reproductive in this manner. Could a power so infinite that it watches these minute details to perfection, create all the great planets and only perform these things on the smallest and most unimportant of them? I am as positive that the planets are inhabited as I am that the earth holds me, and young man when your work is finished on earth you will undergo the change that fits you for an existence on your proper planet, Jupiter. After that in time I believe you will undergo another change and be transmitted to some other planet, for life is eternal in some shape or another."

"Tell me, madam, will I be a plumber on Jupiter, or is the climate so warm that there are no frozen water pipes?"

"What!" she exclaimed, and springing from her chair she grasped my wrist, and gazing into my eyes as if my whole soul was there laid bare for inspection, continued in a sort of Hamlet soliloquy whisper, "would you like to go there now?" There was a bright glitter in her eye, she was inspired, the lines about the corners of her mouth twitched perceptibly with emotion. There was a dangerous vehemence in her manner. Instinctively I looked around for my hat and shifted uneasily on my chair. I thought over all the mean things I ever did, and wiped the perspiration from my brow with my coat sleeve.

Opening my hand she furtively traced the lines along the palm, and then in a sad voice said, "You have not long to stay on this earth; your hours are numbered."

I began to feel that something terrible was about to happen and involuntarily shuddered as I thought of my prospective migration.

At last in sheer desperation I drew my hand away and jumped to the door. It was locked.

"Wait," she said. "I am permitted through the influence of your planet to reveal much of your future. Listen! You are already under the spell of Proserpina who presides over the death of mankind, and if you remain silent I will unveil to you the scenes through which you will pass in the transmission of your soul from earth to your planet, Jupiter."

Closing her eyes she was silent for a moment, and then in a low, plaintive voice began: "You will first perceive a number of terrible forms, disease, old age, terror, hunger, death, the avengers of guilt. On you go to the resort for departed spirits. Among them you mingle. There are those who suicided, victims of love and despair, and hundreds of the sad experiences known to life. Then you will pass into fields adorned with all the beauties of nature — a most delightful recreation to your mind. There are hills covered with fragrant shrubs, grand valleys, flowery plains, shady groves, lucid streams, gentle and unclouded sunshine. Being freed from the passions and prejudices of mortality, you enjoy the pleasures of contemplation, until at the command of Zeno you drink the fatal waters and the oblivious draught causes you to lose all remembrance of the past, so when again you assume the cares and sorrows of humanity on Jupiter elysium is forgotten, the past is obliterated, and amid the new scenes you find nothing strange, for that other life has faded forever from your memory."

"That's very smooth, madam," I managed to say.

"Very smooth, indeed; that's about the appreciation I might from a plumber. You have no more sentiment or imagination in your soul than a stick. However, I have told you all I can, and in closing my seance I conjure you by all means to be ready at any moment to die, for your life is short. One dollar and twenty-five cents please. Thanks! Good night."

A SERVANT GIRL'S VISION

Here is another dream that seems to be sensitive to the ways of the spirit. "Seen in the Spirit" comes from the January 25, 1888, edition of the *Winnipeg Free Press*.

SEEN IN THE SPIRIT
A Charlottetown Servant Girl's Vision of the Fate of a Missing Man

A Charlottetown, P.E.I., despatch says:

Eighteen months ago Charles H. Yeo returned from Winnipeg to visit his relatives in Prince Edward Island. On New Year's Day, a year ago, he was in Charlottetown on his return to Winnipeg. While here he visited the house of a relative, and after leaving it disappeared as mysteriously and completely as if the earth had swallowed him. He had several hundred dollars on his person, and, no trace being obtainable, his parents offered $500 for information of his whereabouts, dead or alive.

That was last summer. Nothing more was heard of it till this week when the grand jury met, and Miss Tuck, a domestic, appeared and told a most extraordinary story. Upon hearing of the reward offered for Yeo's whereabouts, she prayed that she might discover the secret. In answer to her prayer she had a vision.

In the spirit she saw a man walking up and down in front of a certain house. Her description of the man tallies completely with that of Yeo. A man, whom she minutely describes, came out of that house and asked Yeo to go to the rear stable to see a horse. The two were joined by two others while there. The first-mentioned stranger drew a knife and stabbed Yeo to the heart. The murdered man's pockets were searched and a large amount of money obtained and divided among the three men. The body was stowed in an oat bin, and subsequently the bin and the body were taken some distance away in a sleigh, a hole cut in the ice by the same three men and the body thrown in, when the men returned to the city.

This story of her vision has produced a profound sensation. The investigation is still proceeding.

CLAIRVOYANCE

The important particulars of this story are told in its heading and subheading. "The Mirror of Fate" was published in the *Ottawa Journal* on June 8, 1888. Even today it makes lively reading!

THE MIRROR OF FATE
A Journal Reporter's Visit to a Clairvoyant
One Dollar's Worth of Madame Millford,
the Seventh Daughter of a Seventh Daughter—
How She told a Newspaper Man's Fortune

"I wonder what the future will bring forth?"

This is the query that a big portion of humanity frequently ask themselves when they get to ruminate over the past.

The curiosity to probe into the future is born with people and is as natural to a man or a woman as horns are to a cow — except the cow be a mule.

A *Journal* reporter got ruminating yesterday and the result was that with two shining 50 cent pieces in his pocket he called upon a clairvoyant lately arrived in the city, Madame Millford, who claims to be the seventh daughter of a seventh daughter, and all a matter of course is well upon in that species of divination which is able to grasp Fate by the back of the neck and make her disgorge her secrets.

Madame Millford lodges at Mrs. Archambault's on O'Connor street.

She is much like an ordinary woman of forty or thereabouts, has a sharp eye, dark hair and talks very agreeably.

Madame herself answered the door bell when the reporter called. She was sorry she was then engaged with several ladies but if he would call in an hour or so she would endeavor to grant him an opportunity of hearing what the future had in store for him. Be it understood that the reporter did not say he was a reporter. He said he was a theological student.

The second call was a success. Madame was disengaged and with an agreeable air and pleasant smile she showed him into her apartment.

The performance was opened by the newspaper man planking down the fee, one dollar, and taking a seat. Ladies, the Madame said, had their hearts made glad or sorrowful for half the money charged to gentlemen.

The Madame's not a trance performance as some might suppose but gives you "facts" without any other sublunary or celestial aid than your own open hand and a pack of cards. To the sweetly murmured command "Hold out your hands!" the reporter stretched out his time-worn digits, palms upward, and the Madame after a little scrutiny let out a nice little "Oh," she said, "how much alike your hands are!" This statement gave the reporter renewed confidence in Madame's powers. His hands do bear considerable general resemblance to each other, especially after passing through a wash basin. "The lines on your hands are wonderfully well defined," continued the palmist "especially the lines of truth and honesty."

"Great Scott," thought the reporter, "she never saw me with a pair of scissors and a morning paper!"

"You smoke," continued the reader, "there is the line right here."

The lady was sitting close to the reporter, who had just thrown away a cigar and had a seventeen-year-old pipe in his pocket.

After rambling around over his hand for signs and tokens and volubly telling all about how old he would be before he died, Madame dropped into the sweetheart business and picking up a pack of cards and counting out seven which she spread before her, undertook to tell him all about his lady love and his prospective mother-in-law. The mother-in-law racket caught his ears with both hands and every word that dropped from Madame hit the mark every time and sometimes twice.

"There is a dark-eyed, dark-haired, very handsome young lady deeply, very deeply in love with you." This was accompanied by a keen scrutiny of the newspaper man's fact, that made the hot blood leap to it, for her interviewer was a married man. "There is another young lady, a fair lady in a very near similar condition, and you are considerably bothered as to the choice you are to make but I think your preference will go with the dark-eyed girl as she is going to be left a whole lot of money in about ten months. This will come through the death of her father." Here the Madame paused to throw in the suggestion that the money was not to be despised. It was useful especially in providing for a family.

Then she tackled the prospective mother-in-law aspect of the question and held out but faint encouragement on that point. "This mother-in-law of yours will be a perfect Fiji and if she settles on you look out. She is quick at all things, but her tongue is sure death and no antidote."

The Madame in a sympathizing voice, and after giving the cards a fresh shuffle said, "There is a fair-haired man, a great big B flat of a fellow who knows nothing nor will he ever learn, who gives you a good deal of annoyance. He wants people to be impressed with his importance, and tells wonderful stories of his experiences. You see this man hourly. No one believes a word of his great achievements although he thinks people do. Don't bother your head with the creature. He is too flat for anything."

Then without a pause the looker into the future came back to the dark-eyed girl and told the reporter it would be good policy to marry her at once.

Just then a laugh from an adjoining apartment made both the reporter and the diviner look up in bewilderment, and the charm of the whole thing flew out of the window.

The laugh came from the reporter's wife, who unknown to her liege lord had dropped into Mrs. Archambault's parlor on a friendly visit. As the partition between the apartments is but thin, she had heard the whole of the "fortune telling," and not being able any longer to control her merriment, laughed at the idea of advising her husband to commit bigamy and have thrown into the bargain a Fiji mother-in-law. The reporter beat a hasty retreat when the laugh sounded on his ears and Madame's look lost its amiability.

During the preliminary conversational skirmishing, Madame Millford stated that she was doing a rushing business. Government employees she said were the best customers. They wanted to know exactly when they were to get an increase in salary and less work to do, so that they might re-arrange their business affairs on the new basis. One poor fellow, she said, who was working for $900 a year, with only himself to support, had thoughts of suicide unless the future held out hope for better pay.

She also stated that mothers consulted her about their sons, wives about their husbands, husbands about their wives and young ladies about their prospective husbands.

One thing can be said of Madame, however, that she will tell you nothing unpleasant and she will chat with you very agreeably. She hails from the United States and is in Ottawa for the first time making money fast.

By the way the reporter's wife called on Madame Millford later, and was told amongst other things that she was to be a widow. The Madame a few hours previously told the husband that he would be a widower and take a second wife. The young wife tried to reconcile the two statements, but failing, called Madame's attention to the discrepancy.

The Madame broke up the seance with the wife by complaining of a pain in her head.

OLD MRS. COO

Meet Old Mrs. Coo again. She was apparently well known as a prophetess in the Pictou area of Nova Scotia in the last years of the nineteenth century. "The Prophecy Fulfilled" was printed in the *Calgary Herald* on March 2, 1891. There had been an explosion at the Spring Hill mine on February 21, 1891, that resulted in over one hundred deaths.

THE PROPHECY FULFILLED
"Old Mrs. Coo," the Pictou Prophetess, Foretold the Disaster

Montreal, Feb. 25.— Senator George A. Drummond, of this city, is one of the directors of the Spring Hill mines. He showed an official report of the manager of the mine yesterday which tells a remarkable story. It is dated Feb. 16 and in it Underground Inspector Swift says that much uneasiness has been caused among the miners by "Old Mrs. Coo," known in the neighbourhood as the "Pictou Prophetess," foretelling an explosion which was to take place in the Spring Hill mines. Owing to the old woman's story and the consequent uneasiness of the men, a committee of the miners themselves was appointed by the company, and, with Manager Cowans at their head, they began an examination of the mines on Feb. 16. The West mine was examined and on Tuesday last, the North mine was gone through and the most complete examination made of all seams, drifts, slopes and leadings. Everything was found in good shape, with absolutely no presence of danger. The fears of the miners, caused by "Mother Coo," were dispelled by the perfect condition of the mines, except among a very few who hold that she never prophesied wrong. The awful fulfillment of prophecy came Saturday.

DEATH NOTICE

It is a fascinating feature of human nature that men and women yearn to know their future prospects, including what the years ahead hold for them respecting money, love, life, sickness, and death. "A Warning of Death" appeared in the Lethbridge, Alberta, *News* on November 2, 1892.

A WARNING OF DEATH

A curious incident, of recent date, was related to the writer a day or two since by a friend to whom most of those concerned are personally known.

A young lady, sister of Mr. A., an artist of some repute, whose family live in Toronto, came down to breakfast one morning recently and related a singular vision, which had impressed itself more vividly on her mind as she was accustomed to perfectly dreamless slumber.

She had awoke at about seven, and finding by her watch that it was not yet time to rise, had dozed off, waking again very shortly after, and in the interval dreaming this dream. She saw running down the main street of Toronto, as if much agitated and in a great hurry, her friend, Miss M.C., a young lady of about her own age, and subsequently her sister-in-law.

Her friend was dressed in what appeared to be wedding or ball attire, and had orange blossoms in her hair and on her dress. A waterproof cloak was over her head and shoulders, apparently donned in haste or want of a handier covering. Miss M.C. proceeded with great rapidity down the street until, reaching the train terminus, in her hurry she slipped and fell in the mud; and rising again she disappeared from her friend's sight amongst a number of people who were entering a car.

This was the dream; and later on the A. family were informed that Mr. J., stepfather of Miss M.C., had met with sudden death just before four o'clock that morning through falling out of a window at an hotel where he was staying some miles from Toronto, he being a commercial traveller, and that his stepdaughter, Miss A.'s friend, who had been at a ball, was arriving home late, found a telegram awaiting her, had hurried off to take the train for the scene of the accident at the same hour, and habited precisely as seen in the dream.

145

Now comes the second part of the story. A few miles from the town, where Mr. J. met with his terrible death, was a lonely farm kept by a woman with her son and daughter, who were on friendly terms with the traveller, and knew of his stopping at the hotel. The daughter was dressing at a very early hour in order to get her brother's breakfast ready, he being in a stable close by, when a loud triple knock was heard at the front door. The girl promptly jumped into bed again, and excused herself to her mother, who was lying in another room, for not answering the summons, as she was not dressed.

"Then," said the farm-wife, "the loud knocking being here repeated, "I will go myself," whereupon she wrapped herself in a cloak and went down to the door. The farmhouse clock struck four as she went, and just as her fingers were on the handle of the door the three loud knocks were given for a third time with such emphasis as to startle her and elicit the remark, "Dear me, they're in a great hurry, to be sure." But when a moment later the door was opened no one was to be seen. A thorough search was made over the farm premises without discovery, and the son visited a neighbouring farm, it being thought that somebody might be ill there, but found all asleep.

At breakfast the mother said that she had been thinking of Mr. J. all the morning, and could not get it out of her head that some harm had befallen him. The feeling became so strong that, against the wishes of the others, she had the horse harnessed and drove to the town, and on reaching the hotel, found there Miss M.C., who, coming downstairs to greet her, said: "Then you have heard already. How kind of you to come in my trouble."

THE MIDWIFE'S PROPHECY

This extraordinary prophecy was delivered by an otherwise unknown midwife named Madelaine Donat. It was recorded on February 20, 1896, in the pages of the family Bible that belonged to Antoinette and Carl Hartley of Montreal.

The prophecy came to pass in all particulars, according to Robert Tralins, author of *ESP Forewarnings*. Tralins went on to note that the prophecy only came to light following the deaths of the Hartley's children, Carl and Edith. The Montreal-born twins felt themselves to be in telepathic communication; apparently they died at the same time (and on schedule) — at 5:00 a.m. on May 5, 1965. Carl was in Pasadena, California, Edith in Wilkes-Barre, Pennsylvania.

Tralins concluded his account of "The Midwife's Prophecy" with these words: "A search is currently underway for other such 'prophecies' which quite possibly might have been inscribed upon the birth records written in other family bibles of children delivered by this little-known Canadian midwife, Madelaine Donat."

I attest and bear my sign and seal herewith and duly record that on this 20th day in February, in the year of our Lord, 1896, that I have delivered of Mrs. Antoinette Hartley and her husband, Mr. Carl Geo. Clayton Hartley, one fine baby boy and one fine baby girl. The son and the daughter are healthy and sound and do not bear any marks or deformity. The son is to be called Carl Gerald. The daughter is to be called Edith Anne. I predict that they shall live extraordinary lives for three score and eight years and that they shall be blessed with the higher powers of God until the hour of five upon the fifth day of the fifth month at which time one will call upon the other to withdraw from this earth. So be it that this birth record and document shall forever attest to what I, the under-signed hath writ here:

Her Hand And Seal at Montreal, Quebec
[Signature]
Madelaine Donat, Midwife.

BOER WAR DRAMA

No one is quite certain where a dream ends and a vision begins. Both seem to be states of trance that may or may not enable dreamers and visionaries to contact other intelligences. Here is a dream or vision that may be described as "veridical," meaning that it is true to fact. "Saw the Fight in Her Dream" appeared in the March 5, 1900, edition of the *Newfoundland Evening Telegram*. Reports of such experiences (crisis apparitions) are quite common.

SAW THE FIGHT IN HER DREAM

Toronto, Feb. 23.— Miss Vanderwater, the sister of Morris Vanderwater, of 120 Sorauren avenue, one of the wounded Toronto volunteers, relates a strange incident of second sight, and is confident, although she has not yet received a cablegram from Africa detailing her brother's wound or telling of the encounter in which he was injured, that she is in possession of the circumstances under which her brother was disabled.

Miss Vanderwater, who is a trained nurse and a most matter-of-fact young woman, had a vision of Sunday afternoon's fight on Sunday night and saw her brother fall, struck by a Boer bullet.

"I am not at all superstitious," said Miss Vanderwater, "but the vision I had was as realistic as if I had spent the day on the battlefield in South Africa. I was right in the midst of the struggle, and, though close to my brother, could not reach him. The Canadians were charging over the red veldt sand. The Boers were in small kopjes all along their front, and were keeping up a tremendous fire. The smoke seemed to partially obscure the rest of the Toronto boys that I knew, but I could see Morris clearly in the line as they rushed forward. Then I saw a bullet strike him just below the shoulder and I was released form whatever force kept me from him, and I ran forward.

"The bullet has glanced off his ribs," I said to myself as I ran. He staggered and fell into my arms, and we both went down into the sand.

"I tore off the clothes and had just stanched the flow of blood, when I awoke. Next morning I was unable to eat my breakfast, but said nothing to my parents of the wounding of Morris, though I mentioned dreaming that I had been in Africa. When the message came that Morris was wounded, I told my mother Sunday night's dream in its entirety."

Miss Vanderwater is confident that her brother is only slightly wounded, and, though perturbed by the direct news of his injury, is not worried as much as she otherwise would.

She says she is sorry she did not go with the contingent as a nurse.

A VERY REMARKABLE VISION

The flowery language of this account is not to contemporary tastes, but allowances should be made because the incident, if true as described, is a memorable one. "His Spirit Rose in Mystic Light" appeared in the Calgary *News Telegram* on December 15, 1908.

HIS SPIRIT ROSE IN MYSTIC LIGHT
New Brunswick Girl's Disquieting Vision in Her Bed Room

Montreal, Dec. 14.— A very remarkable revelation of the statements of apparently trustworthy witnesses are accepted of a supernormal kind has just been had to a family in New Brunswick who died within the past fortnight near Englehart, on the Montreal River, in Northern Ontario, and whose remains, after disinterment, passed through Bonaventure Station today on their way to Salisbury in the Eastern Provinces.

According to the statement of Jane and Robert McIlwraith, who are accompanying the body to the old home of the deceased, Miss McIlwraith had either a very remarkable vision, in which her brother Joseph appeared to her on the night of Tuesday, Nov. 24, or, as she believes, his ghostly body appeared before her in her room and asked her if she did not know that he was dead. The brother had been away from home two years, at work in the silver region of Cobalt.

She had been in bed for some time and on awakening, as she thought, she saw a light in the room that could not be accounted for by lamp, candle or the moon. "Instantly," she said, "I saw my brother appear before me in a brownish suit of clothes that I had never seen him wear before. He suddenly seemed to start up from nowhere and he asked in a perfectly natural voice, 'Don't you know I am dead?' Having said that he receded back, presumably through the wall. The light also disappeared very shortly.

"I did not seem to be afraid until the light vanished and then I became so frightened, thinking about the appearance of my brother and the message, that I aroused my brother Robert, as well as mother, to whom I communicated the terrible experience."

The family was fearfully agitated, but living some distance away from a telegraph station, they did not take steps for several days after the occurrence to communicate with Joseph. They had not heard from him for about six weeks and he was then preparing for work for the winter or his claim on the Montreal River, which he was to develop with money he had saved at Cobalt. On the Friday they telegraphed and got an answer the following day that Joe McIlwraith had died of pneumonia a few days before, and had been buried. The telegram also stated that he had left fifteen hundred dollars behind.

It was decided that the remains should be disinterred and brought east in order that the deceased might be buried where he spent his early life. His brother went to bring them along, and today was met here by the sister who had the extraordinary experience. They all went east by the I.C.R., Robert and the body having come east over the Ontario Government Railway and the Grand Trunk.

Miss McIlwraith seemed to be a woman of some refinement and exceedingly modest and sensitive-looking, but extraordinary pale — a fact which she attributed to the shock she had received from the singular visitation and the startling confirmation given to the message. The brother found no difficulty in getting the money belonging to the deceased.

From the inquiries that Robert was able to make, his brother died on the day before the sister had the remarkable experience narrated.

"LA PALOMA"

It has long been believed that birds are portents for well or ill. This conviction is probably based on observation, personal associations and traditional imagery and symbolism. Doves represent peace; crows suggest death. The entrails of birds and other animals, properly interpreted, were at one time felt to offer information about the present and the future.

I am indebted to Calgary researcher W. Ritchie Benedict for finding the following story. It originally appeared as "The Unexplained... By Jean Cartwright As Told to Inez Hosie, Regina, Sask." in News of the North (Yellowknife, North West Territories) on June 24, 1964.

This is a true incident that happened in Ontario. My grandparents used to move into Toronto from their farm for the winter months, as grandmother was troubled with rheumatism and had to have warm quarters during the cold days.

They always managed to get a suite of rooms on the second floor of a large house on Balliol Street, which was owned by a friend. The farm, being only a hundred miles east of the city, enabled us to go two or three times during the winter to visit our grandparents, who were always glad to see us, and hear the news about the farm.

It was during the last visit we made at that house, while we were sitting in the front room chatting away, our attention was drawn to a beautiful white pigeon which alighted on the sill outside the window, tapped on the window then flew away.

My grandfather remarked that it was strange that a pigeon would come into the city like that. Soon it returned again, flapped its wings against the window pane, remaining on the sill for a few minutes.

While the bird sat on the sill my sixteen-year-old sister, Wilma, began to sing her version of "La Paloma." "If at the window pane a beautiful dove comes winging, treat it with kindness, for it has come to bear your soul away."

The incident was forgotten for the time being, as our parents prepared to leave for their return to the farm. Our grandparents invited us two girls to stay a couple of days longer, which we were delighted to do, as we planned on doing some shopping.

On the following two days the pigeon came to sit for a brief while on the window sill and to tap on the window pane, and at all hours of the day Wilma persisted in singing the same words from "La Paloma" until it grated on us, and grandfather asked her to stop it.

On the third day, we opened the window to let fresh air into the apartment. Alighting on the sill the bird boldly entered the apartment and, unafraid, flew to the top of the glass cupboard where it sat undisturbed.

We all felt just a little awe at its presence. Certainly its behaviour was not that of an ordinary pigeon. After sitting on the cupboard for a few minutes, it found its way outdoors again through the still-open window.

The third day after the pigeon's initial visit, we prepared to leave, so grandmother accompanied us down stairs to say farewell to the folks below, as she had become friends with them.

151

We visited for half an hour and then returned to grandmother's rooms above. As we entered the door, grandmother called out to grandfather, "Do you think we were gone long?" There was no answer and we heard no sounds.

So we walked into the front room and there slumped over the easy chair was grandfather. We shook him, but he didn't wake. Grandmother became hysterical and Wilma rushed down stairs and phoned a doctor. As the people below hurried up and tried to calm grandmother, the doctor arrived and pronounced him dead.

Friends of ours moved into the same suite where they lived for several years after. I asked them about the white pigeon, if it ever returned, and they said they had never seen it. It had never returned. White or any other coloured pigeons had never been seen near or in the vicinity of that particular house since grandfather's passing.

SOLTYS AND THE GYPSIES

The account that appears here reads more like the curriculum vitae of a professional scientist and academic than it does the personal account of an extraordinary experience. Yet the academic details of Professor Soltys's life provide a sense of drama in light of the predictions of two Gypsy women.

The account comes from a letter dated June 27, 1989 and it was sent to the present editor by the professor's wife, Audrey Soltys, who added the "follow-up."

Before World War II, when I was working as a scientist in the Research Institute in Pulawy in Poland, several of us, men and women scientists, used to meet on Sunday morning in a café bar for coffee or ice cream.

During one of these meetings, a Gypsy woman entered, came directly to me, and told me that I would live abroad in a country surrounded by the sea, and would travel widely and become well known. She said I would marry while I was abroad, and (pointing to the girls) added, "You won't make bread from this flour." I told her to tell the girls their fortunes, but she said I was the only one with an interesting future.

A year later, when I was in the western part of Poland as an army reserve officer in summer training, I was stopped in the street by a different Gypsy woman who told me the same thing, adding that I would have a long life.

When the war started, to escape from the Germans and Russians who invaded Poland, I crossed the frontier with my unit to Romania, and later to France. After the occupation of France, I escaped to Britain. After taking my Ph.D. in medicine I was awarded a postdoctoral fellowship in Cambridge, and then worked as a lecturer in microbiology in Glasgow and later in Liverpool where I met and married the woman who became my wife. From Liverpool I went as the director of a research institute on trypanosomiasis in Uganda, where we spent three years. While in Africa I was invited by the University of Cambridge, where I spent twelve years as a university don attached to King's College. While in Cambridge on sabbatical leaves, I was invited as a visiting professor for a year to Utrecht, Holland, and later to the Sudan. When one of my graduate students became the vice chancellor of Khartoum University, he wanted me to replace him for a years as professor of microbiology. In 1966, I was invited to take a permanent past by the University of Guelph, where we stayed until I retired.

From Guelph, I gave various lectures and seminars at various universities in the United States and Central America, and spent some time as a visiting professor at James Cook University in Townsville, Australia, and the University of Palmerston North, in New Zealand. After my retirement I was asked by CIDA to help Malaysia to organize their veterinary school. After four years there I returned to Canada, and was approached to teach microbiology at a private American university in Dominica, where we spent a year.

During my academic career, I have written three books and over one hundred scientific papers. As an expert on trypanosomiasis (sleeping sickness), I was invited to serve on the World Health Organization in Geneva. Having just celebrated my eighty-second birthday, and been given a clean bill of health by my doctor, I can honestly say that the predictions have been justified.

Follow-up to the above by his wife, Audrey Soltys:

We were in Warsaw in 1978, walking down the busiest main street with fairly heavy summer traffic and crowded sidewalks, when I noticed, on the other side of the street, some Gypsies approaching people. One of them looked in our direction, and started to cross the street, in and out of the traffic, seemingly coming towards us. We were surrounded by other people, and were not conspicuously dressed, but as she crossed, she was keeping us in sight. I asked my husband if we could go into one of the amber shops, and we watched through the window as she looked anxiously up and down the street without approaching anyone else. After some time she crossed the street and rejoined her companions. I wish today I had not so reacted, but it seemed very strange to me. She was much too young to have been one of the Gypsies who had approached my husband years earlier.

SCARED TO DEATH?

The incident recorded here may well be regarded as an instance of a self-fulfilling prophecy. Either that, or it is a testimony to the power of a curse. It takes the form of a letter that appeared in the correspondence column of the *British Medical Journal* on August 7, 1965. The letter concerns the death of woman following routine surgery at North West River Hospital in Labrador, which has since been closed.

The hospital was founded in 1915 by the International Grenfell Association. It was located at North West River, northeast of Goose Bay, Labrador. The physicians who signed the letter reproduced here appealed to "any reader who has had experience of a patient dying under similar circumstances." The two replies that were received are summarized following the initial letter.

I am pleased to be able to offer this verbatim account to my readers. Indeed, I am more than a little relieved, because the story has haunted me for some time. (I sometimes think I am more haunted by ghost *stories* than I am by ghosts!) I first read about it in *Arthur C. Clarke's World of Strange Powers*, written by John Fairley and Simon Welfare. That book was written in conjunction with the popular Yorkshire Television series of the same name, one of the few programs to seriously consider claims of the supernatural and the paranormal, even to the point of examining what evidence exists, pro or con, and regarding it both sympathetically and unsensation-ally. I follow the trail of Canadian mysteries, so I was intrigued to read about the incident at the Labrador hospital. It was new to me, but not to other people.

At a reception in the 1990s, I met a medical doctor from Labrador who had, it turned out, worked at the North West River Hospital in the late 1960s. I asked him about the incident. He said he was familiar with it and added that everyone on the staff at the hospital at the time regarded it as deeply puzzling. He had no further light to shed on the affair, and had no immediate suggestions as to where I should turn for further information.

Fairley and Welfare concluded their account intelligently:

It may be remembered in this connection that fear serves biologically as a defence mechanism which, among other effects, leads to an enhanced activity of the adrenal glands.... The surgeons in the above case drew the conclusion that death was likely to have resulted indirectly from the stress created by the prophecy. While the present case hopefully involves a reaction of exceptional severity, the self-fulfilling pressure on those who profoundly believe in the fortune-tellers' powers is probably far from negligible; and the number of predictions that have been made to come true in this manner no doubt continue to swell the number of adherents.

My research assistant queried the hard-working librarians at the John P. Robarts Library of the University of Toronto who, after much work, located the letter, one of tens of thousands that had been published in the *British Medical Journal*.

SCARED TO DEATH?

A.R. ELKINGTON, P.R. STEELE, D.D. YUN

SIR,— We would like to report a case of an apparently healthy middle-aged woman dying with massive adrenal haemorrhage, following a relatively minor operation, who was subsequently found to have had forebodings of death.

Mrs. A.B., aged 43, mother of five children, was admitted to North West River Hospital, Labrador, on 18 March 1965. She had been complaining of severe stress incontinence for several months. She had been treated during the past three years for anxiety which responded well to reassurance and mild sedation with phenobarbitone, 30 mg., three times daily. There was no relevant past medical history. On examination she was found to be in good health. Vaginal examination revealed a moderately large cystocele and urethrocele. On 19 March anterior colporrhaphy was performed under general anaesthesia. The premedication was pathidine, 100 mg., and atropine, 0.65 mg.; induction with intravelous thiopentone, 400 mg., and Flaxedil (gallamine triethiodide), 40 mg.; maintenance with nitrous oxide, oxygen, and a trace of trilene, accompanied by intermittent intravenous pethidine to a total of 80 mg. The operation, which lasted less than one hour, was straightforward with minimal blood loss. Her blood-pressure remained around 120/70 throughout the operation, and pulse and respiration were normal. She regained consciousness before leaving the theatre.

One hour later she became shocked and her systolic blood-pressure fell to 70 mm. Hg. She remained conscious, but shortly afterwards complained of severe pain in the left hypochondrium. Methedrine (methylamphetamine) was immediately given, 15 mg. intravenously, and 15 mg. intramuscularly, and the foot of the bed was raised. As the blood-pressure showed no response Aramine (metaraminol), 10 mg., was given intramuscularly. An infusion of dextran, 500 ml., with hydrocortisone, 100 mg., was started. Despite continuous infusion with metaraminol and hydrocortisone no improvement was obtained and intransal oxygen was required as the patient became cyanosed. The pain was partly controlled by injections of morphone, 16 mg., given on three occasions. The E.C.G. was normal. Her condition deteriorated and her temperature rose to 103.6°F. (39.8°C.) by midnight, when she became comatose. She died at 5 a.m. on 20 March.

At post-mortem examination the adrenal glands showed extensive haemorrhage. Petachial haemorrhages were found in the stomach, ileum, liver, and in the skin of the nose. There was no other pathology.

Subsequently we learned that this patient had had her fortune told at the age of 5 years, when she was informed that she would die when she was 43 years old. She had told her daughter for many years that she would die at this age. Her forty-third birthday was one week before operation. On the evening before operation she told her sister, who alone knew of the prophecy, that she did not expect to awake from the anaesthetic, and on the morning of operation the patient told a nurse she was sure she was going to die. These fears were not known to us at the time of operation.

We would be grateful to hear from any reader who has had experience of a patient dying under similar circumstances. We wonder if the severe emotional tensions of this patient superimposed on the physiological stress of surgery had any bearing upon her death. — We are, etc.,

A.R. Elkington.
P.R. Steele.
D.D. Yun.
Grenfell Labrador Medical Mission,
Ottawa, Canada.

The letter elicited two replies, which were published in the September 4 issue. The first was contributed by J.C. Barker of Shelton Hospital, Shrewsbury, Shropshire, England. Barker noted that "one is left wondering why a fortune-teller should impart such devastating information to so young a child which was to make such a terrible and lasting impression upon her." He wondered whether "it is possible that were she a hysterical manipulative type her psychological symptoms, stress incontinence and reaction to it, leading to surgery and its attendant complications, might have resulted from her own unconscious efforts to predetermine her demise at the appointed time, having reflected endlessly upon the admonitions of her soothsayer." He concluded, "Perhaps the boundaries of western psychiatry should now begin to be extended to include some of the phenomena of extra-sensory perception."

The second reply was contributed by A. Fry of London. He noted that "the case may represent a version of voodoo death." He observed, "A persistent state of fear can end the life of man," and then drew attention to the influence of a persistent state of fear on the sympathetic nervous system and its role in the control of the patient's blood supply. He concluded, "'Scared to Death' is not an idle saying. A feeling 'I am afraid I am going to die' may actually result in death. The anxiety is not removed even when the patient is anaesthetized. Although asleep, the patient is still suffering from anxiety."

MADAME CURRY'S PROPHECY

John E. Wall, who wrote this remarkable account of a family's history of prophecy, is an editor and researcher who lives in Altona, Manitoba. He has a special interest in anomalous phenomena, especially events of a Fortean nature, particularly those devoted to the field of cryptozoology and pre-Columbian history. He has contributed articles to the journal *Cryptozoology*. The account here comes from the letter written by Mr. Wall to the present editor in the early 1990s.

When my mother was a girl — she may have been a young teenager at the time — she and her mother travelled by train from their home in Glenboro, Manitoba, to Winnipeg, for a day's shopping.

The exact day or even time of year this occurred, I do not know. I do remember, however, my mother telling me that the war was on at the time. Therefore, it could not have been earlier than 1939; it may have been as late as 1941. My mother could have been as young as eleven or as old as thirteen. Whatever her age, the incident I am about to relate impressed my mother so much that she never forgot it.

After spending some time shopping, my mother and her mother decided to rest and have a meal in a Chinese cafe at or near Winnipeg's famous Portage Ave. and Main St. intersection. It was here that they met a tea-leaf reader who called herself Madame Curry. That was not her real name. Possibly she named herself after the Curry Building, in or near which the restaurant was situated. This building still stands and houses a number of stores.

After their meal my grandmother and her daughter decided to have their tea-leaves read. To do this, one downed one's cup of brew to the last drop and inverted the cup over a saucer; a sharp bang of the cup against the saucer and the tea-leaves would come tumbling down. This was done, and Madame Curry proceeded to tell her customers' fortunes by studying the patterns that the leaves made on their saucers.

My mother did not remember the prophecy uttered by Madame Curry for her mother, but she clearly remembered her own. She would one day, predicted the tea-leaf reader, meet a tall, dark-haired man having the initials J.W. She would marry this man and they would have three children, all boys. Their family would move frequently, and after being married to this man for thirty-five years and some days, her husband would die.

In 1951, my father met my mother in a cafe in Glenboro, where my mother was working as a waitress. A year later they married. He was tall (six feet or over) with dark brown hair; his name was John Wall. As a requirement of my father's employment with the Interprovincial Pipeline Company, my parents and their children — three boys — moved frequently in Manitoba and Saskatchewan, finally settling in Outlook, Saskatchewan, where my father became ill with cancer. He died in a Saskatoon hospital one day short of his sixty-sixth birthday. Thus my parents' marriage ended after thirty-five years and five days. Everything that the tea-leaf reader had predicted, possibly forty-five years earlier, had come to pass.

But the irony was not complete. I happened to mention this prophecy to my aunt, who lives in Altona, one evening as I paid her a social call. She asked me what Madame Curry looked like. I described her to my aunt the way my mother had described her to me — a large, loud, buxom woman with white hair. "That sounds like Harry Smith's wife," said my aunt. "She used to live in Plum Coulee."

Mrs. Sharry Smith, my aunt related, had the gift of second sight, prophecy, or so she claimed. Every so often she would go to Winnipeg to read people's fortunes. She lived in the village of Plum Coulee, where my father, his two sisters, and their mother also lived. Mrs. Smith had a loud voice that she used to good effect when calling her children in for supper — one could hear her all over the block. Mrs. Smith was Madame Curry.

I later had independent corroboration of Mrs. Smith's powers from the widowed manager of the Co-op store in Glenboro. She had also had her tea-leaves read by Madame Curry, who had accurately predicted her husband's death as well.

Whether or not the foregoing constitutes the entirety of the tea-leaf reader's prophecy, I do not know. In any event, it is now too late to make further enquiries. My mother died suddenly and without warning of a pulmonary embolism two and a half years after my father's death. Yet she was able to see the fulfillment of Madame Curry's prophecy, uttered half a century or more ago.

6 Powers Beyond Ours

WHO HAS NOT craved the power "to cloud men's minds so they cannot see him"? Who has never yearned to be able "to leap tall buildings
at a single bound"? Who does not desire to "mesmerize" other people
and bend them to one's will? Every reader of this book probably wishes
for an enhancement of an existing power or ability — greater strength,
more endurance, higher intelligence, increased insight — or to gain or
be granted a non-existent, super power: the ability to read minds, control actions at a distance, tell the future, etc. Such thoughts are human —
only too human! The accounts that appear in this chapter are concerned
with enhanced talents: powers beyond ours.

MESMERISM AND OTHER "-ISMS"

Animal magnetism... electrical influence... mesmerism... hypnosis — the words trip
off the tongue so easily. Add to these words the pseudo-science of phrenology, and
you have a form of entertainment that was popular across the country in the nineteenth
century: the evening lecture, usually delivered by a self-styled doctor or professor,
who devoted the evening to amusing demonstrations of mesmeric passes, inductions,
trance states, somnambulism, automatic responses, and so forth.

Current thinking holds that the hypnotic state is a complicit agreement between
the hypnotist and the subject that the former will make suggestions and the latter
will comply with them. Earlier thinking held that the mesmerist's suggestions and
"passes" could operate not only close at hand but also at a distance. Dr. Collyer —
"Doctor" Collyer — may well have used confederates planted in the audience. He
permitted the audience to conclude that he possessed enhanced mental powers,
sharpened through training, but in this instance there are no allusions to accompanying psychical powers. Instead, he employed phrenological explanations to

account for some of the effects he produced. He probably realized them through "cueing." When he told the audience what to observe, he was subtly informing the subject or hypnotee what effect to produce.

"Mesmerism" is reprinted from the December 2, 1842, edition of the *Patriot & Farmer's Monitor.* It is signed "M." Dr. Collyer was popular. He appears not only in this news story, but also in the next one.

MESMERISM

Dr. Collyer, the Professor Animal Magnetism or Mesmerism, delivered Lectures on this subject, in the City Hall, on Friday and Saturday. The audiences were large and particularly respectable, being composed for the most part of the principal families of the City, several Medical gentlemen were also present. The Lecturer commenced by stating that the principle on which the science is grounded is Electricity in one form or another, and the power of one person to communicate the electric fluid to another — he clearly showed that it was impossible for a Professor to Mesmerise every individual who might be placed under his hands, as it requires not only a previous acquaintance but a superiority of influence of one mind over another before the effect can be produced — and from what he stated it would lead us to believe that bodily superiority as well as a greater power of mental force is necessary before the spiritual influence can take effect. We are not prepared to pronounce Mesmerism a science although we call it such — that there is a power which in certain instances can be exerted, there can be little doubt, and the experiments which followed tended most clearly to prove this to be the case.

After entering very fully on the subject — the Lecturer produced his subjects or patients to be operated upon, apologising for doing so, and stating his reasons as above — that altho' he might and most likely would be, successful on the subject selected from amongst the audience, yet that from now having established a previous influence and from the natural state of nervous anxiety with which an ordinary person would be affected on being produced to be experimented on in public, that there were many chances against success, and that the want of success would, by the generality be attributed to deficiency in the science rather than to the true cause.

A Boy of about 15 years old, called Frederick, was now introduced and placed in a chair opposite to the Lecturer,— the boy was tall and thin and of a very unhealthy appearance, looking much like a person who has for a great length of time suffered under the ague.

In the course of a few minutes he was completely senseless, and to illustrate that was so the Lecturer took out his penknife and stabbed it several times into the boy's hand — apparently without producing the least feeling; — in doing this he wounded a large vein which immediately spouted the blood over the floor. This produced such a nervous effect on the operator as to agitate him violently, and the agitation was immediately afterwards perceived in the boy, a violent spasmodic effect in the breathing and contortions of the countenance being produced — rendering it impossible to proceed with the experiments upon him — during the whole of the time it was however perfectly apparent that he possessed no feeling whatever, as with the exception of the spasm and breathing he remained like a person in a complete trance. The Lecturer then demesmerised the boy, who retired. The other patient, a girl of about 16 years old, was then produced. She had the same unhealthy cast of countenance and in the course of two or three minutes, being rendered perfectly insensible.— To prove this, the Lecturer, who appears to possess very little feeling towards human suffering, wished to proceed to the stabbing operation or something to the same effect, but on being prevented by some of the audience who stood by he stamped with his full weight on the poor girl's foot, without the smallest symptom of pain being shewn. He then proceeded with his experiments.

In order to illustrate the doctrines of Phrenology, he placed his head on the organ of Self-esteem in the girl's head, in a few seconds the head was raised, and all the expression of Self-esteem and its concomitants was immediately produced in the face and figure. He then shifted his hands to Destructiveness — all the appearance of an overwhelming wish to destroy was at once shewn, she started suddenly, stamped with her foot and was proceeding to further violence when the operator removed his hands, and the patient sunk back and resumed her corpse-like appearance. Combativeness was then touched — she instantly raised herself up, lifted her arms as if to strike, and would have done so but was reduced to a state of quietude by the removal of the Operator's hands. Veneration was then touched, and from the quiescent state in which she lay she raised herself whilst a most angelic expression over her face, the hands, eyes, and head were raised in a supplicatory posture, and she might have passed for a beautiful statue of devotion,— what was most extraordinary was that, although extremely plain in feature, when in the quiescent state, still when the countenance lighted up from the application of the hands of the operator to the organs of Veneration and Benevolence it seemed as if the soul were beaming from her face, rendering features so ordinary when at rest, almost angelic in appearance when under the influence of the excitement. Other organs were then touched, all followed by the corresponding expression of countenance. On Tune being subjected to the influence, a low sweet tone of voice proceeded from her closed lips, resolving itself into musical intonation. This patient while under the Mesmeric influence is incapable of speaking — this is not the case with the boy, but from what had happened, his powers of speaking were not shewn.— The performances on Saturday evening were attended with even more success than on Friday.

Some persons present who are naturally hard of belief doubted much from the patients or subjects being produced by the Lecturer. Whether the whole was not a splendid piece of staging and imposture, the question however has been completely set at rest by the experiments of a gentleman in Toronto, who has made the science his peculiar study of late, and who is above all suspicion — he has for some time past drawn the attention of many families of the highest respectability to the subject by his conversations and experiments, in many of which he has been successful — whilst in others he has failed from the want of a sufficient influence or communication being established between himself and the subjects operated on. By a late experiment, however, the matter has been set at rest in the most satisfactory manner and by the most convincing proofs.

A lady in this City of good family and great respectability has for some time past been affected with very violent spasms and cramps, so much so as to be for several hours at a time all but senseless, but yet in a state of the most mortal agony. Medicine has altogether failed to affect or relieve her, and the gentleman alluded to, whom for convenience we shall call Mr. C. has applied to see if any relief could be obtained from the Mesmeric influence,— and he kindly consented to attempt it, and after several experimental trials he on Saturday evening last succeeded in producing the absolute Mesmeric sleep, accompanied by a considerable degree of lucidity, or as it is called clairvoyance. The husband of the lady was in attendance, and as soon as the Mesmeric sleep had been produced several friends were admitted into the room, persons with whom the lady was on terms of considerable intimacy — on their approaching or touching her, she frowned and seemed very much displeased, but on their hands being rubbed by the operator Mr. C., she did not object to their approach — or even touching her.

One of the gentlemen present wishing to see whether the Phrenological experiments which had been tried on Friday evening by Dr. Collyer on his patients would be attended with success, proposed that they should be tried, but as Mr. C., the Operator, did not understand the relative positions of the Phrenological organs, the friend placed his hand on the organ of Veneration, but without effect — he then guided the hand of the Operator to the organ and the effect was instantly apparent — the most angelic appearance of feature and supplicatory attitude were produced.— The hands of the Operator were then guided in turn to the organs of Combativeness and Destructiveness, and the changes of countenance and attitude immediately corresponded. Tune was then touched, and the lady, who is very musical, proceeded to sing the Clara Waltz. The Operator then proposed as a further test that he should think of a tune without mentioning it,— and he did so and the patient at once proceeded with God Save the Queen — which was the tune thought of. He then withdrew his hands and thought of the tune "Patrick's Day" — or replacing them on the organ of Tune she instantly sung it, but very incorrectly. The operator then stated that in fact he did not know the tune well, and that he had mentally committed the same errors as the patient did.— These things were repeated several times with the same result.— The lady ordinarily knows the tune well.

Mr. C. then placed a young lady in the room under the influence, and afterwards placed her hand on that of the first patient, asking her who touched her, she replied, Miss C., which was the young lady's name. This was also done with the several other friends — all of whose names were answered correctly. The patient was during the whole of the time insensible to pain and to external objects, except when put in communication with her mesmerically.— Her eyes were fast closed.

The Operator then requested her to walk, and on his pointing his hands towards her closed eyes, she raised herself, followed him round the room and returned to her chair,— all the time her eyes remained shut.

The Operator then returned to another part of the room and took a cup of Coffee, he asked the patient if she tasted anything — she replied, Coffee and very sweet — which was the case, sugar having been added twice by mistake.

Several other experiments were tried, all equally satisfactory, but the details would be too lengthy for an article of this description.— On her being asked if the Mesmeric influence relieved the cramps, she replied yes, and that if she could be operated on a few times more, that she should be free from them for some months.

On being relieved from the influence she had no knowledge whatever of what had passed, but believed herself to have been in a very sweet quiet sleep, or rather a state of the most complete nonentity.

These facts place the question of the reality of the Mesmeric influence beyond all doubt — whether it can be really beneficially exerted remains to be proved, and also whether the amount of good or evil resulting to mankind from the so-called science or influence will be greatest, cannot, yet, of course, be ascertained. That in cases of Surgical operations the effect will be beneficial, there can be no doubt; and also in relieving violent pain, for the time.— Experience however can only show whether the latter effects will be good or bad.

That in the hands of bad men the influence can be wholly abused there can be no doubt, and it behooves all parents to be particular in guarding young persons from the influence, as when once it has been exercised they seem ever after to be much more liable to it. Time, however, the great solver of all doubts, will set this question, with many others, at rest, and in the meantime all conscientious and good persons cannot be too carefully guarded how they conduct themselves if they find that they are really in possession of so tremendous a power either for good or evil.

STAGE HYPNOTISM

Mesmerism is now known by the name of hypnotism. It has therapeutic power, hence its use is regulated by the medical profession. At the same time, the use of hypnotic powers by stage magicians falls under local ordinances and is generally outlawed.

"Mesmerism in Halifax" appeared in the *Nova Scotia Herald* (Yarmouth, N.S.) on August 11, 1843. Phrenology, which goes unquestioned in this article, has no scientific standing, although localization of mental functions in the brain is an established scientific fact. The lively Dr. Collyer — or "Doctor" Collyer — makes another appearance here.

MESMERISM IN HALIFAX

FROM THE *MORNING POST*

We were present, by invitation, at a most extraordinary exhibition, in Dr. Collyer's rooms, on Saturday last. There were present Doctors Grigor, Sterling, Sawers, and Black; and the Editors of the *Royal Gazette*, *Novascotian*, and *Morning Post*; and some Gentlemen whose names we do not at the moment recollect. Two or three ladies, residing in the premises, were also present. The operations were performed on a young woman, who is a servant in the house. Her name is Margaret Ferrel — she is 22 years of age, was born in Halifax, and resided in the city until three years ago, when she took a journey to Pictou, and was absent about 14 months. She had never been very healthy; but was rather worse than formerly during the last two years.

The experiments commenced at half-past five o'clock, P.M. Dr. Collyer sat down before her, and said—

"Now, don't be afraid, Margaret — there will be no experiments which will afterward give you pain — you will not be roughly treated as you were the other evening."

A VISITOR.— "Was that at Mason's Hall?"
SUBJECT.— "Yes sir."

VISITOR.— "Did they hurt you?"

SUBJECT.— "Why, when I was coming home, I felt my thumb pain very much — I could not tell what was the matter with it; but when I spoke of the pain, one of the girls who went with me said that one of the gentlemen in the room must have hurt it in trying to open my hand."

This was said with so much apparent candor and honesty that Mr. J.S. Thompson immediately remarked to us his belief that there could be no deception in the girls — an opinion in which we most cordially agreed.

By this time Dr. Collyer had commenced his operations. He had laid the hands of the young girl on her knees — and covering them with his own — looked full in her face and breathed toward her. In a few moments, her countenance began to move like that of a child bursting into tears. Hysterical motions of the hands and arms succeeded — the lids of the eyes began to fall asleep, there was a sort of catching in the throat, as if she were agitated with deep grief, and almost choking with sobs. In seven minutes after commencing, Dr. Collyer said she was asleep. Her face was now considerably swollen, and she grew calmer as the sleep appeared to become deeper. There were spasmodic motions of the mouth as if she was tasting something bitter; but the motion was not very violent. Her frame now shook like that of an aged person, and on feeling her pulse 12 minutes after the commencement of the operation, when it counted 106 in a minute, the pulsations were found to have decreased to 96 — or ten beats in twelve minutes.

At this time the limbs were not rigid, but hard breathing, and convulsive motion of the hands, nose, and mouth, of the subject continued; and in the conversations which afterwards took place, she spoke with difficulty, and by drawing her breath inward.

DR. COLLYER.— "Margaret, do you see me."

SUBJECT.— (her eyes being closed). "Yes."

DR. COLLYER.— "Where am I? Point to where I am with your finger."

The subject put up her hand and pointed to a distance. Dr. Collyer said that she mistook some other person in the room for him. He stated further that although the young woman was now in a Mesmeric sleep

167

he could not tell what she would do; and requested the gentlemen present to propose experiments. Corresponding action of the body was then tried, by one of the visitors treading on Dr. Collyer's toes; but there was no apparent sympathy in the feet of the young woman.

The next experiment was proposed by J.S. Thompson, Esq., who wished a repetition of testing the sugar and salt, as tried on the previous Wednesday evening. While some person had gone for the salt, however, Mr. T. suggested that a trial might be made with something else, and one of the visitors pulled a piece of tobacco from his pocket. This was handed to Dr. Collyer, who bit a piece off and commenced chewing actively. The countenance of the subject instantly assumed the appearance of strong disgust, like that of a person taking a dose of powerful medicine; and her mouth moved as if trying to spit it out.

DR. COLLYER.— "What is that, Margaret? — What is in your mouth."
SUBJECT.— "Bad — Oh. Ugh!"
DR. COLLYER.— "What colour is it?"
SUBJECT.— "Brown."
DR. COLLYER.— "What is it?"
SUBJECT.— "Oh! it's bad — it's tobacco."

This experiment astonished every person in the room, as there was no possibility of collusion in procuring the tobacco, or in giving the young woman a knowledge of its properties.— Every movement of herself and Dr. Collyer was closely scrutinized: The doctors in the room then commenced pulling Dr. Collyer's hair — when she shook her head, and said, "Oh, don't," and when asked where she was hurt, she raised her hand to her head as if by an effort, and let it drop again very suddenly.

Some sugar was then handed to Dr. Collyer, which he tasted, and she moved her lips as if tasting something. When asked what she had in her mouth, she answered — "Sugar-barley."

A glass of liquid was then given Dr. Collyer — and when, after some demonstration of tasting, the girl was asked what it was, she replied first, "Vinegar" and then "Wine."— She seemed halting between two opinions as to which of these liquids it was.

DR. COLLYER.— "It is wine, but very sour."

We tasted it to satisfy ourselves, and found it to be Madeira, with a strong acid and pungent flavour.

At the request of one of the visitors, by motion, Dr. Collyer commenced pricking his hand with his breast pin, and the operation was answered by the hand of the subject moving quickly as if in pain, but without the power to move very far.

An experiment with some silver pieces, in which Dr. Collyer required the young woman to count the number in his hand, was unsuccessful.

He then stretched out his arm, made passes on it to produce rightly — and taking a visitor's hand, told him to squeeze whenever he wished her arm to begin to fall. So soon as his left hand was squeezed, he stretched out his right and moved it up and down. This was immediately answered by the arm of the subject in an oscillating movement, which brought it lower and lower till it rested on her knee.

Dr. Sawers requested that her arm might be stretched out and allowed to remain so. This was done and the arm remained immovable for three minutes. At the suggestion of Dr. Grigor, the operator then moved his hand at a distance of about a yard, as if he were drawing something from her hand, when the arm dropped suddenly by her side.

It was now three-quarters of an hour after the commencement of operations, and we asked Dr. Grigor to feel the pulse of the subject. He counted 118 beats per minute — or 12 more than at the commencement, and 22 more than the number of pulsation half an hour before!

Some experiments were now proposed in Phreno-Magnetism. The operator placed his fingers on the organs of tune and time, and the subject immediately commenced singing a psalm tune — then, keeping these organs in play, he touched veneration, when the sounds fell into a plaintive cry. He then touched benevolence, and the cry became more sorrowful; and when asked what was the matter, she answered, "Mother's dead."

On compressing an organ in the back of the head, which we could not immediately distinguish, a rapid and complete change overspread her countenance. Her mouth relaxed into a smile — her lips glowed with unusual ruddiness, and the whole features were lit up with an expression of pleasure. The origins of Amativeness and Adhesiveness were those excited:— Mirthfulness was then compressed, and the joyous expression continued.— When asked how she felt, the answer was — "Nice." With this organ, Tune was also touched, and her head began to move quickly. When asked what she was doing, she replied — "Dancing about." On their being further excited with addition of tune, and asked what she was doing or going to do, she said, "Laugh and sing." On exciting the organ of destructiveness, the countenance of the subject exhibited another change. A frown darkened on her forehead, she ground her teeth — and on being asked what was the matter, she replied, with a voice of a person apparently struggling with suppressed anger:— "I am mad — mad!"

This was the last experiment we remained to see — being called away by an engagement. We have described the facts to the public exactly as they met our own observation, under the determination to give Dr. Collyer fair play, while we watched closely to detect delusion. Some of the experiments were failures; abut a very large majority were entirely and strangely successful. We leave the facts open to the judgement of the public. In truth we know not what opinion to offer on them. Mesmerism is to us a puzzling subject; for we can only say that belief in the agency it proposes to unfold is much easier than to suppose any collusion possible with the young woman above referred too — much easier than to suppose that a person in her grade of life has ever been inducted into the doctrines of Phrenology, or has passed through a course of education in systematic humbug, during the short period that Dr. Collyer has been in Halifax, and in only three or four sittings for experiments.

The fairer and more honest course is to believe that there is something in Mesmerism, until the medical gentlemen who were present at the above surprising exhibition shall show the why and the wherefore we should deem its professions unworthy of consideration.

ANIMAL MAGNETISM

Visiting speakers who often called themselves doctors or professors were the vogue in early Canada, travelling from town to town; in town halls or "opera houses" they entertained their audiences with lectures, demonstrations and exhibits of new marvels. They left in their wake satisfied — and sometimes dissatisfied — audience members who would often address letters to the editors of their local newspapers that expressed approval or disapproval. The letters quite often included those lines of *Hamlet* that appear in the letter reproduced below, which originally appeared in the correspondence column of the *Montreal Transcript* on July 9, 1844. In this instance, the member of the audience was satisfied. In fact, he was so completely satisfied, the contemporary reader cannot but help wonder if the letter-writer was a friend or accomplice of Mr. John McIntry, the visiting speaker.

ANIMAL MAGNETISM

"There are more things in Heaven and earth, Horatio, than
are dreamt of in your philosophy."

Sir,— The experiments of Mr. John McIntry, at the lecture room of the Mechanics' Institute, in this city, are beginning to attract attention. A goodly number of very sensible and respectable citizens attended the lecture and experiments, on Saturday evening, with evident gratification. I had myself the pleasure of witnessing these experiments by Mr. M., and must acknowledge that I think still better of animal magnetism, than I did before I saw this gentleman. These experiments have been performed upon two of our own citizens — one a lad, and the other a young man, who, all who know him will attest, would not lend himself to impose upon the credulity of the public. The lad, although a "new subject" and a stranger to the operator, is keenly sensible to the magnetical fluid, and exhibits a liveliness to the influence of the operation of magnetism, far greater than usual. He is prayerful with reverence — musical with music, and would laugh, jump, or make fight, and show invariably an action or movement in keeping with the Phrenological organ which the operator touched. The experiments in clairvoyance were equally successful, and all that I can say concerning this part of the subject is, that I have seen and been astonished — but I am unable to explain the phenomena. The "wherefores" are yet among the occult mysteries of nature. Besides these public experiments, I have witnessed many made in private, and the result of all is that I am fully convinced that by the influence of animal magnetism, the senses of many, if not all of the human race, may be prostrated and subdued, and much pain and suffering thereby alleviated. I ask of all who are still skeptical on the subject, to examine into it themselves — to go and witness experiments in public and private — and I will venture to say that all who do so thoroughly will be convinced. The results produced are so wonderful that we blame no one for resisting any evidence of them not presented to their own senses; but all who doubt ought to enquire. Mr. McIntyre lectures again this evening.

THE MESMERIC INFLUENCE

Swindles like the one described in this column were commonly perpetrated among both the town and country folk in Upper Canada in the middle and late nineteenth century, but the swindles were not often coupled with Mesmeric trances and visions, the past's equivalent of modern-day channelling.

"Mesmerism, at Belleville" appeared in the columns of the *Kingston Daily Whig* on March 30, 1852. (Note: The name of Judge Kilgour is an approximation, as that section of the article is obscured on the microfilm of the newspaper.)

MESMERISM, AT BELLEVILLE

A case is now pending, and to be tried at the next Sessions for this county, which will disclose somewhat of the Mesmeric influence. We forbear giving all the details, lest we might prejudice the prisoner or his trial, nor shall we make any comments. It appears, however, that a man from Rochester, [New York,] named Williams, in company with an individual named Bailey, from Bowmanville, [Canada West,] stopped at D. Vandorvorts Hotel, a few days, some months ago. During this time, Williams represented to Mr. V., that he knew of a Silver Mine, near the Trent Village, which Bailey had discovered to him while in a Mesmeric state. Bailey confirmed this; Williams stated that they were then going round to form a company, and Mr. V., was induced to take one-third of a Share, for which he gave his note for £7 10s., and cash, £2 10s. Several other inhabitants of this County, whose names we know, did the same, some giving a note for the requisite amount, and others cash. We are told of an individual who gave

£17 16s., in cash, and a note for £17 10s. Bailey purchased these notes from Williams, and sold them, subsequently, to a gentleman in Port Hope, for the full value, so B. alleges. The parties who give their notes, were sued at the last Division Court heard by Mr. Robert Kilgour, of Port Hope, and judgement given, in his favour. Bailey was a witness on the counts, and was arrested on a charge of swindling. He was safely lodged in Jail, but has since been admitted to bail, Williams and some others of his companions have not yet been got, nor have the Stock Holders discovered the mine, though several meetings have been held by them at Brighton.

Bailey, in his examination, contended that he was not accountable for Williams' statements; that he himself knew nothing of what he said or did while in the Mesmeric state, and that he was paid by Williams fifty dollars a month for submitting to be Mesmerised; thus the case stands at present.

THE PHENOMENON OF THE TABLE

The stock-in-trade of the spirit-medium a century and a half ago was the little table that moved or tipped all on its own. That is, it was not moved during the seance by the spiritualist. Magicians and sceptics of claims of the paranormal point to conscious manipulation on the part of the spiritualist or his or her accomplice to explain the movement of the table. Psychologists make reference to ideo-motor responses — that is, people sitting around the table, and not the spiritualist, initiate the movements and manipulate the table without realizing they are doing so. Ideo-motor responses are also behind the movement of the planchette that quite often whizzes across the Ouija board, to everyone's surprise. "Table Moving in Toronto" appeared in the (St. John's) *Newfoundland Express* on November 12, 1853.

TABLE MOVING IN TORONTO

The phenomenon of table moving was witnessed by the writer, in this city, the other night. A description of the operation may interest the curious who may not have had an opportunity of witnessing a like performance themselves. The table selected was a common dressing table, of black walnut, about three feet and a half in length and eighteen inches wide. Its

173

weight would be about 30 lbs. The four feet were placed in glass tumblers. Eight persons seated themselves round the table; taking no care either to insulate themselves or the table. They placed the palms of their hands on the surface of the table; but their fingers did not form an actual connection, the nearest hands being often as far as an inch apart, and sometimes more. A good deal of scepticism was expressed by at least one-half the operators; but one or two who had witnessed the success of previous experiments, expressed a confident conviction that the operation would be successful. One of the operators took his hands off the table several times; and by this means caused some delay in the motion. About three-quarters of an hour had elapsed and there was no visible motion of the table.

"I don't believe it will move a bit," one would say; "it's a humbug," another would respond, till at least half the operators had given vent to their scepticism in one form or another. About this time one of the eight, who had witnessed the success of a similar operation before, got down on his knees, and to the great amusement of the company, began to say,— addressing the table,— "rise up on the south-east corner;" repeating his instructions very frequently. In a short time the table began to follow his directions; and the corner rose up so far as to allow the tumbler [to be] taken away. Subsequently the table followed the instructions to rise on the south or the north side, as desired; it also rose on one leg and twirled round the room, the operators going with it and keeping their fingers on the surface. Several questions were asked, and the table instructed to reply by rising up on one side and descending with its two feet rapidly on the ground. Some of the questions and answers were:

"How many apples are there in the basket — on the table?— a rap for every apple."

The table rose on one side and struck its feet against the ground eleven times. The apples were counted and found to be eleven.

"How many pictures and daguerreotypes are there in the room? — a rap for every one."

The number was rapped out correctly; the raps being given at about the rate of one every second.

"How many buttons has Mr. —— on his vest? — a rap for every one."

Four raps; pocket examined, and found to contain only one copper.

"How many chairs are there in the room?"

The answer gave one below the actual number.

"How old is Mrs. ———?"

Raps 27; the right answer.

"How old is Mr. ———?"

Raps 32; the right number. They were also right in two or three other cases of ages.

"How old," asked one of the party, "was my mother's father when he died?— five years for every rap."

Fifteen raps were made, at about the rate of one every second; but the number was deficient by 20.

A great many questions were asked; and the table invariably lifted two legs from the ground to answer them; and it happened that more than half the answers were correct. The first idea that struck the writer was that the principal operator guessed at the answers; and as many of them were such as he would have some knowledge of, he might by some means be enabled to control the motions of the table; for be it understood the table never moved but when directed. How this is to be accounted for is the question. Is it that the minds of all the persons whose hands are on the table are directed to the same object, when one of their number directs a particular motion of the table; and that the united volition of all the parties exerts some unseen power? The table did not move at the direction of every person whose hand was placed upon it, but only of particular individuals. This appeared a singular if not suspicious circumstance. But when the chief director of the movement and three of the others left the table; the writer who had hitherto been merely a spectator of the proceedings, put his hands on the table, and with three others moved it at least a hundred times; it having always obeyed his directions; why or wherefore was as unknown to himself as to any one else present.

It may be, as Professor Faraday asserts, that the motion of the table is produced by involuntary muscular action; but the parties themselves are not conscious of exerting any force upon the table; and it will move when touched only by the tips of the fingers. — *Toronto Leader.*

THE WITCH-HAZEL

The divining rod was commonly used by pioneer settlers who wanted to locate their wells above underground streams, as well as among prospectors and miners who wanted to locate veins of metals on their properties. There are many stories of the effectiveness of the forked branch, which, when held firmly in both hands, dips in the presence of sources of underground water or deposits of specified minerals. Yet the divining rod's efficacy has never been demonstrated under controlled conditions. "The Divining Rod" appeared in the Victoria *Daily Colonist* on October 11, 1867. The mining operations in question took place in Madoc, Canada West (today's Ontario).

THE DIVINING ROD
The Practical Experience of a Medium in Quartz Mining

Editors, *Journal of Mining:*— Gentlemen — Your remarks (in a late issue of the *Journal of Mining*), concerning a work on the subject of the "witch-hazel," has led me to address you on the subject. While operating in mining in Colorado, a few years since, I was let into the mysteries of the "witch-hazel." Previous to that, I was as great a skeptic as any one in regard to it, but my senses of sight and feeling (as fate has ordained me one of the mediums) were too severely worked upon to remain any longer a doubter on the subject. At that time I tested its operations in every way, and was fully satisfied that it was a reality. For the past five months I have been operating in mining at Madoc, C.W., and have continued my experiments with the forked stick (not with the "hazel" alone, as I find most young wood will produce the same effect).

In April last I selected a spot where the stick indicated a vein running northeast and southwest, and set my men to work (where there were no surface indications of a "crevice"). After excavating a few feet, the crevice became very clearly defined, showing two regular walls, about four feet apart, with the vein running perpendicular. By continued experiments when the shaft had reached the depth of nine feet, I found (by the use of the stick) that there was a "lode" running northwest and southeast, crossing the vein we were working, about two feet from the northeast end of our shaft. Immediately directed the men to open the shaft six feet longer in that direction, so as to develop the two veins with the one shaft.

This experiment proved the stick had not deceived me, as the "hanging wall" of a northwest and southeast vein, dipping to the northeast, was exposed, showing, as I expected, another well-defined "lode." I experimented with this system continually, and I am satisfied that it has never yet deceived me, and I venture to say that I can trace any quartz vein as fast as I can walk, taking a Virginia fence course, on the surface. Its operations are singular and worthy of a thorough examination. By walking directly over and in line with the vein, the stick is not affected, but the least deviation to either side causes it to bend towards the person carrying it; or crossing a vein causes it to turn.

Another peculiar feature is that a coin placed in a slit, out in the point of the fork, appears to break the connection, and its operation ceases. These are facts and as I intend to return to the Madoc mines in the early part of September, I shall be perfectly willing to prove them to anyone who will undertake to fathom the mystery. My theory is that it is caused by a current of electricity passing up from the bowels of the earth, through these crevices, and diffusing itself through the atmosphere. As many use the "hazel" to discover water, oil, etc., it may be that electricity is carried by them; or, again, water and oil would more likely be found in or over a crevice, than in or on the solid rock. The operations of the stick, if properly understood, will save a large amount of time and money, expended in various places; in stripping the rocks of the surface soil, to discover a crevice; and in many instances of shafts being sunk, in blind groping for a crevice in the rocks, where the forked stick would have pointed it out in a few moments, without trouble or expense.

It is time this puritanical stigma of witchery was trampled underfoot, and science assume the mastery. I would urge upon you the importance of this matter, and would be pleased to render any assistance in my power towards its development. I do not claim any scientific attainments. My information has been gathered from practical experience in quartz mining.

THE ELECTRIC GIRL

Is it places that are haunted, or people? There are numerous descriptions of haunted houses. There are, as well, many accounts of haunted people, people who could be described as singularly blessed or cursed. Their strange powers are not ours.

A good instance of someone being singled out is Caroline Clare, the "human battery," whose story is told in the suitably titled article "A Human Electric Battery," which appeared in the Saint John, New Brunswick, *Daily Sun* on June 23, 1879. The story was apparently reprinted from the *Hamilton* (Ontario) *Spectator*, but I have yet to locate the story in the columns of the latter paper. Sad to say, there are some other problems with the story of poor Caroline Clare and her astonishing abilities. It cannot be established that anyone with her name lived in this part of Ontario at this time. Meanwhile, the name of "Dr. Tye, of Thamesville" could not be found in any Ontario medical records for the 1870s.

A HUMAN ELECTRIC BATTERY

About two years since a daughter of Mr. Richard Clare, Caroline by name, and then seventeen years of age, living on Lot 25, on the 2nd con. of Rodney, was taken ill. Her disease could not be correctly diagnosed, and had many peculiar features. Her appetite fell off, and she lost flesh till from a strapping girl of 130 pounds weight, she barely weighed 87 pounds. There did not seem to be any organic complaint. The bodily functions were not impaired, the falling off in this respect was not such as in itself would alarm her friends. After a lapse of a few months she took to her bed. Then it was that a change occurred in her mental condition. Formerly she was noted rather for lack of conversational powers, but now fits or spasms would come over her, on the passing away of which, her eyes would become set and glazed, her body almost rigid, and while in that state she would discourse eloquently and give vivid descriptions of far-off scenes, far exceeding in their beauty anything which she had ever seen or presumably ever read of. On the passing away of this state she exhibited a great degree of lassitude and indisposition to move, and was taciturn and surly in reply to any questions. This continued till about a month since, when an extraordinary change occurred.

The girl, although still not gaining flesh, appeared to rally. She became light-hearted and gay, and her friends anticipated an early release for her from the room to which she had been confined so long.

Their expectations were not vain, for she is now about the house apparently as well bodily as ever. But a most remarkable development has taken place: She is constantly giving off electrical discharges, and seems to be a perfect battery. A person, unless possessed of the very strongest nerves, cannot shake hands with her, nor can anyone place his hand in a pail of water with hers. By joining hands she can send a sharp shock through fifteen or twenty people in a room, and she possesses all the attraction of a magnet. If she attempts to pick up a knife the blade will jump into her hand, and a paper of needles will hang suspended from one of her fingers. So strongly developed is this electrical power that she cannot release from her touch any article of steel which she may have taken up. The only method yet found is for a second party to take hold of the article and pull while the girl strokes her own arm vigorously, from the wrist upward. On her entering a room a perceptible influence seizes hold of all others, and while some are affected with sleepiness, others are ill and fidgety till they leave, and even for a considerable time afterwards. A sleeping babe will wake up with a start at her approach, but with a stroke of her hand she can at once coax it to slumber again. Animals also are subject to her influence, and a pet dog of the household will be for hours at her feet motionless as in death.

A curious part of the phenomena is the fact that the electricity can be imparted by her to any article with which she habitually comes in contact. The other day a younger sister, while doing the house work, took up a pair of corsets belonging to Caroline, and on her hand touching the steel she was compelled to drop them with a loud cry and an exclamation to the effect that she had run a needle into her finger. Wooden spoons have had to be made for her, as she cannot touch metal. Altogether the case is a most remarkable one, and attracts scores of visitors to the house of Mr. Clare. Medical men are especially interesting themselves, and it has been stated that Dr. Tye, of Thamesville, will read a paper on the subject of the meeting of the Provincial Medical Association which is to be held in London in the course of this summer. Mr. Clare is the father of a family of seven children, none of whom, except Caroline, show any abnormal qualities.

AN EVENING IN SPIRIT LAND

Here is an engrossing account of a performance offered in Winnipeg by Professor Cecil. Perhaps I should enclose professor in quotes, because the journalist who wrote up this account failed to identify the fellow or his credentials. Perhaps he was a professor of spiritualism or a master of auto-suggestion. "An Evening in Spirit Land" appeared in the August 12, 1879, edition of the *Winnipeg Free Press*.

AN EVENING IN SPIRIT LAND

Every available seat in the city hall was filled last evening — the occasion being Prof. Cecil's widely advertised "Evening in Spirit Land,"— a novel entertainment in this city.

The Professor, after making some explanations as to the nature of the exhibition, invited the audience to name a committee of three from amongst themselves to watch the proceedings on the platform, and Messrs. S.J. Van Rensselaer, A.M. Brown and W.F. Luxton were selected for that purpose.

On stage was a mysterious-looking "cabinet," in which were tambourines, bells, horns and other instruments and two chairs. These, with the ropes to be used, were examined by the committee, and pronounced to be what they apparently were. The Professor and his assistant then entered the cabinet, and being seated on two chairs were tied hand and foot by the committee as securely as could possibly be done. Van was asked to close the cabinet doors, but before he could fasten one, he received a slap on the ear, and for a few minutes enjoyed a Fourth of July pyrotechnical display. Van sat down. Mr. Luxton's turn was next — same result. Mr. Brown, ditto.

However, the doors were finally closed, and immediately the bells began ringing, the horns tooting, the tambourine and triangle joining in the chorus, while hands appeared through apertures in the cabinet doors, and above the cabinet. The doors were opened, and the mediums were found tightly tied.

The Professor had previously announced that perhaps the spirits would work and perhaps they wouldn't — but there didn't seem to be any "perhaps" about it.

The next thing on the programme was the Hindoo box trick — an apparently ordinary heavy chest was locked, tied with ropes and the knots sealed with wax, after having been carefully examined by the committee. This box was placed in the cabinet, and so was the Professor's assistant. The doors were closed, and on being opened one minute afterwards the box was still found there, but the man had disappeared. The box was opened and the man was found snugly ensconced inside. The spirits were evidently working well and the spirits of the audience were also high, as was evidenced by the loud applause which followed this trick-manifestation.

Then the Professor's hands were tied with a handkerchief, and a rope slipped through his tied hands, Mr. Brown holding the two ends of the rope, but the Professor slipped it off without untying the handkerchief or breaking the rope.

Prof. Cecil then entered the cabinet alone with some ropes, and in a very few minutes was found tied apparently more securely than when the committee had undertaken the job — and he only took three-quarters of a minute to do it. The knots were sealed, the cabinet closed, and in a few seconds the Professor was discovered with his coat off. Mr. Luxton's coat was then placed in the cabinet — the Professor being assured that, being a temperance man, there were no "spirits" in the garment — but it didn't make any difference. In a few seconds the coat was on the Professor. Then they sewed it on him, and almost instantaneously it was thrown out of the cabinet, still sewed.

Mr. Brown went into the cabinet with the Professor, and shortly appeared crowned with a tambourine, although he had hold of the medium all the time. Then Van went in — apparently to stay — and firmly grasped hold of the hands of the Professor, who was still tied. Van's coat was thrown out first, then his vest — and on opening the cabinet it was seen that he had still a firm hold on the Professor. The cabinet was closed again, and the spirits commenced taking off Van's unmentionables — but stopped in time to save an awful scene. Van's watch was found in the Professor's pocket. The Professor's mouth was then filled with water, yet he played on a mouth organ and then he released himself from the ropes.

An officer was asked to come forward with handcuffs. Policeman Grady accepted the offer, and appeared with a set of bracelets belonging to the city. These he placed on the Professor, who retired to the cabinet, and shortly appeared entirely free — the handcuffs being found fastened to the handle of a pitcher and the rung of a chair, which were in the cabinet. The Professor was placed in a pillory, which was locked and sealed, but he easily and quickly escaped from his uncomfortable position. He was then tied and a gag placed in his mouth, but he pronounced distinctly any word required of him by the committee.

His young assistant was then mesmerized, and tied in the cabinet, and spirit hands wrote on a slate, a message to Mr. Brown from Katie King reading, "You are a bad man." Spirit faces appeared about and around the cabinet — one being that of Captain Kidd, the pirate, and another of Van's grandmother. The hall being darkened, a ghost came out from the cabinet and sang a song — but his, her, or its voice wasn't much like a ghost's, at least any ghost we ever read about or talked to, the sepulchral tones being wanting entirely.

Then the tricks of the spiritualists were exposed and an explanation given of how he slipped out of the rope in the handkerchief trick, which was very simple — after one knew how — and the entertainment concluded, the Professor promised to expose other tricks this evening.

During the evening, the audience were kept alternately completely mystified and roaring with laughter — as the incomprehensible or the ludicrous was presented. Mr. Ormande presided at the piano, and played some selections with great skill, contributing materially to the enjoyment of the evening. The Professor's entertainment gave unbounded satisfaction to the great majority of the audience, although there were some who expressed themselves that more expositions should have been given. Doubtless these will get all they want tonight.

SOME VERY CURIOUS PHENOMENA

Compassion is what the reader of this account must feel. Heart-rending are the sufferings that were visited upon this little girl who lived in Peterborough, Ontario. Is there any energy left to feel curiosity about her condition? "Singular Phenomenon" appeared in the *Winnipeg Free Press* on November 16, 1882.

SINGULAR PHENOMENON
A Girl Becomes Blind, But Can Tell the Time and See Colours

A girl who has been lying sick in Peterborough for some time is commanding a fair share of public attention there through phenomenal circumstances connected with her illness. Miss Minnie Tracey was employed in the dining room of the Oriental Hotel, and on October 28, she was attacked by some previous sickness, by convulsions and lockjaw. Her sufferings continued till Tuesday, October 31, when she almost recovered.

During the interval Miss Tracey exhibited some very curious phenomena. The patient was unable to see, but surprised the doctor and those present at a particular time by saying that it was 10 minutes to 1:00. No clock was in the room and the time was correct to a minute. Not only was she blind, but even if she were not so, there was no clock for her to see from where she lay. Moreover she was blindfolded and told the time with accuracy. While blindfolded she felt and designated the colour of gloves, distinguished the colour of two sides of a paper, one of which was white, the other red. In fact the parties about her bed were astonished at the marvellous way in which she distinguished colours which she by no possibility could see. The girl even could tell on what part of a paper there was printed matter if there happened to be any.

More than this, she recognized her friends by touching their hands, and if the person presented to her was a stranger she readily recognized the fact. A reporter of the Peterborough *Review* visited the girl and he was astonished. Below is an extract from his remarks on the occasion of his visit:

"Was it this angel that told you the colours and the time and other things you told us yesterday?" asked the reporter.

"Yes, it was the same angel," she replied; "when I touched a colour it would tell me what it was, and it would tell me the time. When Dr. O'Shea brought in his cousin I could not see him and never knew him, but the angel told me who he was."

Again was her statement confirmed by Mrs. McIntyre and the doctor, in so far as they said Dr. O'Shea's cousin did call to see her, and although his name was not mentioned, she told at once that he was a cousin of the doctor. "On Monday evening," she said in answer to a

183

question, "I could not see any one, and it was then the angels first came to me, and they stayed with me until I could see last evening, and then they said 'goodbye' three times, and have not returned. I cannot tell anything now, only by my ordinary sight."

THOUGHT TRANSFERENCE

I wish I knew more about Professor Tyndall and his lecture circuit across the Northwest Territories (the northern reaches of the prairie provinces). As is so often the case with reports of this vintage, we don't know what Tyndall was a professor of, so it might be wise to refer to him as "Professor"! The correspondent uses Tyndall's "advances" as an occasion to comment on the state of affairs regarding the Society for Psychical Research, as well as his own efforts to investigate psychical phenomena.

"Mind Reading" appeared as a letter to the editor in the *Regina Leader-Post* on March 31, 1891.

MIND READING

To the Editor of *The Leader.*

Sir,— Professor Tyndall's advances through the Territories may make a brief account of the significance, history and present scientific status of mind reading not uninteresting to your readers. Before proceeding, however, it is necessary to state that the phenomenon is more properly termed thought transference than mind reading. It is evident that it is not the mind reader, but the person whose mind is read who is the active factor in the process. This is expressed in the names "percipient" and "agent." The percipient reads the agent's mind, but the agent transfers his thoughts to the percipient.

The significant question to which this phenomenon gives rise is thought. Can thought be transferred from one mind to another, through other channels than the senses? This question is engaging the attention, not merely of those whose interest is purely scientific, but also of theologians, indeed of every intelligent friend of religion and culture. Not only would an affirmative answer throw very important light upon spiritualism, but would also seem to afford a very valuable sensuous demonstration that the mysterious something we call the self, the ego, the soul, transcends sense, is imperishable, immortal.

The phenomenon of transferring thought to persons in hypnotic sleep is as old as the ages. The Egyptian sorcerers, the Indian fakirs, the Grecian oracles, the Roman sibyls, the mediaeval magicians — the secret of all their supposed supernatural power is the force which attracted so much attention one hundred years ago as mesmerism or animal magnetism and which is now more scientifically called hypnotism. The mesmerizer or hypnotizer can "suggest" any idea to his subject and it immediately appears to his mind. But the possibility of transferring through to certain wide-awake persons was only discovered as late as 1875. Since that time several societies have been formed for investigation, one of which, the London "Society for Psychical Research" has recently published a voluminous report of its proceedings.

Thought transference when accomplished by contact has no value for science. So long as the agent in any way touches the thought reader there is always the possibility that his movements lead him on the right track. But some of the experiences of this society performed without contact and with every precaution would seem to place the genuineness of the transference beyond a shadow of a doubt, e.g., the agent and percipient were placed opposite each other with a screen between them. The agent gazed intently upon a figure or paper and the percipient correctly reproduced it. At another time there were two agents having different pictures in mind, and both were reproduced. The work of the society has, however, been subjected to a very searching review by D. Stanley Hall, the leader of the Experimental Psychological movement in America, who points out innumerable possibilities of error of which there is no evidence that the society was even aware, and concludes that the theory of telepathy, though by no means impossible in some sense, is as yet "crude and premature," lacking "everything approaching proof save to amateurs and speculative psychologists," and should be allowed to "lapse into forgetfulness."

E.N. Brown.
Maple Creek, March 22.

MENTAL TELEPATHY

"Thought Reading" appeared in the columns of the August 10, 1886, edition of the *Winnipeg Free Press*. It is an account of a stage act performed by an accomplished stage magician and mentalist. I have no doubt that the Reverend Mr. Gordon mentioned in this report is none other than the Presbyterian minister and author who published his popular novels of Prairie life under the pen name Ralph Connor.

THOUGHT READING
Mr. Stuart Cumberland's Marvellous Experiments in Victoria Hall

Mr. Stuart Cumberland yesterday evening gave a marvellous exhibition of his power of mind reading in Victoria Hall to a somewhat small but very attentive and enthusiastic audience. A committee of the best-known people in the room was selected to sit on the platform and keep things along. This committee included the Rev. Mr. Gordon, Hon. Dr. Wilson, Mr. Bedson, Mr. F. W. Buchanan, Mr. Pearce, and others.

Mr. Cumberland began his seance by a difficult experience. He wanted a gentleman to pick out in the audience some lady, and think of her constantly; he on his part undertook to find the lady while blindfolded himself. To make the experiment somewhat parallel to the classical story of Paris and Stonore, he produced an apple, which he said would be given to the lady so selected as a souvenir of the occasion.

There was this difference between the two circumstances, he said, that while Paris had only to select the fairest of three ladies, the critic in this case would have to choose from a galaxy of beauty. After some difficulty in getting a man to make a selection Mr. Cumberland pounced on Mr. F. W. Buchanan. The latter, having chosen the lady, retired to the anteroom with the Rev. Mr. Gordon and to the latter confided the name of the person picked upon. Then the experiment began.

Mr. Buchanan was told to concentrate his thoughts on the lady. Mr. Cumberland, then blindfolded, placed Mr. Buchanan's wrist on his temple for a moment during which time he stood wavering. Suddenly he made a dash for one of the aisles, down which he rushed, dragging

Mr. Buchanan after him; then hesitating for a moment he branched down a line of seats and made his way directly to where Miss Mingaye sat. Mr. Gordon then announced that Mr. Buchanan had selected Miss Mingaye prior to the experiment. The mind-reader was rewarded with the most enthusiastic applause.

After the experiment he was quite blown and exhausted as though he had received a severe nervous shock. He several times took occasion to state that there was nothing supernatural in anything he did: Natural laws controlled his experiments, and their success was in exact ratio to the intensity with which the person operated on concentrating his thoughts on the subject of the experiment.

All his experiments were marvellous, but some were more wonderful than others. For instance, he wanted someone in the audience who had a pain somewhere in his body to come forward and let him blindfolded find it. No one appeared, because, as Mr. Gordon remarked, this was a very healthy climate, so Mr. Cumberland said that a pain would have to be manufactured, and deputed Mr. Gordon to take Mr. Bedson out of the room and prick him with a pin. This was done, and Mr. Cumberland, having blindfolded himself, seized Mr. Bedson's right hand, held it to his temple, and then began searching for the pain. He went up the arm and touched the face, but was not satisfied. He was heard to say "most peculiar"; then dropping Mr. Bedson's right hand he took his left. This time he went directly to the right hand, and lingered for a moment at the back, but he was still unsatisfied. He then asked Mr. Gordon, who had made the picture, to give Mr. Bedson his left hand and him his right. This time he went directly to Mr. Bedson's right hand and almost instantly located the spot on the side of the hand at the base of the little finger — "the exact spot" to use Mr. Gordon's phrase.

Mr. Cumberland then explained the cause of his hesitation. When he first tried to find the pain with the right hand it was impossible to do so because the pain being in the hand moved along with it. At the spot on the back of the hand where he had first stopped, there was an old sore which had been paining Mr. Bedson for some days.

Another experiment was the drawing on a blackboard of an object thought of by a person whose hand he held. The person was

Mr. Secretan, and Mr. Cumberland, blindfolded, slowly drew the out-
lines of a dissipated looking bottle, with a bit cork and a label "Gin"
on the side.

The final experiment was the most difficult, as it certainly was the
most interesting and amusing of the lot. It was the enactment of a mock
murder scene. First a man was to be selected as the murderer; Mr.
Cumberland was then to retire, and the murderer was to stalk down from
the stage, seize a victim, drag him on the stage, and there despatch him
with one of six knives. Two robbers were then to go through him and
hide the swag in various parts of the room. He, blindfolded, was to pick
out the victim among the audience, take him up to the stage, despatch
him over again with the same knife and in the same spot. He was then
to take the robbers and find the hidden articles.

Having outlined the programme, it then became necessary to select
the murderer and the robbers. Mr. James Fisher was proposed as the
murderer and Mr. Leacock as the victim, but finally Mr. Pearce was
selected as the horror and Dr. Wilson and Mr. Buchanan as the professional robbers. Mr. Pearce in selecting a victim hit on an unwilling one,
who refused to be dragged from his seat. Quite a wrestling match
occurred, greatly to the delight of the audience. A more willing person
was found and the entertainment was in every way a success.

Tonight Mr. Cumberland will give another seance when he will write
out on a blackboard the number of a bank note thought of by any person.

TRANSMUTATION OF METALS

"The Transmutation of Metals Accomplished by an Ottawa Teacher" is the title of a
feature article reprinted from the Calgary News Telegram of March 13, 1911. The
lone inventor working in his makeshift basement laboratory was rather more
commonly encountered in the past than he is in today's era of academic and
corporate research and invention. Mr. Keogh's "lab-top" work recalls the charade
of "cold fusion" in the 1980s. One wonders if any readers of this article bothered
to respond to the scientific alchemist's generous offer.

THE TRANSMUTATION OF METALS ACCOMPLISHED BY AN OTTAWA TEACHER

L.R. Keogh, Instructor in Chemistry in Collegiate Institute,
Claims to Have Discovered Secret Sought for Centuries —
Makes Interesting Demonstrations

OTTAWA, March 13.— L.R. Keogh, teacher of mathematics and English in the Collegiate Institute here, claims to have discovered the secret of transmuting the elements or metals. He says he has changed copper into iron, a secret which chemists have been trying to discover since the study of chemistry began.

Six months ago Mr. Keogh stated he had made this amazing discovery. His statements aroused much interest in Canada and the United States. However, the matter soon dropped without an adequate test of his claims being made.

The public forgot but Mr. Keogh continued his experiments with more diligence. And now he comes out with the startling statement that he has succeeded in changing copper into nickel and also in making lead.

Before some noted chemists Saturday, Mr. Keogh carried on a test. Although his experiment was not entirely convincing, it was exceedingly interesting.

To summarize in brief the result of experiment, Mr. Keogh had a solution which he claimed contained partially transmuted copper in an abnormal state, along with considerable zinc, and a small quantity of iron, which he said, had been gradually forming in the solution. There was also, probably, he added, a trace of iron from the zinc used. This solution he showed by the usual tests to contain copper in large quantities, and that if iron were present, it was not revealed by the usual tests with ferro cyanide and ferri cyanide of potash. He also showed the presence of the zinc in large quantity. He then boiled the solution with caustic potash, which precipitated and redissolved the zinc, and which he claimed changed the abnormal copper of the solution into hydroxide of iron. To prove this, he filtered off the precipitate. He then proved the presence of the zinc in the filtrate and proved the absence of the copper in the filtrate. He then dissolved the precipitate, and proved that the solution so obtained contained large quantities of iron, and not enough copper to be revealed by the ordinary tests.

The experiment was sufficiently satisfactory to be instantly interesting and to open up marvellous possibilities.

He is willing to submit to a test which would prove absolutely whether or not his claims have any foundation on these conditions; he will allow himself to be shut up in a well-equipped laboratory, with every trace of iron, and all salts of iron, or solution containing iron, removed. He will guarantee to transmute copper into iron.

TO WORK SOME TELEPATHY

Roger Burford Mason taught in the private school system in England for twenty years before immigrating to Canada in 1988. He settled in Toronto, worked as a journalist, and eventually founded *The Danforth Report*, a community paper. Over the next decade he published two collections of stories, *Telling the Bees* (1990) and *The Beaver Picture* (1992); a book of travel sketches, *Somewhere Else* (1996); a book of travel sketches; the biography of a book dealer; and *A Grand Eye for Glory* (1998), a life of painter Franz Johnston. He was a lively fellow who died much too soon. One day, Mason told me about an unusual incident that occurred during his teaching career. It involved telepathy or chance. I asked him to write it down for me. He did. Here it is.

I was teaching at a comprehensive high school in Luton, about thirty miles north of London in the early 1970s.

One morning, the period before lunch, I was covering a class for an absent colleague, and since there were no class notes, I was left to temporize for thirty-five minutes with a class of twelve-year-old students. Having finished whatever class work they had outstanding, and whatever homework they had already been assigned for the day, they still needed to be shepherded through the last fifteen minutes of class, so I decided to play a game with them to while the time away.

I sent a boy out of the classroom and then told the others that we were going to work some telepathy on him. Writing "eggs and bacon," or it might been "bat and ball," on the blackboard so that everyone could read it, I then cleared the board and asked the boy back inside. He stood facing the corner while I told the class to try and think the brief phrase into his mind.

Nothing worked with this boy, as I recall, and we had patchy luck with the next two or three children, but then a girl answered five or six correctly in succession, and as far as I could see, without cheating or being given help or clues.

As the bell rang to end the period, the girl had become tearful and frightened, and subsequently, I learned, had been unsettled and unable to sleep that night. Her mother complained about the game to the school principal. The educational psychologist for the school board was called in, and I was told not to conduct games or experiments of that kind again.

NOT TO QUESTION ANYTHING IN INDIA

Bob Buckie, a librarian who lives in Hamilton, Ontario, is a man who enjoys the pleasures of travel. He contributed this short memoir, under the title "The Delhi Mail," to a collection of odd-but-true stories called *The Great Canadian Anecdote Contest*, published in 1991 and edited by George Woodcock. I have given the story its present title. Buckie's experience constitutes yet another episode in the ongoing epic known as "The Mysteries of the Great Subcontinent."

The overnight Calcutta–Delhi express jerked to a halt in a small, nameless town outside of Patna. As the setting sun cast long brown shadows, I took the opportunity to stretch my legs and ship *chai* from a tiny earthenware cup. Twenty carriages of eight compartments; at least six people to a compartment, I tallied. Over a thousand people, about half now milling about on the platform.

Weaving purposefully through this crowd, a young Indian dressed neatly in flannels, white shirt and a thin V-neck cricket sweater made his way toward me. "Good afternoon, sir," he introduced himself, shaking my hand, "my name is Kumar." Without waiting for a reply, he continued, "You are Canadian. You have come from Kathmandu, returning to Delhi. Do not go there. Go instead to Majestic Hotel in Varanasi. They will ask twenty rupees but say you will pay only ten."

With that he left.

"How the hell did he figure that out?" I wondered. There were no telltale maple leaves, no labels; my bag was Indian-made, my accent was Scottish; if anything, I looked German or Scandinavian after my rather severe haircut. But I knew already not to question anything in India. So, heeding his advice, I broke my journey and sought out the Majestic, demanding half the asked-for price.

A knock came and Kumar appeared. "In Varanasi I am your guide. Very cheap. Tomorrow, we will hire a rowboat. Dawn is best time to see Ganges," he stated laconically and disappeared once more. We did not see the sun rise, however, as there was a terrific thunderstorm. "Quite auspicious," he observed, drawing on his student knowledge of Victorian literature.

The Ganges was peculiarly devoid of people and the churned water a dark khaki. As he pulled on the oars, Kumar insisted that the water was quite drinkable. This I did not question. He did show me unusual aspects of this most remarkable city, for which I gratefully added a little bonus, but it was time to get back to the Guptas in New Delhi.

"Booki-ji!" Gupta shouted on my return. "Where have you been? We were so worried."

"Sorry about that, Mr. Gupta, but I can look after myself, you know," I protested. He thrust the previous day's newspaper at me, the headlines blaring, *Delhi-Mail Crash. 7 Killed, 84 Injured.*

Gulp! — my train. Auspicious indeed, Kumar — almost suspicious.

THE SPOON BEGINS TO BEND!

These two e-mails come courtesy of Marcello Truzzi, a friend and a noted sociologist with a special interest in the principles of conjuring and the history of stage magic. These messages refer to the visit to Toronto made by Uri Geller, the controversial Israeli-born psychic, who single-handedly — or single-mindedly — made "spoon-bending" a household word.

The first e-mail was written by Allan Slaight, the broadcasting executive who has also published books that illustrate the magical effects of Stewart James, the postman from Kortright, Ontario, who was incredibly inventive when it came to originating magical effects. The letter is dated January 28, 2000.

The second was written by David Ben, a lawyer and noted magician, who (with director Patrick Watson) devised a successful "period" magic act called *The Conjurer* which was presented as part of the Shaw Festival in Niagara-on-the-Lake, Ontario.

Slaight and Ben are two very observant people, so I would hesitate to try to bend a spoon in their presence! In their e-mails they refer to Ray Hyman, the psychologist and noted skeptic; James Randi, the Toronto-born illusionist and critic of claims of the paranormal; the magician's publication, *Linking Rings*; and other subjects of interest to illusionists and sceptics.

Hold me responsible for "this premature attempt to make a miracle out of nothing."

I've been in magic since 1939. I've toured in western Canada with an evening show of magic and mind-reading. I immodestly state that I came across as a real psychic with uncanny powers. I wrote, with Howard Lyons, *Stewart James in Print*, and am now finishing up, with the invaluable assistance of Max Maven, a ten-year, two-volume effort called *The James File*, which will run to more than 1,600 pages.

I scoffed at those early Geller reports. I was 100 per cent on Randi's side. I watched Geller blow his brains out on the Johnny Carson show. Then I forgot all about the guy until Marcello e-mailed me in mid-October and suggested I might like to meet Uri, who was in Toronto on a publicity tour for his *Mind Medicine* book. I contacted him at his hotel, and arrangements were made to pick him up at noon on Saturday, October 16.

The two of us are in my car. After a very brief "nice to meet you," he immediately pulled a coffee spoon from his pocket. I am instantly suspicious. "It's from the hotel," he says. "Please make sure it's normal." I take the spoon and test it for any type of pre-weakening. Nothing. Solid as can be. It would have taken a considerable, two-handed effort to bend that particular spoon.

As I watch carefully (stare is a better word), Uri takes the spoon back. No switch. He holds the bowl between the forefinger and thumb of his left hand. Thumb underneath and the finger inside the bowl. He *gently* strokes the spoon with the first two fingers of his right hand. No effort. No exertion. No tensing of muscles. Just a very soft caress of the handle of the spoon.

Before my eyes, the spoon begins to bend! It seems to *droop*. It bends not quite 45 degrees. He puts the spoon on the dashboard of my car and sits back in the passenger seat. The effing spoon continues to bend. He picks it up and hands it straight to me. It is now bent to right angles — 90 degrees. The metal is cold. Uri signs the spoon and gives it to me. (And all of this is reported to Marcello.)

Weirdly, and for reasons I now can't explain because for years I had lost all interest in Geller, I had ordered the Margolis book and it arrived the day before I met Uri. Prior to that incident in my car — which I reported that evening to a number of people, including magicians David Ben, Daniel Zuckerbrot and Mark Mitton — I was not aware that there were "after-bending" reports. When I raced through the Margolis book the following day, I was staggered to encounter the part where a Margolis-owned spoon bends somewhat, is placed on the author's 14-year-old son's hand, then continues to bend.

That same Saturday evening, Geller joined some of us at a fund-raiser for the Children's Own Museum, a cause dear to the heart of David Ben and his wife. David will receive this letter. I urge him to write up his account of a second spoon bending incident and forward it to this group.

Ray, I was the world's toughest skeptic until that bloody spoon bent before my eyes. I know the magician's methods — or most of them — and I have books and videos on spoon- and key-bending. What I witnessed is well beyond all that!

You have done a dandy job, from your vantage point, in airily dismissing my account, and those of others. You write: "...the question of scientific interest is not how many people claim to have 'seen' the item continue to bend but whether it did indeed continue to bend without physical contact."

The spoon now in my possession sure as hell did!

I agree with your commentary that Uri has had thirty years to prove his powers via photos or video and has not done so.

And you rightly point out that, as an amateur magician, I am not exempted from "the human equation."

Mind you, I thought you were doing just fine until you cited those first five examples. I would have quit when I was ahead — or at least not behind!

It would be nice to meet you sometime. Your one-man parade in the *Linking Ring* those many years ago was one of the very best.

Allan Slaight

★

To Whom It May Concern:

I was one of the magicians Ray Hyman alluded to in his extensive missive regarding Uri Geller and the bending spoon. I too witnessed Geller bending a spoon. Soon after it occurred, Marcello Truzzi asked me to describe what took place in more detail. The bending took place at a gala dinner that I was hosting for the Children's Own Museum in Toronto. Here is the body of my letter to Marcello.

Here is what happened to the best of my recollection. I introduced and invited Geller to come to the stage to address the audience. I wasn't sure whether he would perform or just tell a few stories. He said he would do three minutes and then leave because he had to get to a radio interview via telephone to a U.S. station.

I introduce Geller. He tells a charming story about when he first recognized his powers. *Very self-effacing.* Charming. Said with an "I can't believe it is true because it is so trivial" posture that he first became famous for bending spoons.

He asked everyone (450 people) to pick up their spoons. (It was a black-tie gala dinner.) I gave him a handheld microphone, but it apparently wasn't working properly. He started to speak from the podium but moved into the audience. I got the microphone to work and followed him into the audience with the microphone directly under his mouth at all times. I was always standing to his right side. We moved from table to table.

I am unclear on the next point because it happened so fast. Initially I seem to recall that he picked up a spoon from the table. (He may have had it on his person but my recollection is that he picked it up from the table.) He kept on apologizing to say that it may or may not work. Imagine a large dance floor jutting out into the space with tables situated on three sides with the stage area for the band bordering one side. He picks up the spoon from the stage-left side of the dance floor. Holds it in his left hand — high — my side. We sweep past the table bordering the left side and downstage sides of the dance floor. He holds the spoon by his fingertips to the right. Can't recall if he moved his right fingers over the arm of the spoon or just held the spoon with his left fingers.

Commented that sometimes the spoon will bend. I see a slow movement of the arm of the spoon. *Not 90 degrees.* He gracefully shows the spoon to a variety of people stating, "Look... you can see that it is bending."

We backpedal to the stage-left side of the band's stage where the lectern is located. He comments he will offer the spoon for auction as a fund-raiser for the children's museum. Plants the seed that another spoon he bent sold for $25,000 at an auction in N.Y.C.

He takes out a pen and signs and dates the spoon. He comments that at times the spoon has continued to bend even after he has gone but that it *always* stops (he can't explain it) at a 90-degree angle. He says that he will leave the spoon on the lectern where it may continue to bend. I am standing to the left of the lectern and he is standing to the left of me.

He reaches over to place the spoon on the lectern. It slides off because of the incline for speakers' notes. He picks it up and gently places over the molding at the top of the lectern. It is balanced precariously. It does not appear to be at a 90-degree angle at this time. (I made a mental note of this because Slaight had already tipped me to the dashboard episode. I wanted to see if it really bent any further.) It did not appear to be 90-degrees when he placed it on the lectern.

He departs (from my left, as I am in between him and the lectern and the spoon). I take the handheld mike and thank him on behalf of the audience. He departs to large applause. I immediately pick up the spoon from the lectern and place it into my pocket so that no one can steal it before I have the opportunity to auction it off. I notice that it is now at a perfect 90-degree angle — a different physical appearance than what I recall seeing when he placed it gently down on the lectern. I secretly shake my head because it is now different and I did not see him do one thing that was suspicious, with speed, without grace or charm. It was flawless. I have no idea what he did.

I now have the spoon at my home. It is perfect. I have seen many spoons bent by so-called experts. Uri is in a league of his own. The curvature of the bend is beautiful — not forced. I have said to many people that the curvature reminds me of a single line drawn by Matisse. It is a work of art. You can tell that it was created by a master. Quite wonderful. And he is a very gracious guest, and quite charming. I would open my home to him and his brother-in-law at any time.

What is even more interesting, however, is our conversation about David Blaine and David's posturing for the media. I thought that his comments, more than anything, raised doubts about any particular powers he may have professed to possess. Geller was very approachable, humane and — wink, wink — wonderfully ambiguous.

I'm a fan.

Now, I would like to add a few further comments. Although I am not an expert in the paranormal, I am an expert in sleight of hand. I would stack up my knowledge and ability in sleight of hand against anyone in the world. I do not believe that Geller used sleight of hand to bend the spoon. (I have seen most of the spoon bending experts created by the magic community and their work is not very elegant when compared with Geller.)

Further, with no disrespect to Mr. Hyman, I find the explanation of the shift in focus to account for the visible bending of the spoon to be rather simplistic. I was briefed earlier in the day to watch for this should Geller attempt to bend a spoon. It was not at 90 degrees when it was placed on lectern. It was at 90 degrees afterwards.

You can probably sense from the tone of my letter to Marcello that I am not convinced that Geller has paranormal powers. I am rather indifferent. He may or may not. I am not prepared to state that he is a genuine psychic just because he performed something that I cannot explain. It was just a beautiful performance.

I do find, however, the actions of most skeptics repugnant. They seem such a rude and ungracious bunch. I would not want to perform for them even if I had psychic powers. I have certainly turned down well-paying work because the potential client was obnoxious. I would not blame Geller for doing the same.

David Ben

Miracles and Other Cures

THERE IS NO question that the mind may influence matter. It is a matter of will. But so far in human history there are only partial answers to the question, "How is it that matter is influenced by mind?" Are belief and faith able to act directly on the human body and thereby bring relief from pain and heal the body?

Faith healing and miraculous cures go hand in hand, as do visits to "miracle shrines," of which Canada has more than its share. Accounts of pilgrimages to the shrine at Ste-Anne-de-Beaupré outside Quebec City are well represented here. Members of the medical profession look askance at reports of those "miracle cures" that follow visits to shrines or grottoes, and they regard them as unsubstantiated and underreported (as to the medical conditions both before and after the supposed cures). At the same time, there are medically authenticated cases of "spontaneous remission." Who knows the potencies of the mind, the unfathomable powers of prayer? There is always hope...

THE POOR LITTLE CHILDREN

This account was titled "Extraordinary Superstition in New Brunswick" when it appeared in the *Quebec Daily News* on October 18, 1862. Apparently it is reprinted from the *St. John's News* (Saint John, N.B.). In this account of a local superstitious practice, "whooping cough" was spelled "hooping cough."

EXTRAORDINARY SUPERSTITION IN NEW BRUNSWICK

The *St. John's News* says:— There is a woman in Duke-street, owning a donkey (if you know what that is). and it appears that it got bruited abroad that if a child having the hooping cough were to crawl under the animal's belly, or that of any other donkey, a speedy cure would be the result. Incredible as it may seem, crowds of women with afflicted children from "York Point" and Portland have been going over to this donkey-woman for some days past, and the poor little children (hooping at an awful rate) have been crawling under the animal's body in a continuous stream. The pressure became so great that the owner of the Doctor at last commenced to charge a York-shilling fee; and on Monday she did a handsome business in this way. We talk of the infidelity of the people of India, and wonder at their ignorance; but here is an amount of superstition in a Christian community which it would puzzle better philosophers than we are, to account for.

STE-ANNE-DE-BEAUPRÉ

The shrine of Ste-Anne-de-Beaupré east of Quebec City is the largest Roman Catholic shrine of its kind in Canada or the United States. Each year it attracts tens of thousands of pious pilgrims and not-so-pious tourists. The pilgrims kneel before the statue of St. Anne, the mother of the Blessed Virgin Mary, and pray for cures for their pains or relief from their infirmities.

"St. Anne de Beaupré" is reprinted from the *Irish Canadian*, November 20, 1878. It originally appeared in the *New York World*. Some spellings have been regularized.

ST. ANNE DE BEAUPRÉ
How Her Intercession Saved the Fishermen of Cape St. Ignace

FROM THE *NEW YORK WORLD*

The pilgrimage season at the shrine of St. Anne is over. The election campaign kept many of the faithful at home, nevertheless 30,000 devotees have visited the shrine and many miracles are reported. Of those that have been formally attested one of the most extraordinary is the cure of

Emilie Plamondon, daughter of M.J.B. Plamondon, of St. Sauveur. Emilie, a girl of fourteen, began her devotion in the chapel where the precious relic of the saint is treasured, at the foot of the hill looking across the river, on the 18th of August. About a year ago an abscess that defied medical skill broke out in her foot. At first she felt a stinging pain; then her foot began to swell, and at length a terrible sore opened, and the bones came away in small pieces. In the beginning of August the doctors gave her up, and the priest administered the last Sacrament. She lay for some days apparently at the point of death, but rallied on the 9th and entreated her father and mother to take her on a pilgrimage to St. Anne. They granted her request, and on the 18th, as stated, she paid the first visit to the shrine. She was carried into the church by her parents and placed in front of the high altar. She could not kneel, but supported herself while she prayed with her crutches. Over a hundred pilgrims were in the chapel, and after the rosary all joined in the canticum of St. Anne. They were singing the first verse

Glorieuse Ste. Anne,

Daignez prier pour nous,

A fin qu'un jour nos aimes

Au ciel soient aver vous,

when suddenly Emilie dropped her crutches, and, to her amazement, stood erect, and found that every trace of the abscess had disappeared, not even a scar remaining. The doctors who had seen her a few days before were summoned. They examined the cure and pronounced it miraculous, and the witnesses of the miracle duly attested it. Emilie is at this moment preparing to enter the Sodality of the Blessed Virgin, in the parish of St. Anne, having resolved to devote herself to the service of God. She can be seen in the chapel every day, and hundreds have heard from her lips her marvellous story.

On the 11th of July the young people of the congregation of the Holy Virgin of St. Sauveur made their annual pilgrimage to the shrine under the charge of the Oblate Fathers. They numbered 400. Just as they reached the chapel they met several hundred pilgrims from the parish of Cape St. Ignace coming out. Two of the St. Ignace pilgrims, however, had remained — an old man named Forget and his wife, the latter suffering from spinal disease. The St. Sauveur pilgrims filed into the church and began their devotions. They noticed the old couple praying devoutly at the altar steps. By and by the priest, Father Sirois, of the Ignace, mounted the pulpit and exhorted the worshipers to persevere zealously in their supplications. While he was speaking Mme. Forget rose from the couch on which she lay and holding up her hand, cried out, "O, blessed is St. Anne! Father, I am cured." Father Sirois stepped down and approached her, but she walked forward with a firm step and met him. All present saw the miracle, and, amid the joyful tears of the pilgrims, the choir sang the "Magnificat," and at the close Mme. Forget was escorted home by the congregation.

On the 17th ult., Father Blais, the curé of the parish of St. Raymond, with several of his parishioners brought to the shrine a woman named Pilon, the wife of a blacksmith. She had been attacked with typhoid fever, which left her completely blind. The doctors said the optic nerve was paralyzed, and that her blindness was incurable. On being told this the sufferer implored the Almighty, if it was his will, to take her out of the world, for she had four young children and her husband was a poor man and she knew she would be a burden upon them. The priest sought to comfort her, but for a time she was inconsolable. At length he induced her to commit herself into the hands of God and bear her dreadful affliction with resignation and humility. When her mind had become settled, he called her neighbors and asked them to join him in a pilgrimage with Mme. Pilon. On their arrival at the chapel Father Blais instructed her to say, "Lord restore my sight for the sake of my children and my husband," and to sing immediately after the hymn of St. Anne which every French-Canadian child is taught:

O tendre Mère,
Ste. Anne, en ce beau jour;
Nôtre prière
Reclame ton amour, &c.

She obeyed her instructions to the letter, and prayed and sang with much devotion. Towards evening she grew faint, for she had been fasting that she might approach the Eucharist, and the neighbors took hold of her arm and led her out of the chapel. As they passed a statue of St. Anne, on the middle Altar, she said, "Would to God, my friends, that I could see." She had scarcely uttered the words when she stopped and exclaimed, "I am cured! I am cured!" and, throwing herself at the foot of the Altar, returned thanks to the saint — the priest and neighbors, and over fifty other devotees, joining in her thanksgiving.

On the 1st inst., during a fierce gale, two fishermen, named Lemay and O'Connor, of Cape St. Ignace, were driven down the river in their smack, which dragged its anchor, and the villagers standing on the shore were powerless to save them. This was shortly before 6 p.m., and the darkness soon hid the drifting boat. The villagers spent the night on the shore, praying to St. Anne, the patroness of mariners, and the morning found them still engaged in the pious work. At 9 a.m. the two fishermen entered the village on foot, and were hailed as men from the grave. They related that at 10 p.m., while they were drifting down before the tempest, unable to steer the craft, and expecting to be swamped every moment, they saw a light ahead. At first they took it to be that of an inbound steamship, and saw with horror that it was bearing down upon them rapidly. All at once, however, it lit up their boat and the angry waters, and they knew it was a supernatural light. In an instant the gale abated, and, though they did not touch the rudder, the boat turned sharply out of mid-channel and ran into the anchorage of Ste. Anne de Témoignage, nearly twenty miles from Cape St. Ignace. They had barely made the craft secure when the storm again set in with fearful violence. The two men, with the villagers, at once made a pilgrimage to the shrine of the saint and returned thanks for their great deliverance.

These are perhaps the most striking of the many miracles reported this season. The fame of the shrine has gone out through the continent, and where none but French Canadians and Indians used to worship there are now seen during the summer scores of Catholics from the United States, many combing from New Orleans and Baltimore, and even from the Pacific coast.

203

A MANITOBA MIRACLE

"A Manitoba Miracle" appeared in the *Winnipeg Free Press* on September 26, 1885. Apparently, the article is a translation of one that had been published in the French-language publication *Le Manitoba*.

A MANITOBA MIRACLE
Account of a Cure through the Prayers of Saint Anne

A correspondent of *Le Manitoba*, writing from Sainte-Anne-des-Chenes under date of the 11th inst., makes the following statements:—

An extraordinary cure has taken place in the Church of Sainte-Anne-des–Chenes. In the course of last spring Edward Hebert, son of Felix Hebert, was attacked with a malady which rendered him nearly blind. His whole face was covered with sores. The physician had advised our priest to treat with care the poor patient, who was really to be pitied. His sufferings were dreadful. The doctor of our parish had declared that if the young sufferer should ever be restored to health he would very probably be left blind. From this the anguish of his good and respectable parents may be seen. Human remedies continuing to be ineffectual the parents, by the advice of our priest, had recourse to the power of the good Saint Anne. A nine days' devotion was performed in her honor, and scarcely had it been finished when the sores began to heal, his eyes, which had been horribly swollen, resumed their normal condition, and the poor child, the loss whose sight the physician had feared, is now rejoicing in good health, can engage in study, and attend school; his eyes are perfectly healed. Glory and honor to our Lord, who, through the intercession of the good Saint Anne has granted to this poor child a cure which may be regarded as very extraordinary. He invoked with confidence the patron saint of his parish and his prayers were heard.

AT THE SHRINE OF ST. ANNE

The principal shrine in Canada is the Roman Catholic church at St. Anne de Beaupré outside Quebec City, Quebec. For more than three centuries it has been the destination of pilgrims, tourists, and congregants who seek its "healing" ways. It has been the subject of countless news stories.

Here is a typical, unsubstantiated story. "At the Shrine of St. Anne" appeared in the *Medicine Hat News*, 27 Oct. 1898.

AT THE SHRINE OF ST. ANNE
Wonderful Cures Reported from Beaupré
Cripples Throw Crutches Away

Montreal report: "At this season it is usual to hear marvellous tales of miracles wrought at the shrine of St. Anne de Beaupré. Thousands of pilgrims go there every year, and though all are not cured of their ailments, the percentage of those who derive some benefit is said to be large. The ladies of the parish of St. Jean-Baptiste, whose beautiful church was destroyed by fire last winter, returned yesterday morning, and their pilgrimage seems to have been unusually prolific in thaumaturgy.

There were over 650 pilgrims in charge of Curé Auclair, pastor of the parish, and several other well-known clergymen. On arriving at St. Anne a procession was formed and proceeded to the church, where there was general communion and a low mass. "Up to this point," wrote a pious correspondent of *La Presse*, "St. Anne had received us as strangers, but after mass a young girl of fourteen or fifteen, whose name we could not ascertain, decided to come into close favour with the wonder worker. She went to the rear of the church, near the pyramid of offerings, with some friends, and took off a sort of harness in which she was wrapped for some years because of a weakness in one leg, which she was utterly unable to bend and which caused her great suffering.

"Trusting to herself, she directed her steps towards that statue of St. Anne. At the first step everyone hastened to support her, for she seemed to sink from the acuteness of her pain, but she asked to be left alone. She recovered, took another step, a third, a fourth, and finally, having reached the statue, 200 feet farther on, she was cured. After a short thanksgiving, she went to the Calvary, so difficult of access even for those in good health, and climbed it without difficulty. Her cure is complete, except for a slight difference between one leg and the other.

"Another favour, if not a miracle, was the cure of a child of 4 years old, who in his prayer in the Basilica cried out, 'St. Anne, cure me.' He left an iron shoe behind, and came back walking firmly on both feet. Another little boy left his crutch and promised St. Anne that he would leave his shoe next year. A lady named St. Vincent, suffering from paralysis, felt that she had received much benefit.

"But what touched the pilgrims most was the offering made by Miss Lamarche, who obtained a perfect cure from St. Anne nine years ago. Since that time she goes every year to return thanks and to promise that at the end of the nine years she would accomplish the promise she made in order to obtain the cure. Miss Lamarche had obtained a great favour, and consequently promised a great sacrifice to St. Anne. During the consecration of the great wonder worker, Miss Lamarche cut off a magnificent head of hair, which she left at the foot of the saint. The sacrifice was well chosen, for we believe that it is the last thing which a girl of 21 would like to lose. This demonstration threw the pilgrims into admiration and fervour. The most of them even shed tears. All profited by the good example and learned that St. Anne is generous to those who are generous in sacrifice."

A SIMPLE CURE

It may well be with relief that the reader is able to turn from devotional practices, ones that lead to miraculous cures of debilitating conditions, to folkloric remedies of ongoing problems.

Superstitious practices of the kind described in this article are rapidly disappearing from the oral tradition. The new "art-preservative" is the written tradition, not the oral one based on transmission from generation to generation.

Physicians regard warts on human bodies with great wariness, for they seem to have a life of their own. "Wart Cures" appeared as part of a write-in column headed "Canadian Folklore" which appeared in The (Toronto) Globe on June 24, 1911.

WART CURES

Dear Rose Rambler,— In Saturday's *Globe* I noticed some cures for warts in your folklore column, and I thought I would send two of which I have heard, one curing me entirely of a small wart on the side of my thumb.

I was told to rub the wart with my tongue each morning on waking up. I have a bit of Scotch blood in my veins, and I was quite young at the time, so believed in the remedy. I did this each morning for a month or so, and one day was surprised to see that the blemish had entirely disappeared, whether from the prescription or not, I cannot say. I did not notice the wart getting smaller or gradually disappearing; it seemed to go all at once.

Another cure which I have heard of is to place a piece of meat in a bag and hide this between two stones. It is believed that by the time the meat is entirely decayed, the wart will have disappeared.

Another superstition regarding the white spots on the finger-nails is: (running from the thumb to the little finger) — a friend, a foe, a gift, a beau, a journey, and, of course, the more white spots, the more of each one will have.

A hairpin on the street, pointing to you and picked up, is a sure sign that the first gentleman you meet and speak to is your future husband.

Your folklore column is extremely interesting.

Autumn Woods

THE POWER OF SUGGESTION

The contributor of the following short article is Dr. Peter Steele, a physician in medical practice in Whitehorse, Yukon. His article appeared under the title "A Testament to the Power of Suggestion" in the *Medical Post* of May 30, 1995. It is reprinted with permission.

I'm a very conventional doctor — no iridology, a touch of homeopathy, little chiropractic — but I have had remarkable success with charming warts. My apogee of success was a child of nine who had forty-seven painful verrucae on the soles of his feet.

We went through my routine, with the essential connivance of the parents, of going to the bank to withdraw one new penny for each wart, going down to the Yukon River and throwing each of the pennies over the shoulder while saying the magic word *Tikkitikkitembonaseremboberiberibushkidankerwallamannapannakofemaskoshotz*, which I have printed out on a label stuck on a wooden tongue depressor for the child to learn at home.

Since I started, I have had at least fifty successes, mainly with children between the ages of six (when they can understand my mumbo-jumbo) and twelve (after which they think I'm a jerk). I attribute this to their suggestibility in a matter I think is mostly attributable to self-hypnosis.

I find it marvellous that in these days of hi-tech science the charming of warts is so completely inexplicable. But I have a theory, completely empirical. Warts are small tumours caused by the human papilloma virus. Tumour behaviour can be modified by the immune system, and the immune system can be triggered by hypnosis.

I suggest that in charming warts we are inducing a state of self-hypnosis, whether it be by juice of celandine, frog legs under a full moon, or by my magic word. It is interesting that the only adults with whom I have had success are highly suggestible.

The mundane scientific fact is that it doesn't matter what your incantation, potion, or sacrifice, you must believe to trigger your immune system to alter the metabolism of the papilloma virus in your skin. Then, Presto!

Dr. Peter Steele, Whitehorse, Yukon

8 Inquiry into the Bizarre

HERE IS AN inquiry into the bizarre. It is also a bizarre inquiry, for it comes to the reader by way of a supermarket tabloid.

These lively weekly publications, which are displayed at supermarket checkout counters, are easily dismissed by serious-minded folk. Indeed, the sensationalistic headlines of "the tabs" speak for themselves: *Girl Sees Her Child in UFO*; or *Alien Bodies Found in Alaska*. But as psychologist Kenneth Ring noted, "If you treat the tabs as folklore, they make remarkable reading."

What can be said for the publishers of the tabs, if not for the publications they edit, is that they know what sells. Their editors, reporters and correspondents have taken to heart the interests of unsophisticated North Americans and concocted stories tailored to them. Subjects that interest ordinary Americans (and Canadians) include paranormal powers and especially the idea of alien beings and abductions.

The *National Enquirer*, the leading tabloid, conducted its own "Psychic Survey" in April 1978. It was not in any way a scientific survey, but it was a careful one, which asked its readers to complete a questionnaire about their psychic experiences and to describe any inexplicable or improbable experiences they had had. The questionnaire was prepared in consultation with Joel Whitton, a psychiatrist and researcher in Toronto who has a special interest in psychical and parapsychological matters, and the late Professor A.R.G. Owen and Iris M. Owen, founders of the New Horizons Research Foundation in Toronto.

The survey comprised eleven questions requiring yes or no responses. Each reader was asked to check the appropriate reply. If the reader answered yes to a question, he or she was asked to describe each experience on a separate sheet of paper. The instructions continued, "To the best of your recollection, please try to include the place, date and time of the experience; whether you were fully awake, asleep or in an in-between state; the kind of medication you were taking at the time, if any; your mental state (from feeling depressed to feeling happy); your physical health; whether the experience was associated with someone else; whether others were present and what they experienced; whether you had the same experience more than once."

Finally, each reader was asked to fill in the blanks on the form for name, age, sex, address, telephone, occupation and number of years of schooling, and to send the replies to the *Enquirer*'s office in Lontana, Florida. The replies were then forwarded in bulk to Dr. Whitton and Professor Owen. Dr. Whitton noted: "Nothing of this magnitude in analyzing psychic phenomena has ever been attempted before. Indeed, the last major survey of this type was conducted by the British Society for Psychical Research, and it was a door-to-door poll of some 17,000 people. The BSPR's study found that ten percent of respondents said that they had had a psychic experience."

Professor Owen added, "Until now, nobody has ever really attempted to answer a very important but quite unsolved question: How many people really have experienced psychic phenomena?" There is no answer to that question, as replies from the *Enquirer*'s questionnaire were not examined for their statistical significance. But it is apparent from the volume of mail — some 2,500 responses — that psychic experiences are quite common. Most of the replies were quite brief, but some were quite long and detailed.

The questions posed by the survey were:

1. Have you ever seen, heard, smelled, felt or tasted anything that was not due to any physical cause?
2. Have you ever had a dream or vision which came true?
3. Have you ever bent or moved an object solely by using the power of your mind?
4. Have you ever had the experience of floating away from your body?
5. Have you ever sent messages to someone else or received messages using only the power of your mind?

6. Have you ever accurately made a prediction about an important event prior to its actual occurrence?

7. Did you ever get the strong feeling an event was actually taking place at that exact moment and then found out later it did in fact happen?

8. Have you ever healed an injury or successfully treated an illness or ailment of someone else using mind power?

9. Have you ever seen objects move mysteriously by themselves or seen ghost-like figures or heard unexplained sounds?

10. Have you ever had experiences or memories of a previous life?

11. Have you ever experienced any other strange, unexplained phenomenon?

More than one hundred readers from Canada filled out the questionnaire. For the most part, these responses were the same as those submitted by Americans. But there was one odd difference: a large number of American accounts reported psychic experiences that featured flashes of light. This feature, to which no particular significance can be ascribed, was not characteristic of the Canadian accounts.

After reading all the accounts, Professor Owen concluded: "This is the most exciting survey ever attempted in the field of psychic research."

The accounts of a number of the psychic experiences of Canadian readers are being reproduced here for the first time. In publishing them, pains have been taken to disguise the names and addresses of respondents and to eliminate identifiable personal details; in their stead, appropriate equivalents have been substituted. Routine copy editing has regularized punctuation, removed repetition and enhanced the narrative flow. Nothing of consequence has been added or subtracted.

The reader will do well to bear in mind that most informants offered not one single instance of a paranormal experience, but two or more instances of such episodes. It seems these experiences are commonly reported in quantity by a limited number of people. To ensure variety, each respondent has generally been limited to a single experience. Finally, fuller accounts of characteristic experiences have been selected in preference to impressionistic accounts of unclassifiable incidents. The biographical information at the end of each account is, in the opinion of the editor, insufficient to identify the informant.

Certainly, the experiences reproduced here make for exciting reading, and I am grateful to Professor Owen for drawing these accounts to my attention and allowing me to use them in this way.

ASTRAL TRAVELLING

I had gone upstairs to have a drink of orange juice and then returned downstairs to the recreation room, where I slept that evening. I was half asleep when I seemed to feel a large black cloud cover me, and then I felt I was being swept upwards with the speed of lightning, as though I was going through a long tunnel. I could not open my eyes, or I didn't want to.

When I finally opened my eyes, I found myself standing beside a very large wicker basket with a top on it. Directly in front of me was a bunk bed with a child (male) around seven or eight years old, sleeping with his back facing me. I also remember royal blue ozite on the floor with bicycle skid marks in white just in the centre of the floor.

My eyes closed again for the second time and I started to rise slowly. I opened my eyes and saw I was going to go through the ceiling, so I braced my arms around my head to ward off the blow. However, I passed through the ceiling with no difficulty and found myself being swept upwards again. I found myself in another room (it could have been a bar where drinks were being served) and staring at a woman dressed in a black coat and black head kerchief. I thought I knew her and put my arms around her, only to discover it was someone else. I cried out.

Again my eyes closed, and by this time I was getting very frightened I found myself walking through walls and then, for the third time, I was swept upwards and then felt someone or something grab my ankles and swing me back and forth like a pendulum. I felt as if I were going to be hysterical and called out, "God help me — get me back home." As I said this, I was back in my recreation room, looking desperately for the colours of certain items to make sure I was in the right room. I felt very relieved when I found I was back home safe. I had

212

great difficulty going back to sleep, as I certainly didn't want to repeat the experiences I had just gone through.

E.F., Winnipeg, Man.; female, age 46, self-employed, 10 years schooling

HAUNTED HOUSES

THE FIRST HAUNTED HOUSE

When I was a child of eight, we — my parents, two brothers and two sisters and I — lived in a haunted house. And, Mr. Man, I mean haunted!

When we went to bed, as soon as the lights were put out, it seemed as if a whole family took over for the night shift. I could hear dishes being taken out of the cupboard and being set down on the table. I could hear footsteps — different, weighted steps. Other members of the family heard the walking, too. Nothing else happened.

About town it was said that every family that had lived in that house had lost one member through death before the family moved from that house. My parents never discussed the matter, at least not in the presence of us children. However, we moved out of the house as soon as another house was available in town.

During World War I, a vacant house was unusual in the town of Collingwood, Ontario, because it was a very busy shipyard town. But within a few months, the house we had moved into was sold and we had no choice but to move back into the haunted house again, at least until the big stone house my father was having built eight miles west of town was completed in the spring of 1919. But before we moved from the haunted house the second time, mother gave birth to a baby girl — stillborn.

THE SECOND HAUNTED HOUSE

The second haunted house was in Toronto, Ontario. I had just one experience.

213

It was June and I had been studying for exams. My sisters and brothers, all younger than I, had already gone to bed and were asleep when I was ready to prepare for bed. As I started to go upstairs, mother said, "Good night — I am going out at eight-thirty and I'll lock the doors."

By the time I had washed, brushed my teeth, etc., I noticed that the street lights were on. There was a lamppost just across from my bedroom window. I realized that it had gone on at 9:00 p.m., but in June it was still light outside. When I got into bed beside my sleeping younger sister, I lay on my left side, with my face to her back, which meant that my "good" ear (I have always been completely deaf in my right ear) was lying on the pillow.

I was no sooner settled down than I heard my mother call me. The thought occurred to me, "That's funny, mother said she was going out at eight-thirty and it's past nine now." Then I heard her call again. I quickly rose up to answer her, when I saw a woman in a shroud-like gown sitting on the side of the bed, her head looking into my sister's face. The woman straightened up, turned her head and looked directly at me, but said nothing. She stood up and turned and walked toward the bedroom door. Then, within about two feet of the door, she seemed to disintegrate right through the floor.

Later, at breakfast, I described the "ghost woman" to mother she looked stunned. She said, "Why, that is the description of my mother to a T."

I guess our grandmother must have known at that time the health and other problems that were lying ahead for my sister.

THE THIRD HAUNTED HOUSE

The third haunted house we lived in was also in the city of Toronto. Like the first one, it was somewhat noisy, but it was much less of a joke to me. My mother had bought this nice old brick house with ten rooms on two floors. Mother was in real estate, and when she bought a house the first thing she did was have the locks changed on the doors. But the locksmith did not complete the front-door changeover the first day, so we ended up putting a chair against the door, wedging it under the knob. However, my sister went out to supper with her boyfriend, while I chose to get a few jobs done and have supper. By the time I was ready for bed, my sister had returned and we went to bed.

This was in late March or early April and there was a lot of snow on the ground. This night there were big snowflakes coming down. There was the sound of the snow being shovelled. After an hour or so of the sound of the shovelling, which never seemed to be getting any farther away, I had got up to see who was doing all the shovelling, but no one was there. We finally went to sleep.

The next day our cousin Ruth came from Grafton, Ontario, to spend the night with us. I told Ruth about our experience of hearing the continuous shovelling. That night there was the sound of the shovelling again. She asked about it and said that it seemed to be going on and getting closer. All at once Ruth gave one great yell: "What was that?" Then she said, "May I come into your bed?"

My sister Catherine said, "No! There's two of us in one bed now." But then, in a few moments, my sister became hysterical, so I said, "All right, Ruth, you can come in now."

When she came on the run and closed our bedroom door quickly, she slammed it on part of her nightgown. She gave one scream that would almost have wakened the dead. She thought somebody had a hold of her gown from the back. If she'd had the heart problem then that she has now, that would have no doubt been the end of her.

The next day I was doing a bit of shopping at Mealing's Grocery and Butcher Shop. I was telling the owner about our experience of our first nights in the house that we'd just moved into. He said, "Oh, you must be the new people at 202." I replied that we were. He said, "Oh, yes, well, a man was shot in that house."

He explained: "It seems the couple who lived in the house had a guest, a man, who lived upstairs. He came downstairs to spend time with the lady while her husband was on the night shift. The man always put the coal in the furnace and banked it up for the night for the lady. The husband became suspicious and began checking. As I understand it, the husband came back one night and shot the man through the back of the neck. He did it from the stairs. The man was in the basement shovelling the coal for the furnace."

I said, "I guess he must have come back to finish the job. We heard the shovel against the cement for two nights now. I took the sound to be a neighbour shovelling snow from our sidewalk."

End of haunted house experiences for me!

R.B., Collingwood, Ont.; female, age 69, retired housewife,
high school (nights), university extension (nights)

CRISIS APPARITION

Our air crew was engaged in the bombing of Frankfurt-on-Main on the Ruhr River system.

During an air battle, we were engaged by enemy fighters and anti-aircraft guns, along with searchlights. We were repeatedly struck and were badly fragmented by flak. (A later check indicated we had been struck forty-five times.)

At one point, the engines suddenly stopped. This was caused by the vacuum of an explosion of flak, starving the engines from fuel feed.

The captain called for everyone to prepare to abandon the aircraft, mentioning something about the "Weiners and Kraut" we'd have for breakfast!

We were all very much terrified by the running battle, and I had begun the recitation of the Lord's Prayer. The crew quickly joined me in the prayer.

While saying the prayer, I was very personally comforted by an apparition, now indescribable, but then imagined to be a spirit. That apparition introduced me to the family kitchen at home in Sydney, Nova Scotia.

The family began to enter the kitchen, one by one, in a sad frame of mind. They said nothing, except someone said, "Jimmy is in trouble."

The incident took place 0500 Greenwich Mean Time on the morning of September 20, 1942.

Years following the war, the family affirm that on the night of September 19, at midnight, "something" aroused them, each separately, and they "gravitated" to the kitchen.

The two incidents happened at the same moment.

It was the night for which I was awarded the Distinguished Flying Cross by King George VI for "courage, skill and 'devotion' to duty"!

It was also the incident that put me in the hospital. Yet when the telegram concerning my condition was delivered to the family at home, they "already knew" that I was okay!

J.C.L., Port Stanley, Ont.; 57, male, publisher, postgraduate

PRECOGNITIVE DREAM

It was in 1952, when I had just opened my first beauty salon, back in Germany. I was very afraid of the future because the business was very low. I had a dream one night, which gave me a very positive feeling, but I did not know why. The dream showed me a very straight road. I was about to walk down it. I saw little houses, with front yards, in every detail, but all was very unfamiliar. I came to Canada in 1966 and moved into a small apartment which was about a mile away from the next big shopping centre. The first time I went to do my shopping, on my return I was waiting for the bus to take me home. I looked down the road, and there it was: the road of my dream fourteen years ago.

M.S., Eganville, Ont.; female, age, work, and education unspecified

THE HAUNTED PENITENTIARY

This happened in Halifax, Nova Scotia, sometime during July 1937. I'm not sure what day it was that I became the caretaker of the old Imperial Penitentiary on the eastern side of the Northwest Arm, next to Halifax on its western side. At that time the old penitentiary was in ruins. It has been torn down since then.

My wife, our daughter, my wife's younger sister and I moved into what had been the Governor's House, a huge three-story place. We all knew the story of the large Newfoundland dog that was supposed to be

217

haunting this house. The story was that the former caretaker's fourteen-year-old daughter had suffered a nervous breakdown because of him. They said that when the family would be eating their meals, he would come and lie in the doorway of the room. If one of them moved toward him, he would go into the hall and disappear.

We took another man and his wife and their two sons in with us for company. When we moved in, we could lock the front door, but not the back door as the lock had been broken. The house had two porches in the back, an outside one and an inside one. Both doors opened out. I said to my wife that evening, "I'm going to put a couple of door hooks on the inside porch door so that we can secure it before retiring for the night."

That evening I got two door hooks and eye bolts. I screwed the hooks into the door-top and bottom, and the eye bolts into the side of the door frame, top and bottom. That night, before going to bed, I closed the door and hooked it, top and bottom. The door fit into the frame so tightly that it was impossible to push a piece of paper between door and frame.

The next morning, when we got out of bed, the door was wide open. The eye bolts had been torn out of the door frame and were hanging on the hooks in the door. The same thing happened three nights in succession. So I said to my wife, "Okay, if they want the door left open, it can stay that way. I'll put a sliding bolt on the inside of the hall door and see what happens."

That evening I went to my tool chest and got a hand drill, a screwdriver, a centre punch, a pencil, the sliding bolt and catch, and nine screws. I asked Archie, the chap who was living with us, if he would help me. He held the bolt in place while I marked the places for the screws. I picked up the drill and drilled the holes for the screws. With Archie helping, I started to put the first screw in place, when there were three knocks on the back door. I opened the door and looked out, but there was nobody to be seen. So I closed the door and started on the screw again. I had the screw about halfway in when the knocks came the second time. Again there was nobody there when we looked, so I said to Archie, "That's some damn fool playing a joke on us. If they come again, you go out the front door and I'll go out the back door, and if anybody is out there we'll corner him."

When the knocks came the third time, Archie ran out the front door and I went out the back. We ran around the house, but there was nobody around. So I said to Archie, "Okay, let's go back in, and if they want to knock on the door, they can knock all night. I'm not going out again."

I went in and had got one screw set up and was starting on the second, when something hit the back door. I opened the door and went out and looked around, but could see nothing. Then I looked behind the door, and sticking into the door was a three-cornered bayonet like the ones they used in the First World War. It had been thrown with such force that it was nearly driven through the door. It was still quivering when I looked at it. I plucked it out of the door and took it inside and showed it to the others. (I still have it in a box in my basement. When anybody asks me about it, I tell them it was given to me by a ghost. I don't know where it came from or who threw it at the house. There were several people in the old prison, but the side door of the prison was a good five hundred feet from the back door of the house, if not more than that.) I finished putting the bolt on the hall door without any more trouble.

Now, I'll speak about that Newfoundland dog I mentioned earlier. Shortly after the appearance of the bayonet, I was alone in the house. All the rest were out for the afternoon. The third floor was called the attic and it had not been swept or cleaned for years. There were cobwebs and dust everywhere one looked. So that afternoon I decided to clean it up. I locked the front door and set the bolt in the back door. All the windows were locked so that it was impossible for man or beast to get it. I got a paper box, some old cleaning rags, the broom and dust pan, and went upstairs.

On each floor there were three bedrooms and a bathroom. I started in on the bathroom. After I'd finished there, I moved into the back bedroom and cleaned that. Then I moved to the two front bedrooms. I did one and I went into the other one. This one was located over the room where my wife and I slept. On the floor of the room there was a pile of lumber and a hot-water tank that lay on its side. Many a night my wife and I would lie in bed and listen to that tank rolling back and forth over the floor. We would hear the lumber being moved about. But when we got up in the morning and looked, everything would be in its place.

As I started in on that room, I heard an animal coming upstairs. It never occurred to me to wonder how an animal could be in the house with all the doors and windows locked and secured. I heard him come up from the ground floor, trot around the stairwell on the second floor, and start up for the attic floor. When he came in sight, he was the most beautiful Newfoundland dog I had ever seen in my life. His coat was glossy black and curly. He came into the room where I was and looked at me out of his lovely large brown eyes. He lay down on the floor with his red tongue hanging out of his red lips. I walked over to him and patted him on his lovely big head and said, "Hello, old fellow. Where did you come from?" I ran my hand down over that beautiful glossy coat. He just lay there and watched as I cleaned up the room.

When I had finished, I looked around to make sure everything was all right. I picked up the broom, put the dust cloths in the paper carton with the dust and dust pan. I picked up the box and said, "Okay, old fellow, let's go downstairs." As if he understood me, he got up and started down the stairs ahead of me.

I took my time following him. I watched as he went down to the second floor and started for the ground floor. Suddenly I became aware of the silence in the house. There was no sound of the dog moving around, and then it hit me. How in the name of heaven could he get into the house, with everything secured like it was? I raced downstairs and searched everywhere — in the bathroom, under the bath and behind it, in the back and front parlours, behind the furniture, in the closets, in the kitchen, behind the stove; everywhere I could think of, but no more dog.

And I never saw him again. I don't know where he came from or where he disappeared to. All I know is that he was there with me for a short while, and then he vanished.

H.J.G, Halifax, N.S.; 78, male, retired caretaker, six years schooling

CRISIS VISION

I had a vision that came true.

I came home from work a little tired, a little after midnight. Everyone I thought was in bed asleep, so I settled down to watch the late show on TV. The movie was quite interesting, and all of a sudden the picture changed and I could see my sixteen-year-old son lying on the ground by his trail bike. There were rocks all around. It startled me, so I went in to talk to my wife and tell her about it. She told me that he had left to go to a friend's house, so I dismissed it and settled back to watch TV.

About ten minutes later we had a call from the hospital. The RCMP had found him and taken him to the hospital, where he was detained overnight. The next day I visited the place where the accident had occurred, and everything was as I had seen it that night.

G.M., Gander, Nfld.; 40, male, driver, 11 years schooling

THE FARMHOUSE POLTERGEIST

I can't remember the exact dates, but the time was between August 1975 and April 1976. We had rented a house on Drummond Road in Niagara Falls, Ontario. It was an old farmhouse that had been remodelled inside. From the time we moved in, I heard noises in the upstairs hall. But as I wasn't used to a large house, I put it down to nerves.

The next morning, as I was dressing my daughter, Bridie, I happened to turn quickly toward a dresser that was near the doorway and just caught a glimpse of a little girl watching through the rails of the banister.

We had five bedrooms in the house, so a friend of ours, named John Kusma, who was in his fifties, came to board with us. My husband worked steady nights and did not like us being alone, even though we still had our boxer dog. So John being there made us all feel safer.

I hadn't said anything to John about the noises. About two weeks after he moved in, John and I were in the kitchen having coffee, when suddenly he asked me if the girls were asleep, as he could hear heavy footsteps in the hall overhead. I went to check and when I returned I assured him they were fast asleep. It was then that he told me that he had heard the footsteps ever since he had moved in.

Little did we know that the footsteps were just the start. Twice a day we found Bridie's bed stripped of its sheets and the blankets and top mattress lying on the floor. This went on for a week. When we asked Bridie to do that for us, she didn't even know how to go about it.

221

John's bedroom door was always pushed open, even after he had closed it. The downstairs bathroom door, which could only be locked from the inside, was locked, and my husband had to take the frame off to get at the lock mechanism.

My husband and I were watching T.V. and John was upstairs shaving when we heard him yelling, "What do you want?" When we asked him what he was yelling about, he said that he had heard a woman calling him, two or three times, and he thought that it was me. When Tim, my husband, told him that I had not said anything, John went white. He stood at the top of the stairs, staring down at us as if he didn't know whether he should stay up there or come downstairs.

My mother-in-law and a friend of hers came to see us one night and we sat in the front room. It wasn't too long before the smell of flowers, mixed with some kind of spice, drifted in around one part of the room. At times it would get stronger and then fade. This went on for about an hour or so.

Another night, my sister and John and I were in the kitchen when we heard the footsteps start upstairs. John went to the foot of the stairs to see if he could see anything. When I heard him call me twice in a loud whisper, I answered, "What?" My sister said that she also heard me being called, but that it wasn't John. I told her that it was so, and that I would ask him when he came back into the kitchen. When John returned, he said that he had heard the loud whisper, too, but that he had not called me.

At one o'clock in the morning, John and I were having coffee in the kitchen when we heard a child calling for her mother. I went and checked my girls, but they were sound asleep. I knew it wasn't one of mine because the child we heard had the voice of a child of about eight or nine years, and my girls were only two and five years of age at the time. Also, this child was calling "Mommy," and my children call me Mummy.

One morning John came running out of his room and asked Tim and me who was pounding on the walls. It sounded as if the house was being smashed down, and yet no one else heard anything.

On another occasion I was talking to my friend Ruth on the phone upstairs. I heard something crash in the kitchen downstairs. I went to see what it was and saw that a picture that my daughter Tracey had made was lying on the floor. The string on the back of the picture was still in place, and so was the nail that was on the wall.

The dog and our two cats had followed me downstairs into the kitchen but would not come back up with me. I tried to get them to come up, but the dog just whined and the cats ran and hid. About half an hour later, I was still on the phone. There was a crash that sounded like someone had taken every breakable piece of glass and dishware in the kitchen and had thrown it against the kitchen wall. At that point I called John and we searched that house, from cellar to attic and even outside, but there was nothing broken anywhere.

A few times there was the sound of doors opening and closing, followed by muffled conversation between a man and a woman, but you could never make out what they were saying.

One night I was reading in bed when I felt something come into my room. If you have ever felt something totally evil, then you will have some idea of what I felt. It seemed to hold me down for about ten minutes. When it finally left, I ran to John's door and asked if I could sit there for a while. It was two hours before I could go back into my room.

Then, for about two weeks, things seemed to quieten down. Just before we moved out of the old farmhouse, the footsteps started again and the bedroom door kept opening.

We moved at the end of April, before our lease was up.

L.A.M., St. Catharines, Ont.; 28, female, housewife, 10 years schooling

A SENSE OF PRESENCE

My father, A.D.N., passed away July 30, 1957, at the age of eighty-four, in Toronto, Ontario. He was a chiropractor, and I had worked for him as an assistant for eight years, so I felt very close to him.

Dad was very psychic and had always been interested in the occult, so at a very early age I too became very interested in psychical things, reading everything on the subject I could get my hands on.

We had many discussions about life after death and whether a person who had died could come back and make his presence known. Dad said,

"I'll come back and tweak your ear or something so you'll know it's me."

At the time of Dad's passing, my husband and I owned and operated a summer resort about 150 miles north of Toronto. My brother phoned in the early evening to tell us the news, and I took it very hard.

It was necessary to make arrangements for some others to take over running the resort while we would be away. So we weren't able to leave for Toronto until the next afternoon.

In the morning, as I was preparing breakfast, tears streaming down my face, I felt a very light touch on the left shoulder blade. I didn't think much about it until it had happened several times, every two or three minutes.

Suddenly, I realized: this is Dad, making his presence known. It was a very comforting feeling. This happened hundreds of times during the next few days, then gradually the sensation decreased, but I still felt it many times a day.

Gradually, over the months that followed, it decreased further. But always at Christmas, Easter, birthdays and special days, I still feel it a few times. Two or four weeks before there is a death in the family, depending on how close the person is, I feel it many times a day.

A.M., Scarborough, Ont.; 63, female, cafeteria manager, 13 years schooling

PAST-LIFE EXPERIENCE

My first past-life experience came with a bang.

I drove my girlfriend down to Niagara Falls to spend the day and part of the evening. I was nineteen and working, just starting to feel a little bit independent. We borrowed my parents' second car for the day. When we got there we had a marvellous time shopping and sightseeing.

Rita suggested that we go into Madame Tussaud's, and I was quite agreeable. Inside we were enjoying ourselves very much and Rita asked me to accompany her into the Torture Chamber or Chamber of Horrors because she was afraid to go alone. As I had been in that part of the exhibit some years previously and had not been impressed, I protested that heads with eyeballs hanging out of them and statues of infamous people weren't nearly as interesting — besides being very distasteful to look at — as some of the truly magnificent exhibits that could be seen upstairs.

Nothing would do but that we had to go into the horror chamber. I remember being dragged along disinterestedly and occasionally going into shouts of laughter at some of the more lurid exhibits. We began comparing some of the figures to people we worked with, saying the figures displayed some of their least attractive habits. With Rita a little way ahead of me, I turned a corner and came upon an exhibit labelled The Hook of Algiers.

The instant I clapped eyes on this exhibit, I froze on the spot. The contents of my stomach became lodged in my throat, and I experienced what I later termed a "flashback." The exhibit itself showed a man suspended by the abdomen from a giant meat hook. A paragraph or two explained the method of torture and execution. I later forced myself to read the explanation, but all I can now remember of it is that if the victim was cut down within three days, he often survived.

What actually happened went like this. As soon as I saw the exhibit, Madame Tussaud's disappeared. I found myself outside a walled city. I was watching a person being suspended from a hook. Other people were around and I was terribly upset. I wasn't positive if the victim was a man or a woman, but I "knew" that this person was in some way connected to me and that I was involved with him/her. I felt that I was a woman and was dressed in the flowing garments of that period.

It was full daylight and the city walls seemed to be baked clay or very dusty stone. The ground was either dust or sand. I could hear what sounded like a large crowd going about its daily affairs. The other people around were all dressed in flowing robes of various colours. There seemed to be other people whom I felt to be like a "family" around me.

The victim was in a small cleared space in front of the wall and the rest of us in a semi-circle around him. It was a small crowd and I got the impression that this was no big deal — just a minor matter. There were two or three men who were inside the semi-circle and I felt them to be officials of some kind.

The most distinctive feature of this happening was the waves of feeling that engulfed me. I was horrified and terribly afraid. Before this happened, I could read about or see movies of people being hurt or

225

mutilated and it never really affected me. After this incident anything like that makes me very sick and repulses me so strongly that I almost become ill at the thought.

Anyway, the whole experience must have taken less than a minute. Then I found myself in Madame Tussaud's again. I tried to rationalize the incident by forcing myself to look at the exhibit and read about it, but I was so upset that I simply had to leave — fast. I grabbed my girlfriend and we left.

I don't remember driving home. But when I got home, my mother, after one look at my face, asked, "What happened?" I told her, and it was she who suggested that the experience might have been that of a past life.

I agree with this theory because no one can shake my belief that I was actually there outside those city walls.

L.M.B., Mt. Hope, Ont.; 29, female, clerk and housewife, 12 years schooling

OUT-OF-BODY EXPERIENCE

Place: Southwest corner of Warden Avenue and St. Clair Avenue East,
        Scarborough, Ontario
Date: Approximately Spring 1955
Time: Approximately 11:00 a.m. to 1:00 p.m
Age: 41
Medication: None
Health: Excellent
Mental State: Happy, excited by the occasion
Others present: My five children; and a sprinkling of the populace of
        Scarborough
Occasion: Queen Elizabeth's motorcade was to pass by during her first
        visit to Canada as the reigning monarch.

I had a very busy morning getting myself and my children ready. Then the two youngest were put into the carriage and we all trudged the two miles. We were early enough to get a good front-row spot among those people waiting eagerly to see the Queen. My eldest daughter (fifteen years old)

226

held up her one-year-old brother, while I held my two-year-old daughter in my arms. My nine- and six-year-old daughters stood in front of us.

As the motorcade passed by at thirty miles per hour, the Queen appeared ethereal, exquisite in a grey, upturned hat, which allowed her delicate skin and fine features to be seen to best advantage. Just before the open limousine passed us, she turned and appeared to look directly at us with a kind, warm expression. It seemed as if she looked deep into my eyes. I floated up and away above my family as I felt a profound sensation of joy. I had been deeply moved to think that this young girl could be persuaded to come from her home in England to let her subjects in Canada see her. It was a profound and wonderful privilege for me to be able to take my children to see their Queen.

M.F., St. Catharines, Ont.; 64, female, 16 years schooling

THE EXPERIENCE OF FLOATING AWAY

I have had the experience of floating away from my body on several occasions. Usually I have had it when I was in a state between being awake and being asleep. I do not really remember these times, but on the night of October 19, 1975, at about 10:30 p.m., I was involved in an accident where my left hand was amputated just above the wrist.

I remember pushing the saw away from my arm and looking down at my wrist. When I saw what had happened, I remember saying, "Oh, my God!" and the next thing I knew, I was standing behind and to the left and about six inches above my earthly body. My arms, in this out-of-body experience, were sticking straight out from my body. There was a pale yellow light in the room, and everything was very quiet. I could hear no sounds whatsoever. The saw was still running, but I could not hear it. I remember looking down at myself, standing in front of the saw, and then I remembered what had happened to my left wrist. As I looked to my left arm, which was still outstretched, I suddenly found my floating self and my earthly self reunited, and I was back standing in front of the saw.

This was the most vivid and memorable out-of-body experience that has ever happened to me. At the time of the experience, I was in good health and taking the occasional vitamin pill. While I was floating out of my body, I felt a great sense of well-being and the sense that everything was going to be all right.

I am typing this with both hands, so you can see that everything did turn out all right.

T.R.K., Union Bay, B.C.; 27, male, self-employed, 13 years schooling

PREMONITION OR INTUITION

My psychic experience occurred back in 1943, or thereabouts, while I was serving in the U.S. Navy.

We had a poker game going in the barracks and a hand of five-card draw had been dealt. I called the opening bet when I found I had three small hearts in my hand. This gave me probabilities for either a straight or a flush.

I was utterly astonished when, as my two cards were dealt me, I found myself absolutely certain that they were both hearts. That such a thing could be possible, I couldn't believe. Still, I knew they were hearts. Since I was playing poker, I hid my reaction and simply placed the cards on top of the others, hoping to make the other players think I had three of a kind.

After a couple of raises, I won the hand when I turned over the five hearts that I knew were there.

I don't think a lightning strike would have been a more memorable experience. But why such a significant event should have occurred in such an insignificant thing as a poker game has puzzled me ever since.

E.McD., Surrey, B.C.; 54, male, bricklayer, college

A CASE OF CLAIRVOYANCE

In May 1977, a young mother was murdered in a shopping mall in Bramalea, a suburb of Toronto. This occurred the night before my thirtieth birthday — Friday, May 13th. When I first heard about the murder on the radio, I received a picture of a man in my mind. It was a very detailed picture. It included dirty blond hair, pockmarked face, and even his height.

This information bothered me very much all that evening and into the next day. I finally told my husband about it and gave him the description of the young man I saw in connection with the murder. We also related this information to friends at dinner that evening.

My husband is the manager of the ambulance service in that area. The following Monday the police arrived in his office to see him to get the report from his attendants who had picked up this woman at the scene. While talking to my husband, the policeman said that they had a description of a suspect from two young boys who were going to the mall that Friday night to "hang out."

The boys said a man ran past them, and the look on his face scared them so much that they went home instead of to the mall. They told their parents who came forward when the police appealed for assistance. As the policeman gave my husband the yet-unofficial description of the suspect, my husband must have had a strange look on his face because the policeman asked if he knew the man he was describing. My husband said, "Well, sort of." He was the same person I had described to him the day following the murder. The police didn't think this was a joke and, in fact, accepted the assistance of several psychics, but without success. The murderer is still free.

This is not the first time I have a psychic experience, but it is the first time that I have received such a very clear, accurate and definite "picture." It was almost as though the young mother was reaching out to anyone sensitive enough to receive her message, telling us who killed her. To the best of my recollection, I was fully awake, taking no medication of any kind, and my mental state was completely normal at the time.

N.B., Woodbridge, Ont.; 30, female, office manager, 12 years schooling